Skepticism

Skepticism
The Central Issues

Charles Landesman

Blackwell Publishers

Editorial Offices:
108 Cowley Road, Oxford OX4 1JF, UK
   Tel: +44 (0)1865 791100
350 Main Street, Malden, MA 02148-5018, USA
   Tel: +1 781 388 8250

First published 2002 by Blackwell Publishers Ltd, a Blackwell Publishing company

Library of Congress Cataloging-in-Publication Data has been applied for.

ISBN 0-631-21355-4 (hardback); ISBN 0-631-21356-2 (paperback)

A catalogue record for this title is available from the British Library.

Set in 10 on 12.5 pt Photina
by Ace Filmsetting Ltd, Frome, Somerset

Printed and bound in Great Britain
by T.J. International, Padstow, Cornwall

For further information on
Blackwell Publishers, visit our website:
www.blackwellpublishers.co.uk

In memory of Howard Kahane

Contents

Preface

Skeptical ideas can be found in many texts of ancient Greek philosophy; they reappear in modern philosophy in new versions and continue to have influence up to the present time. Skeptical arguments have been used to support philosophical views that, while not fully skeptical, lean in that direction; terms such as relativism, conventionalism, constructivism, anti-realism, pragmatism, and subjectivism are some current examples. Many philosophies that do not march under the banner of skepticism have actually incorporated skeptical themes.

Global or radical skepticism doubts the very possibility of knowledge of the world and presents arguments intended to demonstrate that we are not in possession of the knowledge we think we have. Local varieties apply skeptical arguments to restricted domains of human inquiry and interest, such as religion, common-sense belief, ethical and aesthetic value, scientific inference, and the self. We live in a skeptical age, and the clamor we hear about the indispensability of faith, the need to accept eternal verities, and the attainment of objective knowledge testifies to their vulnerable condition. Although almost everyone agrees that Descartes' quest for certainty is no longer a valid program, the need to live with uncertainty, with negative capability as the poet John Keats has called it, has created a general nervousness throughout our culture.

A complete discussion of skepticism would include its history from ancient times to the present day, an account of its cultural significance, an analysis of its main arguments, and a defensible theory of human knowledge that can be used to evaluate its claims. This book, however, is merely a sketch of that inclusive project, a prelude to a historical-philosophical synthesis. Its aim is to introduce the subject, to explain what philosophical skepticism is, to identify and interpret some of the most historically influential skeptical arguments, to convince the reader that skepticism cannot be easily dismissed, and finally to show that its extreme claims denying we are in possession of knowledge cannot be sustained. I have tried to make the book self-contained so that it is accessible to those who have no prior knowledge of the subject, and I have attempted to make it philosophically contentious so that it will be of interest to those who are concerned with the problems and history of the theory of knowledge.

Briefly, this book agrees with the skeptical claim that we cannot establish by sound logical means that we actually have knowledge, and it disagrees with skepticism when the latter says that we do not have knowledge and even that knowledge is impossible. I have attempted to show what is right with skepticism and what is wrong with it, and to develop an approach to the problem of knowledge that enables us to escape the full force of the powerful arguments of ancient and modern skeptics.

The first chapter serves as an introduction. It presents some of the main historical actors, and it identifies the theme of realism as an essential part of the debate between skeptics and anti-skeptics. The second chapter discusses a historically important local skepticism according to which certain of our common perceptions – those of color, for instance – fail to represent accurately things as they are in themselves. It introduces the theme of the shakiness and uncertainty of our common sense beliefs. Chapter 3 discusses the difference between a belief's being justified and being true. Chapters 4, 5, and 6 discuss ancient skepticism, with an emphasis upon the central skeptical argument against the criterion. This powerful argument is intended to show that we fail to have knowledge because one of its essential preconditions – a criterion of truth – cannot be established.

Chapters 7 through 12 are concerned with the problem of our knowledge of the external world and explore in some detail what Hume called skepticism with regard to the senses. The famous skeptical arguments that Descartes introduced at the beginning of his *Meditations* – from dreams and from the possibility of a malicious demon – are interpreted and criticized. The main vehicle of criticism is G. E. Moore's ways of defending common sense, particularly his proof of an external world. Although Moore's proof is unsatisfactory as it stands, it can be amended and elaborated to reveal the failure of Descartes' arguments. Chapters 13 and 14 discuss two examples of local skepticism – Hume's doubts about induction and doubts about the possibility of self-knowledge. The method of arguing against skepticism that was developed with Moore's proof as a basis is applied again to defend the possibility of knowledge in both cases. The final chapter discusses whether it is possible to combine skepticism with positive philosophical activity; using the examples of Hume and Quine, it shows that skepticism need not undermine

1

Skepticism and the Retreat from Realism

Seek out reality, leave things that seem. (William Butler Yeats)

The Skeptical Tradition

The word "skeptic" is derived, via Latin, from a Greek term meaning one who inquires or examines. This ancient meaning, however, fails to capture either the nature of the initial stages of the skeptical tradition in Greek philosophy or the current usage of the term in everyday discourse and in the philosophical literature. Certainly, the skeptic inquires into various topics, but what is distinctive about his or her inquiry is that it focuses upon the question of whether or not we can have knowledge of the topic under examination and concludes either that knowledge is not possible or that, even if we are in possession of knowledge, we cannot establish that we are. Philosophers are concerned to inquire into the possibility of knowledge; within Western philosophy, the skeptical tradition, using powerful and plausible arguments, favors a pessimistic outcome.

I have spoken of the skeptical tradition, so a word is in order about the propriety of even applying the notion of tradition to such an individualistic enterprise as philosophy. We find skeptical ideas scattered throughout Western philosophy from its very beginnings in ancient Greece to the present day. With what right do we amalgamate them under a unified heading?

Historians of philosophy have developed a standardized though somewhat vague and ambiguous vocabulary for describing philosophical points of view. Such terms as idealism, materialism, realism, empiricism, rationalism, skepticism, and many others are used to classify philosophers and their ideas into handy pigeon holes. They enable us to group philosophical ideas together based upon similarities among them and to distinguish classes of similar ideas from ideas that differ in important ways. They sometimes indicate the influence of one group of thinkers upon others. This terminology has its limitations. Consider, for example, the variety of philosophers who are frequently classified as empiricists because they place the foundations of human knowledge in experience: Aristotle, Aquinas, Bacon, Hobbes, Locke, Berkeley, Hume, James, Mach, Carnap, and Quine. While careful scrutiny will reveal certain empiricist similarities among them, lumping them together overlooks vast differences and obscures their affinities with philosophers who are listed under different rubrics. Philosophical classifications are not like labels for political parties that people officially join; at best, they point to a salient feature that systems that differ in many other ways have in common. Such groupings fail to rise to the level of natural kinds; they are closer to what Wittgenstein thought of as concepts based upon family resemblances. They should be understood as handy devices for abbreviated reference rather than as the product of a deep analysis of a philosophical tendency.

Sometimes these labels are applied so ambiguously as to be misleading unless prefaced by explanatory remarks. For example, Plato, Berkeley, Kant, and Hegel are often called idealists, yet the points in which they differ are even more interesting than their points of similarity. There are cases in which a philosopher applies a label to himself and then lives to regret it. For example, Charles Sanders Peirce adopted "pragmatism" as the label for his conception of inquiry, but when he saw that the term was being used with a sense different from his own, he replaced it with "pragmaticism," a word which, he said, "is ugly enough to be safe from kidnappers" (Peirce, 1965, p. 5.414).

With these remarks in mind, be forewarned that when I refer to the skeptical tradition, I am grouping together a variety of thinkers whose point in common, no matter how else they differ, is that they have provided reasons for doubting large classes of beliefs that are deeply entrenched in the minds and actions of mankind. Some members of the tradition have exerted influence upon others. One major thinker in the tradition, Descartes, considers himself to be the first philosopher who has provided an adequate refutation of skepticism; he belongs to the tradition by virtue of having formulated, as a prelude to his refutation, powerful arguments of a skeptical nature intended to undermine all established belief; he was giving the devil his due so that his refutation would be seen to be directed against the most powerful forces of the enemy.

Philosophical skepticism should not be confused with the specific doubts directed toward particular beliefs that arise in everyday life as well as in scientific inquiry. Copernicus and others had doubts about the view that the earth was the center of the solar system and succeeded in replacing it with the heliocentric hypothesis. Freud made people doubt whether they knew themselves as well as they thought they did. These are doubts engendered by the production of evidence against an established view. But they do not put into doubt the prevailing conception of evidence or lead us to suspect that we have no knowledge or justified belief about anything.

As distinguished from these specific doubts, philosophical skepticism aims to make us question the very framework within which particular inquiries occur. It asks not only whether this or that specific belief counts as knowledge, but whether this type of inquiry is capable of producing any knowledge whatever. It raises doubts about the adequacy and reliability of the prevailing methods of fixing belief and about whether we are ever justified or warranted in believing what we do. It questions, also, whether our basic concepts have application to things as they are. As Stroud has pointed out, "the threat of skepiticism is what keeps the theory of knowledge going" (Stroud, 1987, p. 293).

Global Skepticism

Within philosophical skepticism we must distinguish global from more local varieties. The global skeptic questions whether any knowledge or justification is possible at all, no matter what the subject matter. Some of the dialogues that Plato wrote present Socrates as wondering whether anyone is in possession of any worthwhile knowledge. The skepticism that Plato ascribes to Socrates is sweeping though vaguely demarcated. The fact that some of his dialogues end without a determinate conclusion suggests the possibility that inquiry, no matter how relentlessly pursued, will, in the end, fail to find answers. A number of Plato's texts deny that our ordinary non-philosophical beliefs actually count as knowledge (see Groarke, 1997). In the famous allegory of the cave (in *The Republic*, book VII), Plato suggests that most people resemble prisoners in a cave who take the shadows cast on the wall to be real things. Only the few who are able to leave the cave have a correct idea about what the world is really like. Reality is hard to know, and most are doomed to live in the realm of shadows forever.

Despite these intimations of global skepticism in Plato's portrait of Socrates, few would go so far as to pronounce Plato himself to be a global skeptic. The great skeptic of the third century CE, Sextus Empiricus, writes in his *Outlines of Pyrrhonism*: "Even if Plato evinces doubt about some matters, yet he cannot be a skeptic inasmuch as he shows himself at times either making assertions about the reality of non-evident objects or preferring one non-evident thing to another in point of credibility" (Sextus Empiricus, 1955, I.225).

Note the distinction implicit in this passage between those objects that are evident and those that are non-evident. The evident, such as the ways things appear, are those we are entitled to feel certain about, whereas we may doubt that we have knowledge of the non-evident because our beliefs about them are the conclusions of shaky inferences even when their premises refer to what is evident.

In this passage, Sextus suggested one version of global skepticism: we do have some knowledge (of evident objects), but we have no knowledge at all of anything transcending what is evident, such as how things are in themselves independently of how they appear to us. This skepticism about the non-evident does not go so far as to deny that we are in possession of any knowledge whatsoever. I shall use the term *epistemic nihilism* for that extreme form of global skepticism that denies the possibility of any and all knowledge, and even justified belief. Nihilism has a special difficulty of its own, since if the nihilist presents arguments in favor of the claim that there is no knowledge of anything, he cannot consistently claim that his arguments and their premises contain knowledge, and thus he undermines the basis of his own position. The more modest skepticism about the non-evident claims that the premises and arguments that are offered as reasons for doubt are drawn exclusively from what is evident.

Forms of global skepticism constituted an important current of thought in ancient Greek philosophy. Sextus Empiricus' use of the term *Pyrrhonism* for his version of skepticism refers to Pyrrho of Elis (*c*.360–270 BCE) Although Pyrrho himself left no writings, some information on his life and thought is contained in *The Lives of Eminent Philosophers* by Diogenes Laertius, who lived perhaps in the third century CE. Diogenes is not thought to be a reliable source of information so we cannot count on the historical accuracy of his life of Pyrrho. However, the stories and ideas he presents were widely circulated and were used by others in their reflections on skepticism.

Although the skeptical schools of ancient Greece produced a large body of writings, only a few texts have survived. What we know of ancient skepticism is contained in the compilations of Diogenes Laertius, Cicero, and Sextus Empiricus, as well as in the writings of its opponents, such as St Augustine, and in scattered references from a large variety of sources. The skepticism formulated in these writings had little impact upon medieval thought after Augustine and, in fact, they were largely unavailable until they were recovered in the fifteenth and sixteenth centuries. The writings of Sextus Empiricus appeared for the first time in Latin translation in the mid-sixteenth century, and it was these texts that contributed most to the emergence of skeptical thought in early modern philosophy, especially in the writings of Montaigne (1533–92), Descartes (1596–1650), and Bayle (1647–1706) (see Popkin, 1968, chapter 2; Schmitt, 1983). Such was the power and impact of Descartes' philosophy that the issue of how to rebut skepticism became one of the top items on the agenda of modern philosophy. The problem of skepticism became a permanent feature of the philosophical thought of succeeding centuries until our own time as a result of the profound writings of David Hume (1711–76), who carried the logic of the skeptical arguments found in Sextus and Descartes to their extreme nihilistic conclusions.[1]

Two landmarks in the effort to overcome that logic are to be found in the works of Thomas Reid (1710–96) and Immanuel Kant (1724–1804). In his *Inquiry into the Human Mind* and *Essays on the Intellectual Powers of Man*, Reid offered a particular diagnosis of the basis of skepticism: if we assume that knowledge of the external world is based upon inferences from mental representations (or ideas, as they were termed in the writings of Reid's predecessors), even if these ideas are among the objects that are evident to us, the inferences are too shaky to justify the body of our common sense beliefs. Reid thought that Hume reasoned correctly from the assumption of this theory of ideas and that global skepticism was the logical outcome of this starting point. Since global skepticism is absurd just because it violates our common sense beliefs as well as the mental rules by which they are generated, we should simply reject the theory of ideas and the representational theory of knowledge that was based upon it.

Kant, on the other hand, had no sympathy with the common sense refutation of skepticism offered by Reid and others.

> To appeal to common sense when insight and science fail, and no sooner – this is one of the most subtle discoveries of modern times, by means of which the most superficial ranter can safely enter the lists with the most thorough thinker and hold his own. But as long as a particle of insight remains, no one would think of having recourse to this subterfuge. Seen in a clear light, it is but an appeal to the opinion of the multitude, of whose applause the philosopher is ashamed, while the popular charlatan glories and confides in it. (Kant, 1783, p. 5)

---

1   Hume appears to shrink from fully embracing nihilism since he claims that we do have knowledge of our sense impressions. However, for him, our knowledge is only of our *present* impressions, since we have no good reason to trust our memory (Hume, 1739, p. 265). On the other hand, he seems to endorse the arguments for "total skepticism," which "leaves not the lowest degree of evidence in any proposition" (Hume, 1739, pp. 183, 268, 267).

Although Kant belittled philosophers who appeal to common sense, his intemperate blast is unfair to Reid, who was an able philosopher and not in the least superficial. We shall see below that the appeal to common sense in the thought of G. E. Moore (1873–1958) is a powerful antidote to skeptical challenges. But Kant is correct to this extent: that merely affirming what we already believe without accompanying that affirmation with an account and justification of the worth of common sense has no weight against skeptical argumentation.

In contrast to his estimate of Reid, Kant held Hume's philosophy in the highest regard and testified to its particular importance for his own philosophical development: "I openly confess that my remembering David Hume was the very thing which many years ago first interrupted my dogmatic slumber and gave my investigations in the field of speculative philosophy a quite new direction" (Kant, 1783, p. 5). Indeed, for Kant, skepticism marks an indispensable stage in the development of philosophical thought on the problem of knowledge. "The first step in matters of pure reason, marking its infancy, is *dogmatic*" (Kant, 1781, A761). While making grandiose claims to know the nature of reality, the dogmatist fails to determine whether his claims count as knowledge because he "has not surveyed the sphere of his understanding, and therefore has not determined, in accordance with principles, the limits of possible knowledge." Instead of fixing his beliefs in a principled way, the dogmatist simply muddles through, relying upon "the simple method of trial and failure" (Kant, 1781, A761, 768).

The second stage is skepticism, an examination of our claims to be in possession of knowledge together with a firm rejection of all those beliefs that fail to pass the test. Kant calls this stage "the censorship of reason."

> The sceptic is thus the taskmaster who constrains the dogmatic reasoner to develop a sound critique of the understanding and reason. . . . While, therefore, the sceptical procedure cannot of itself yield any *satisfying* answer to the questions of reason, none the less it *prepares the way* by arousing reason to circumspection and by indicating the radical measures which are adequate to secure it in its legitimate possessions.

Once a skeptical examination has undermined all dogmatic claims, philosophy has been prepared for the third stage, which is

> to subject to examination, not the facts of reason, but reason itself, in the whole extent of its powers. . . . This is not the censorship but the *criticism* of reason, whereby not its present *bounds* but its determinate [and necessary] *limits*, not its ignorance on this or that point but its ignorance in re-

gard to all possible questions of a certain kind, are demonstrated from principles, and not merely arrived at by way of conjecture. (Kant, 1781, A769, 761)

Kant identifies dogmatism with the method of fixing belief by trial and error. Skepticism cures us of our penchant for muddling through by making us see the importance of a principled, permanent distinction between what we can and what we cannot know. It accomplishes this by showing that, in the absence of a principled distinction, we are not entitled to our claims to be in possession of knowledge.

For Kant as for Reid and the followers of common sense, skepticism is a useful but unstable point of view. It prods us to adopt a critical standpoint and to discover the correct principles that generate knowledge from experience.

Scepticism is thus a resting-place for human reason, where it can reflect upon its dogmatic wanderings and make survey of the region in which it finds itself, so that for the future it may be able to choose its path with more certainty. But it is no dwelling-place for permanent settlement. Such can be attained only through perfect certainty in our knowledge, alike of the objects themselves and of the limits within which all our knowledge of objects is enclosed. (Kant, 1781, A761)

Kant is aiming at certainty and is unsatisfied both with muddle and with doubt. He is the chief advocate of the idea that by using the *a priori* methods of philosophy, one can determine for all time the extent and limits of human knowledge.

There is no consensus that Kant has actually shown that skepticism is not "a dwelling-place for permanent settlement." Kant had great respect for skepticism and especially for Hume's version of it. In fact, he was a kind of skeptic himself even though he claims that his critical philosophy enables us to deflect skeptical arguments.

Realism and Idealism

Kant's critical philosophy attempted to overcome skepticism by assimilating it rather than by simply refuting it. One of the starting points of his philosophy is the distinction between "things as objects of experience and those same things as things in themselves. . . . The object is to be taken *in a twofold sense,* namely as appearance and as thing in itself" (Kant, 1781, Bxxvii).

Consider any object whose existence does not depend upon our own mental activity. For example, the computer on which I am writing these words is not a product of any mental act of mine even though the mental image of it formed when my eyes are closed is a product of my will. I can think of the computer as something that exists in causal independence of my will. When I am looking at it, it acquires a relation to me which consists of its appearing to me in a sensuous form and of my becoming aware of it. In the one case it is a thing in itself; in the other case, it is an appearance.

With this distinction in mind, Kant enunciated a basic thesis about human knowledge: "We can . . . have no knowledge of any object as thing in itself, but only in so far as it is an object of sensible intuition, that is, an appearance" (Kant, 1781, Bxxvi). What this means, in the first instance, is that in order for us to gain knowledge of any object, that object must enter into a relation to us mediated by our senses; that is, it must appear to us. Kant is here affirming a version of *empiricism* when he claims that our knowledge of the external world is founded upon and limited by our perceptual access to objects. If there should be objects to which there is no perceptual route (e.g. God or Plato's forms), we are forever barred from gaining any knowledge of them.

On first reading, Kant's claim that our knowledge of objects is limited to the appearances seems to be the banal and obvious truism that in order to know something we must establish some relation to it, a relation that involves our sensory apparatus. But there is a further level of interpretation that interjects something more controversial. Suppose that, in processing the information gained from the senses, the mind organizes the data of sense according to principles and rules of its own without regard for how things are in themselves. In that case, the appearances would exemplify features and structures which may or may not match the features and structures they exemplify as things in themselves. Since our knowledge is limited to things as they appear, we may never be able to know those features and structures which they exemplify in themselves and which are lost and replaced in the course of mental processing. Here are intimations of a form of global skepticism. But, as we have seen, skepticism, for Kant, is a resting-place but not a dwelling-place, so he proposes that we adopt a point of view that enables us to deflect skeptical doubts about the possibility of knowledge:

> Hitherto it has been assumed that all our knowledge must conform to objects. But all attempts to extend our knowledge of objects by establishing something in regard to them *a priori*, by means of concepts, have, on this

assumption, ended in failure. We must therefore make trial whether we may not have more success in the tasks of metaphysics, if we suppose that objects must conform to our knowledge. . . . If intuition must conform to the constitution of the objects, I do not see how we could know anything of the latter *a priori*, but if the object (as an object of the senses) must conform to the constitution of our faculty of intuition, I have no difficulty in conceiving of such a possibility. (Kant, 1781, Bxvi–xvii)

According to Kant, as philosophers reflected upon the problem of knowledge, they had assumed that "all our knowledge must conform to objects." What this means is that things as they are in themselves have a certain nature or character and that the task of inquiry is to gain knowledge of this independent nature or character.

Kant calls this traditional approach to the problem of knowledge *transcendental realism*,

which regards time and space as something given in themselves, independently of our sensibility. The transcendental realist thus interprets outer appearances (their reality being taken for granted) as things-in-themselves, which exist independently of us and of our sensibility, and which are therefore outside us. (Kant, 1781, A369)

The transcendental realist (or realist, for short) claims that inquiry attempts to gain knowledge of things as they are independently of our sensory apparatus (sensibility) and forms of thought (categories of the understanding).[2] If, in the course of processing sensory information, the mind adds features to the appearances which fail to be exemplified by things-in-themselves, one of the tasks of inquiry is to determine just that fact about mental processing and to subtract those psychic additions to attain an adequate and true representation of the object.

Kant, however, thinks that realism is a form of dogmatism and leads to skepticism:

After wrongly supposing that objects of the senses, if they are to be external, must have an existence by themselves, and independently of the senses, [the transcendental realist] finds that, judged from this point of view, all our sensuous representations are inadequate to establish their reality. (Kant, 1781, A369)

2   "Seek out reality, leave things that seem" (W. B. Yeats, "Vacillation").

In order to avoid the inevitable skeptical consequences of assuming realism from the start, we must make a new beginning by assuming that "objects must conform to our knowledge." This new point of view Kant calls *transcendental idealism*, according to which

> External objects (bodies), however, are mere appearances, and are therefore nothing but a species of my representations, the objects of which are something only through these representations. Apart from them they are nothing. Thus external things exist as well as I myself, and both, indeed, upon the immediate witness of my self-consciousness. . . . In order to arrive at the reality of outer objects I have just as little need to resort to inference as I have in regard to the reality of. . . my thoughts. For in both cases alike the objects are nothing but representations, the immediate perception (consciousness) of which is at the same time a sufficient proof of their reality. (Kant, 1781, A370–1)

Transcendental idealism (or idealism, for short) deflects skepticism rather than refutes it. Instead of adopting the realism of our usual understanding of the human condition as far as our knowledge is concerned and showing that, contrary to what the skeptic argues, the inference from the sensory data to the existence and character of the object is valid, idealism adopts the idea that no such inference is necessary in the first place. The objects of inquiry are given in the appearances themselves; inquiry is an effort to grasp things not as they are in themselves, but only as they appear to us.

Kant thus retains an element of skepticism: if our knowledge depended upon a shaky inference to things as they are in themselves, then the skeptic would be correct in concluding that knowledge of objects is impossible. Skepticism is thus parasitic upon realism. But if, instead, it can be shown that the object to be known is evident (to use Sextus' terminology), if inquiry is actually content with the ways things appear, the problem, for Kant, disappears.

After Descartes, the dominant challenge that skepticism raised was to find a proof of the existence of the external world. Kant interpreted skepticism in this way when he wrote that

> it still remains a scandal to philosophy and to human reason in general that the existence of things outside us (from which we derive the whole material of knowledge, even for our inner sense) must be accepted merely on *faith*, and that if anyone thinks good to doubt their existence, we are unable to counter his doubts by any satisfactory proof. (Kant, 1781, Bxl, note)

With the adoption of the point of view of idealism, Kant thought that the scandal to philosophy had been terminated for good. We have genuine knowledge of and not merely faith in the existence of the external world. Such knowledge does not depend upon a shaky inference from the ways things appear to their character as they are in themselves, for the external world just consists of the appearances in their systematic interconnection.

However, there is a significant residue of skepticism remaining in Kant's philosophy. After all, he did not deny that there are things-in-themselves, and he did not deny that they may very well have a character different from the character they present as they appear to us. And if they differ in character, what that difference amounts to can never be known by us because it transcends all possible experience. Both in his acceptance of an unknowable thing-in-itself and in his rejection of realism as the way of understanding the object of inquiry, skepticism remains a "dwelling-place for permanent settlement" in Kant's thought. Such is the cost of deflecting rather than refuting the skeptical arguments. We can see in Kant's thought the beginnings of a current approach to the challenge of the global skeptic, which is to avoid assuming at the outset the truth of transcendental realism, a position now frequently called *anti-realism*. If gaining knowledge of things as they are in themselves is not the aim of inquiry, then our knowledge-producing activities may be confined within the domain of the appearances without any apparent loss. In that case, Kant thought, skeptical arguments can gain no leverage.

Local Skepticism

Between the global skepticism of Sextus and Hume and the particular doubts about existing beliefs engendered as a result of the discovery of new evidence in particular inquiries lie various forms of local skepticism that have had vast cultural significance and retain philosophical importance. I will mention just one instance in this chapter, and another will receive extensive discussion in the following chapter.

The instance I have in mind is the skeptical undermining of traditional forms of religious belief. Biblical religion obtained essential philosophical grounding during medieval and early modern philosophy. The chief form of support consisted in the formulation and defense of various arguments for God's existence. If one appeals merely to faith to explain the basis for one's belief in God, one is met with the affirmations of different and opposed faiths and one's own faith appears contingent and arbitrary. But if one can depend upon philosophical arguments whose logic is valid and whose premises are undeniable, the accusation that one's belief rests upon a house of cards is defeated. Faith by itself is a feeble basis for religious belief once the multiplicity of objects of faith is recognized, but when it is allied with reason, it justifiably gains in self-confidence.

Religious skepticism is the product of a number of different intellectual currents in modern thought. The break-up of Christian unity in the Reformation created a number of opposing faiths; the fact that people could disagree about religion and that this disagreement appeared irreversible and insoluble led many to examine the foundations of faith and to find it wanting. Biblical criticism undermined the tendency to treat the books of the Old and New Testaments as if they were indubitably accurate historical narratives. Philosophers such as Hume and Kant examined the traditional proofs of God's existence and concluded that they are unsound. Scientific explanations of numerous phenomena convinced many that religious belief had no plausible explanatory role to play; naturalistic explanations gradually replaced appeal to the supernatural.

Global skepticism had its own specific contribution to make to the decline of religious belief. The appearance of ancient Greek skeptical texts in early modern philosophy contributed to making people aware that there actually is a problem concerning the basis of human knowledge. These texts raised the question of whether there is any way of defending the prevailing methods of fixing belief. The texts of Sextus, Descartes, and Hume showed that even the most entrenched beliefs are vulnerable to skeptical probing. Reflections on the basis of human knowledge convinced many people that the senses provide the only source of information about the world and that metaphysical beliefs that transcend the limits of sensory information and logical inference possessed no warrant and, perhaps, no meaning.

David Hume recommended that we adopt a kind of *mitigated skepticism* "which may be the natural result of Pyrrhonian doubts and scruples." Given that he thought that the arguments of global skepticism are unanswerable, Hume recommended "the limitation of our inquiries to such subjects as are best adapted to the narrow capacity of human understanding." The imperfections of our cognitive capacities as revealed by the skeptical tradition is reason enough for us to confine ourselves "to common life and to such subjects as fall under daily practice and experience" (Hume, 1748, p. 162). The anti-metaphysical outcome of Hume's reflections upon the problem of knowledge and upon global skepticism are brought home in this famous passage, which brings his *An Enquiry Concerning Human Understanding* to an end:

When we run over our libraries, persuaded of these principles, what havoc must we make? If we take in our hand any volume; of divinity or school metaphysics, for instance; let us ask, *Does it contain any abstract reasoning concerning quantity or number?* No. *Does it contain any experimental reasoning concerning matter of fact and existence?* No. Commit it then to the flames: for it can contain nothing but sophistry and illusion. (Hume, 1748, p. 165)

A few sentences earlier Hume had remarked that the "best and most solid foundation [of the belief in God and the immortality of the soul] is *faith* and divine revelation" (Hume, 1748, p. 165). Neither of these beliefs can be established, for Hume, by either abstract or experimental reasoning. It would appear that Hume is advocating a form of fideism according to which religious belief is more a matter of faith than reason. But it is not clear that he is actually recommending faith, because, whether these beliefs are advocated in books of divinity or school metaphysics or in sermons encouraging the believers to be faithful, they would still be examples of "sophistry and illusion." His remark should be interpreted as an ironical aside intended to deflect the attacks of religious dogmatists and the fury of the intolerant.

It is interesting to note that the revival of skepticism in early modern philosophy was initially used to support fideism rather than unbelief. For a fideist, skeptical arguments were useful in undermining the claims of reason to constitute the foundation of religious belief. Faith enters the picture to fill the gap between what reason is capable of validating (and if Hume is correct, reason is capable of validating very little) and what Christian belief requires. Thus, after forcefully presenting the arguments of the Pyrrhonist skeptic, Montaigne asserts:

All things produced by our own reason and ability, the true as well as the false, are subject to uncertainty and debate. It was for the chastisement of our pride and the instruction of our wretchedness and incapacity that God produced the disorder and confusion of the ancient tower of Babel. All that we undertake without his assistance, all that we see without the lamp of his grace, is only vanity and folly. The very essence of truth, which is uniform and constant, we corrupt and adulterate by our weakness when fortune gives us possession of it. (Montaigne, 1965, pp. 414–15)

For Montaigne, Pyrrhonism shows that man "is a blank tablet prepared to take from the finger of God such forms as he shall be pleased to engrave on it. The more we cast ourselves back on God and commit ourselves to him, and renounce ourselves, the better we are" (Montaigne, 1965, p. 375). Montaigne was kinder to metaphysics and philosophy than Hume when, instead of pronouncing it to be sophistry and illusion, he remarked that "philosophy is but sophisticated poetry" (Montaigne, 1965, p. 24).

With Pyrrho, suspension of judgment was the most reasonable outcome of global skepticism; with the fideists, religious belief seemed appropriate; with still others, unbelief was the outcome. Although skepticism purports to show that we fail to have the knowledge we think we have, the question of what beliefs to settle upon is left open. Hume pointed out that although our common sense beliefs cannot be justified by either abstract or experimental reasoning, our nature would still lead us to adopt those beliefs necessary for our existence. "Nature is always too strong for principle" (Hume, 1748, p. 160). The question of the ethics of belief, of what we ought to believe or are entitled to believe, is not settled by skeptical argumentation. Our nature assures us that we will believe enough to survive but leaves open the question of whether we should settle for mitigated skepticism, as Hume thought, or religious faith, as Montaigne recommended. Later we shall discuss at greater length the implications of skeptical arguments for the question of the fixation of belief.

2

The Great Deception of Sense

The Book of Nature

It has not only been the skeptical tradition that has been concerned with the question of the reliability of the senses. The fact that the senses sometimes deceive, that things are not always what they seem, that illusions and hallucinations occur, that the senses are capable of delivering misinformation as well as information about the external world has been a topic of discussion throughout the Western philosophical tradition. On the one hand, common sense admits the possibility of error but claims, nevertheless, that our senses usually are reliable. Global skeptics, on the other hand, seized on such facts in order to raise the question of whether there is any reason at all to trust the senses. In this chapter we shall discuss a major episode in modern philosophical and scientific thought that raised the question of the accuracy of the information that the senses deliver. Skepticism with regard to the senses leads us to wonder about the extent to which the ways things look, feel, sound, taste, and smell accurately represent the ways things are actually constituted. The issues in this chapter are a step toward extensive doubts whether we have any knowledge at all of the external world.

Philosophical thought in the seventeenth century was particularly concerned with the issue of whether the unreliability of the senses is systematic. This concern was generated in part by the revival of the ancient atomic or corpuscularian theory of matter in opposition to the Aristotelian theory that had been dominant in late medieval thought. According to the atomic theory, the objects that are large enough for us to see are composed of material particles too minute to see; their essential features, such as their size, shape, mass, motion, and number, are those that are studied in geometry and in mathematics generally. Galileo (1564–1642) remarked that the book of nature is written in "the language of mathematics, and its characters are triangles, circles, and other geometric figures without which it is humanly impossible to understand a single word of it; without these, one wanders about in a dark labyrinth" (Galileo, 1623, p. 230).

But what of the qualitative features of nature such as colors and sounds, tastes and smells, heat and cold? How can they be made to fit into this picture? Here is Galileo's answer:

> People in general have a concept of [heat] . . . which is very remote from the truth. For they believe that heat is a real phenomenon, property, or quality, which actually resides in the material by which we feel ourselves warmed. Now I say that whenever I conceive any material or corporeal substance, I immediately feel the need to think of it as bounded and as having this or that shape, as being large or small in relation to other things, and in some specific place at any given time; as being in motion or at rest; as touching or not touching some other body; and as being one in number, or few, or many. From these conditions I cannot separate such a substance by any stretch of my imagination. But that it must be white or red, bitter or sweet, noisy or silent, and of sweet or foul odor, my mind does not feel compelled to bring in as necessary accompaniments. Without the senses as our guides, reason or imagination unaided would probably never arrive at qualities like these. Hence I think that tastes, odors, colors, and so on are no more than mere names so far as the object in which we place them is concerned, and that they reside only in consciousness. Hence if the living creature were removed, all these qualities would be wiped away and annihilated. (Galileo, 1623, p. 274)

This remarkable passage contains a whole world of philosophy within itself. Let us review its main assertions.

The Nature of Matter

In the first place, Galileo claims that the geometrical and mathematical features of bodies are inseparable from the bodies themselves; they are, he says, "necessary accompaniments." It is of the very nature of bodies to have size and shape, to have location in space and time, to be in either motion or rest, to be in contact with some bodies and spatially separated from others, and to be numerable. If you take away these features (what Locke later called the *primary qualities*) from bodies, you remove the bodies themselves. Our very conception of what it is to be a body incorporates this list of characteristics. We may wonder whether other types of objects (numbers, God, minds) possess some or all of these features, but there can be no question that bodies possess them because possessing them is just what it means to be a body.

Second, the qualitative features (what Locke called the *secondary qualities*) of bodies are not "necessary accompaniments." We ascribe these qualities to bodies because our sense experience compels us to. Reason, unaided by the senses, would not lead us to impute them to bodies because they are not implied by our conception of the nature of body. That, for example, lemons are yellow or, for that matter, that lemons have any color whatever is purely contingent; relative to our notion of body, lemons might lack color. It is only because lemons look yellow to most people most of the time that we are convinced that they are yellow.

Whereas these two points that Galileo affirms are perhaps consistent with the common sense of the matter, the third point is quite extraordinary and goes against the grain of our original understanding of matter. It says that not only is it imaginable or conceivable that bodies lack secondary qualities but, as a matter of fact, they do lack them. When I assert that lemons are yellow, I am using the name "yellow" to describe them, but there is nothing there corresponding to the name. Strictly speaking, when I say that lemons are yellow, I have said something that is false, even though, at the moment I say it, I am convinced of its truth. Judgments that affirm secondary qualities of bodies are "very remote from the truth."

According to Galileo, then, we are quite justified in being skeptical with regard to many of the judgments of the senses. Although he is not a global skeptic, he thinks that the ways in which our senses cause things to appear are systematically unreliable as far as the secondary qualities are concerned. It is not merely that experience convinces us in certain particular cases that things are not what they seem. Rather, with regard to the qualitative features of bodies in general, things are never what they seem. We have, Galileo thinks, excellent reasons to doubt large classes of perceptual beliefs. This is a form of local skepticism with regard to the secondary qualities.

The Subjective Turn

Although Galileo says that bodies lack secondary qualities, he does not go so far as to say that nothing exemplifies them. He claims that "they reside only in consciousness." By "consciousness" here, Galileo is referring to the ways things appear through the senses. The fact that lemons look yellow is a fact about human consciousness or sense awareness. When we speak about the appearances, the ways things look, sound, taste, smell, and feel, it is always appropriate to ask to whom these things look, sound, taste, smell, and feel in the way they do. That lemons look yellow is a fact about most human beings and, perhaps, some animals. That this lemon looks yellow to me here and now is a fact about me (as well as the lemon).

So talk about the appearances brings in the point of view of those who are aware of bodies; the ways things appear are ways in which we become aware of bodies. I shall call this the *subjective point of view* because it refers to the subject to whom things appear and allows us to wonder whether the ways things subjectively appear correspond to the ways they objectively are. There can be no appearances without living creatures to whom the things appear. Therefore, according to Galileo, "if the living creature were removed, all these qualities would be wiped away and annihilated."

The secondary qualities, then, reside only in sense awareness, and if all creatures capable of sense awareness were removed, these qualities would be annihilated and only the primary qualities would remain. There is a certain ambiguity in Galileo's account, an ambiguity that has permeated almost all discussions of the subject, even up to the present day. There are two major interpretations of the claim that secondary qualities "reside only in consciousness." One of them takes this claim literally; when, for example, it is said that something is yellow, Galileo could mean that there is some item that is a constituent of consciousness that literally is yellow. So when this lemon looks yellow to me, the fact that its yellow color resides only in consciousness implies that there is a yellow something or other that I am aware of. I shall use the term *sense datum*, popularized in the writings of Russell and Moore, to indicate this type of constituent of consciousness that is supposed to exemplify those very features that bodies only appear to have.

The second interpretation denies that there is something literally yellow in consciousness when something looks yellow to someone. That something looks yellow does not imply that it or anything else for that matter is yellow. There is no conceptually valid immediate inference from "looks yellow" to "is yellow." Whatever is going on when something appears to someone, there is no subjective or mental entity that exemplifies the primary or secondary qualities that appear. This second interpretation leaves it open how the phenomenon of subjective appearance should be understood. Its main intent is to deny the sense datum approach. In any case, Galileo's phrase "reside in consciousness" fails to settle which interpretation he might favor.

Sense Data

The literal or sense datum interpretation has been the most popular approach to understanding perceptual consciousness in the history of modern philosophy, although it has few explicit advocates at the present time. It says, for example, that when I see something that appears to me to be yellow, I am directly aware of something, a sense datum, that is yellow, and my thought that some physical object really is yellow is triggered by my awareness of the sense datum. Various terms have been used by those espousing the sense datum approach – ideas of sensation, impressions of sensation, sensa, qualia – and there are many versions of the theory; in fact, it should be understood as a family of theories whose distinguishing feature is that in sense perception there is some entity, a sense datum, that we are acquainted with, that literally possesses the sensible features that something appears to have.

Since there is no valid immediate inference from "appears yellow" to "is yellow," the question remains how to bridge this conceptual gap. One attempt to do so is provided by H. H. Price:

> When I see a tomato there is much that I can doubt. I can doubt whether it is a tomato that I am seeing, and not a cleverly painted piece of wax. I can doubt whether there is any material thing there at all. Perhaps what I took for a tomato was really a reflection; perhaps I am even the victim of some hallucination. One thing however I cannot doubt: that there exists a red patch of a round and somewhat bulgy shape, standing out from a background of other colour-patches, and having a certain visual depth, and that this whole field of colour is directly present to my consciousness. (Price, 1954, p. 3)

For Price, sense data are the termini of the process of doubt. He can find reason to doubt that there is a tomato there because he could be having just that experience even if there was no tomato at all in the place he was looking at – reflections and hallucinations are explanations he offers about how such error is possible. What he cannot find reason to doubt is that he is directly conscious of a red bulgy patch having not only the two dimensions of length and height but also the third of depth.

It is instructive to note that others have been able to doubt what Price finds indubitable. Here, for example, is Berkeley on the perception of depth: "It is, I think, agreed by all that distance, of itself and immediately, cannot be seen. For distance being a line directed end-wise to the eye, it projects only one point in the fund of the eye, which point remains invariably the same, whether the distance be longer or shorter" (Berkeley, 1709, para. 2). Berkeley here offers an argument explaining why the third dimension of depth or distance cannot be immediately seen. If we refer to Sextus Empiricus' concept of an evident object, Price and Berkeley disagree about whether depth is evident. One of them must be mistaken. But how can one be mistaken about that which one is certain of? To say that one is certain, that one assents to a proposition that is indubitable, is to exclude the very possibility of mistake.

Perhaps Price might be willing to retreat and assert only that even if he is mistaken that there is a three-dimensional object of which he is aware, nevertheless there is, without doubt, something red of which he is aware. But why is that beyond doubt? As we have seen, the proposition that something looks red fails to imply that something is red. So even if he cannot be mistaken about how something looks, he is not entitled to infer the existence of a sense datum from that alone.

In fact, there is a reason for doubting the existence of sense data as items in addition to bodies that exemplify sensible qualities. The reason is that sense data simply fail to fit into our picture of the world. Where are they located? Are there non-physical patches of red existing somewhere in space? Or in the brain? Or in the mind? None of these alternatives is plausible at all. Of course, there are arguments in support of sense data. A friend of sense data could insist that they should be simply added to our world; a place could be found for them. Or instead, he might try, as many philosophers, Berkeley and Russell being outstanding examples, have tried, to construct a different picture of the world in which sense data could find a home.

I do not wish to consider these possibilities any further other than to point out that once the issue of sense data does not simply remain a question of reporting what we are directly aware of but turns into a matter of argument, of the pros and cons of different theories and interminable discussion about them, then Price's argument goes by the board. There is no reason to suppose that there is such an evident terminus to the process of doubt about what is seen. One never knows what one will find reason to doubt. So there is no reason on the basis of Price's argument to prefer the sense datum interpretation of the nature of the appearances. One wonders whether we should not also suspect the applicability of Sextus' notion of the evident, of the very idea of the indubitable. But more of that later.

The Great Deception of Sense

Although philosophers have worried about the ways in which sense experience could mislead us with respect to the perceptual judgments it triggers, considerations of the sort that persuaded Galileo of the ways in which the senses could be systematically misleading led Thomas Hobbes (1588–1679) to say: "Whatsoever accidents or qualities our senses make us think there be in the world, they are not there, but are seemings and apparitions only. The things that really are in the world without us, are those motions by which the seemings are caused. And this is the great deception of sense" (Hobbes, 1650, p. 7). Hobbes here distinguishes between the "seemings and apparitions" which cause us to believe in the objectivity of the secondary qualities, and "things that really are in the world without us" that cause these appearances. "The great deception of sense" consists first in the fact that the qualities presented via the appearances do not correspond to any qualities of the "things that are really there in the world," for the only qualities present in these things are the motions of bodies and whatever primary qualities are implied by the fact of motion. Second, it consists in the fact that beliefs ascribing secondary qualities to objects are one and all false; that is, the qualities "are not there."

Projection

How are the appearances able to fool our faculty of judgment in such a pervasive and systematic way? On Galileo's view, the conception that people have of the secondary qualities "is very remote from the truth." How is it possible that our sensory apparatus, created (by nature or God) for the purpose of guiding our conduct amidst "the things that really are in the world without us," could be so prone to error? Let us consider an example. The cover of the book I am now looking at appears red all over and I judge, without doubt or hesitation, that it is red. Why am I so sure of its color? Because not only is the red color presented to me in the appearances, it is presented as completely overlaying the facing surface of the cover. Color is not presented as disjoined from colored bodies; what are presented are bodies as colored. Thus when I report that the book is red, I am simply reporting what I think I see.

But, according to Hobbes and Galileo, the color does not in fact overlay the cover. Colors, for Galileo, reside only in consciousness; for Hobbes "they are not there." Its overlaying the cover is a mere appearance. But the qualities presented in the mere appearances seem to be located where they are not. I shall use the term *projection* for the mind's activity of bringing it about that the secondary qualities appear to have a location where they are not. Projection explains why the senses are systematically unreliable with respect to the secondary qualities.

Hobbes attempted to explain how projection occurs.

> The cause of sense is the external body, or object, which presseth the organ proper to each sense, either immediately, as in the taste and touch, or mediately, as in seeing, hearing, and smelling; which pressure, by the mediation of nerves and other strings and membranes of the body, continued inwards to the brain and heart, causeth there a resistance, or counterpressure, or endeavour of the heart to deliver itself; which endeavour, because *outward*, seemeth to be some matter without. (Hobbes, 1641, chapter 1, para. 4)

The outward endeavor of the heart explains the outward appearance of the secondary qualities. This is just guesswork on Hobbes' part, and we still do not know anything about the mechanism that underlies projection.

Hume, on the contrary, was averse to speculating about the physical mechanisms that produce various mental tendencies; he was content simply to identify the mental propensity itself: "The mind has a great propensity to spread itself on external objects, and to conjoin with them any internal impressions, which they occasion, and which always make their appearance at the same time that these objects discover themselves to the senses" (Hume, 1739, p. 167). For Hume, projection is the mind's tendency to "spread itself on external objects," to "conjoin with them any internal impressions." Something mental is projected upon something physical. The subjective is objectified. Thus, secondary qualities are merely psychic additions that are produced by the mind by a mechanism unknown to us.

Although the process of projection seems quite mysterious, before we conclude as to its impossibility, we should recall to mind one familiar instance of it. Consider the case of a visual after-image. After gazing for a few seconds at a bright light, I am able to see an after-image of a different color projected against the wall. The image seems to be on or near the surface of the wall, but, in reality, it is not there. A quality is caused to appear at a location at which it does not actually exist. So projection does occur, although we still await an account of it.

In Hume's formulation, the theory of projection belongs to the subjective turn in philosophy brought about by Galileo's reflections on secondary qualities. Internal impressions are "spread" upon external objects. The theory of psychic additions was not without its critics. Here is Whitehead's sardonic characterization:

> Thus nature gets credit which should in truth be reserved for ourselves: the rose for its scent; the nightingale for his song; and the sun for his radi-

ance. The poets are entirely mistaken. They should address their lyrics to themselves, and should turn them into odes of self-congratulation on the excellency of the human mind. Nature is a dull affair, soundless, scentless, colourless: merely the hurrying of material, endlessly, meaninglessly. (Whitehead, 1925, p. 54)

Not only does the theory of psychic additions conflict with common sense, it disenchants nature itself. While philosophers might agree with it, Wordsworth and the other romantic poets would heartily dislike it.

The Human Epistemic Condition: The Original Understanding

We have yet to encounter any good reasons why we should take the subjective turn along with Galileo, Hobbes, and Locke. Their picture complicates the rather simple account embedded in our naive or original understanding of the human epistemic condition that we have acquired without the benefit of philosophical argument or scientific instruction. According to the original understanding, it is just not true that the secondary qualities "reside only in consciousness." On the contrary, they are exemplified by perceptible "things that are in the world without us," and their causal connections to other things provide us with access to those things as well. Our sensory consciousness is the way in which we obtain a direct access to nature and to nature's qualitative features, as well as to its quantitative aspects.

Even if we should agree with Galileo that the secondary qualities are not "necessary accompaniments" of corporeal substances, even if they are mere "accidents" of bodies as Hobbes understood them, it does not follow that they "reside only in consciousness." To say that the yellow color of this lemon is an accidental feature of it merely implies that this lemon might not have been yellow. But that implication is compatible with the lemon's actually being yellow.

Moreover, according to our original understanding, such accidents are closely allied to the primary qualities. The color of the book is integrated into its surface and is inseparable from its shape. As Berkeley emphasized, you cannot separate the primary from the secondary qualities.

But I desire anyone to reflect and try, whether he can by any abstraction of thought, conceive the extension and motion of a body, without all other sensible qualities. For my own part, I see evidently that it is not in my power to frame an idea of a body extended and moved, but I must withal give it some colour or other sensible quality. . . . In short, extension, figure, and motion, abstracted from all other qualities, are inconceivable. (Berkeley, 1710, para. 10)

In effect, Berkeley was simply rejecting as incompatible with principles evident to us the claim that secondary qualities are mere accidents. Once you have a corporeal substance, you must have both primary and secondary qualities.

The Human Epistemic Condition: The Scientifically Instructed Understanding

In his first epistemological works, Berkeley undertook to defend what he took to be our original understanding against the new understanding of nature that had been developed earlier under the influence of the revival of atomism and the development of a mechanical conception of nature. According to this new understanding, the sensory organs of the human body are continuously bombarded by streams of imperceptible particles that produce changes within the brains and nervous systems of sentient creatures. Sense awareness of "the things that really are in the world without us" is the mental effect of these underlying physical events. The atoms themselves possess only primary qualities; the secondary qualities are psychic additions that "reside only in consciousness." The human mind is endowed with the ability to interpret inner sense experience as signs of external bodies and events.

Locke formulated this picture in the language of ideas: "For since the Things, the Mind contemplates, are none of them, besides it self, present to the Understanding, 'tis necessary that something else, as a Sign or Representation of the thing it considers, should be present to it: And these are *Ideas*" (Locke, 1689, Book Four, chapter xxi, para. 4). According to Locke's argument, knowledge of the external world is possible only by means of the awareness or contemplation of items that are "present to the understanding." But corporeal objects are external and hence not present to the understanding. Therefore, they can be known only on the basis of the signs or mental representations (ideas) that are present to the understanding.

Locke thought it obvious that ideas are and bodies are not present to understanding. The underlying argument, I think, is that natural philosophy or natural science has shown that knowledge of nature is possible only if nature itself, through its impact upon the sense organs, leaves its traces upon the human mind. These traces (or ideas, in Locke's terms) are directly accessible to the human mind just because they "reside in consciousness." Physical nature is only accessible by means of interpretations of these traces or mental representations. The fact that these traces are present to the understanding explains the fact that we have unmediated access to them.

The picture becomes confusing because projection makes it difficult to distinguish between features that are external and those that are present to the understanding. Price's argument above appeals to the method of doubt to sort them out and to identify those that are present. Arguments of that sort, stemming ultimately from the philosophy of Descartes, attempt to connect that to which we have direct access with that which is indubitable. Such a connection is not inevitable provided we have some other way of identifying what is present to mind. It would be better for this philosophical picture if there were some other account because we have already found that appealing to the indubitable is problematic.

Locke would not have been impressed with Berkeley's argument for the inseparability of the primary and secondary qualities. That one cannot form a visual image of an extended body without endowing it in imagination with some color or other simply speaks of the limitations of the imagination, and this does not constrain the modes of existence of external objects. The mind does not dictate to nature, so the fact that something is unimaginable to us imposes no limits upon the possibilities of connection and disconnection within nature itself.[1]

Although our conception of nature and of the minute particles of which perceptible bodies are composed has changed significantly since the influential reflections of these seventeenth-century thinkers, Locke's *representative theory of knowledge* remains as an alternative to the picture embedded in the original understanding. Science informs us of the basic features of matter, the primary qualities, and they are used to explain the nature of the causal chain that ultimately produces the traces or mental representations that the mind uses to infer the very explanations of their origin. For the friends of mental representations, the original understanding fails to provide a deep grasp of how knowledge of nature is possible. It offers only the most superficial account of how I am able to see an object's color – I simply open my eyes and look at it – that is all it has to say. The scientifically instructed understanding, on the other hand, introduces entities postulated by a well confirmed scientific theory to go on from there. It provides a narrative whose main characters are postulated entities acting in accordance with verifiable

---

1   For example, our visual imagination endows all imagined objects with color; yet there is not the slightest reason to think that sub-atomic particles are colored.

laws. Even if we are still unsure how the transition from the physical to the mental comes about, the occurrence of mental representations (ideas, appearances) plays an indispensable part in the story. We do not have to know how to bridge the gap between the body and the mind in order to know that events on both sides of the gap are necessary to make knowledge possible.

The Problem of Color

The subjective turn says that secondary qualities reside only in consciousness. We have seen that the sense datum interpretation of this claim is not at all promising. The best way of understanding it is to say simply and without bringing sense data into the picture that although things appear to exemplify secondary qualities, such appearances are deceptive. There are two ways of understanding the deception. Using color as the example, we can interpret it as meaning that we have good reason to doubt the reliability of our color perceptions: although the lemon looks yellow, that is not enough for me to be justified in thinking it is yellow, and I have no further reason to believe in the objectivity of color. Call this type of local skepticism *color skepticism*. A stronger claim is that we have reason to think that nothing has color, neither physical things nor mental things. Call this *color nihilism*.[2] One who sticks to the common sense view that physical things have color is a *color realist*.

My rejection of the sense datum approach eliminates from consideration the idea that there are colored mental things. The surviving question concerns the colors of bodies. There are two powerful reasons that we can find in the philosophical tradition in favor of color nihilism: one is a causal argument and the other is an evolutionary argument. Let us consider these in detail.

The causal argument

In order to explain in a scientifically instructed way why things look to have the colors we impute to them, we make reference to various observed and

---

2   Color nihilism should not be confused with the view that there are no colors. One who believes in the existence of unexemplified properties would say that colors could still exist even if nothing were colored. Call this view *color Platonism*. The argument for color Platonism is founded on the fact that terms for unexemplified properties have meaning and that this could only be understood if the properties meant exist. Color Platonism plays no role in the discussion that follows.

unobserved entities, such as physical objects, their microstates that account for the fact that they reflect or emit certain light waves and absorb others, the light waves themselves (or whatever other entities such as quanta that replace light waves as physical theory evolves), and events in the sense organs and nervous system. The explanatory theories used for this purpose incorporate a substantial commitment to a variety of unobservable entities whose existence has been confirmed by the success of these theories in both pure and applied science.

Nowhere in the list of the causes of the appearances of color do the names of colors themselves occur. Colors drop out of the explanatory picture; they play no role among the causes of appearances. All the causal work is exerted by imperceptible physical properties and events. Color itself is causally inert. Thus, the statement that lemons are yellow does not appear within the body of statements used to explain why lemons look yellow. In this respect, colors differ from shapes. One would have to refer to the shape of the facing surface of a lemon to account for the fact that it looks to have this shape from this angle of vision.

According to the causal argument, since color has no explanatory role to play, we have no good reason for believing in the existence of colored objects, strange as that may seem. The hypothesis that there are colored objects could be dropped from our system of belief, and it would make no difference whatever to our scientifically instructed understanding of phenomena. Things would still appear to have colors, and that is what is important to us.

We must keep in mind that the appearance of a quality does not entail that there are any physical instances of it. Since colors are inert, there is no causal argument in support of there being any physical instances. So it looks as if we have reason to doubt the reality of colored objects. Therefore, color skepticism is justified.

The argument makes use of *Ockham's razor*, which says, in Peirce's words, that "a hypothesis should be stripped of every feature which is in no wise called for to furnish an explanation of observed facts." (Peirce, 1997, p. 115) Since colors play no role in any explanation of observed facts, our system of beliefs should be stripped of any constituent which implies that there are colored objects. There is a stronger principle that I shall call *Ockham's guillotine*, according to which we are justified in disbelieving in the existence of any entities that play no such explanatory role. Relative to this principle, color nihilism is justified. Now for the evolutionary argument.

The evolutionary argument

There is evidence that different species of animals see different colors. There are differences among species in the ability to discriminate objects of different colors. The retinas of different species respond differently to light stimuli.[3] So let us pretend that, whereas lemons look yellow to us, and, therefore, we think they are yellow, they look green to tigers, who, consequently, have different thoughts about the matter. Who is right? Humans or tigers? Or perhaps neither? Both cannot be right because nothing can be both green and yellow in the same respect and at the same time.

Perhaps there is something wrong with the question. From an evolutionary perspective, it is reasonable to suppose that animal color perception evolved in the way it did because of its utility in the struggle for existence. Color vision helps animals to search for objects that are useful and to avoid those that do harm. Species differences in color vision evolved because different objects possess different utilities to different animals. The utilities are founded upon those features of objects that cause events that matter to the animals involved. These features – their nutritional properties, for example – are based upon the primary qualities. So it looks as if the ability to discriminate colors – that is, the capacity to have color experiences – is a genetically based capacity for response to primary qualities rather than a capacity for an objective grasp of secondary qualities. This capacity for response is the capacity of the nervous system to obtain information about the environment by transforming physical stimuli into a form (sensory appearances) that the animal is able to assimilate.

As far as the animal knows, it is its sensory experience that enables it to detect the useful features of bodies. It knows nothing of the underlying neural processes that transform information into a useful form. It may have no clear idea of the features of objects that make them useful to it. For example, why certain objects have nutritional value are things that most humans and no tigers know anything about. As Hume was found of saying, nature takes no chances. Animals that fail to be programmed to take advantage of the cues that their experiences provide about the dangers that lurk in their surroundings will not survive.

---

3   That different animal species have different forms of sense experience is not a new idea, or a product of modern biology. Sextus Empiricus, for example, points out that "the same impressions are not produced by the same objects owing to the differences in animals" (Sextus Empiricus, 1955, I, 40).

In brief, the evolutionary argument tells a story that makes it plausible to suppose that what matter in the lives of animals are the appearances of colors, not the colors themselves. It is the appearances that do all the work in guiding behavior. Colors themselves drop out of the picture. Despite the fact that Berkeley ruminated on these issues 150 years before Darwin, he got it right:

> Can it be imagined that their sight [the sight of very small animals] hath not the same use in preserving their bodies from injuries, which appears in that of all other animals? . . . Is it not therefore highly probable, these animals in whose eyes we discern a very different texture from that of ours, and whose bodies abound with different humours, do not see the same colours in every object that we do? From all which, should it not seem to follow, that all colours are equally apparent, and that none of those which we perceive are really inherent in any outward object? (Berkeley, 1713, pp. 175–6)

By causing colors to appear to be inherent in outward objects, projection allows color vision to be advantageous. Even though the beliefs that projection triggers, such as that this lemon is yellow and that tomato is red, are, strictly speaking, false, they are useful falsehoods that we cannot help believing are true. The senses are unreliable as far as the secondary qualities are concerned, but their deficiencies in this respect do not matter because, for those species that have managed to survive, they provide information about useful features of bodies. Ockham's guillotine once again leads to color nihilism.[4]

The Concept of Color

Before we turn to the arguments on behalf of the color realism of common sense, it would be useful to gain some clarity about what it is that is the subject of dispute. Confusion about our concept of color only muddies the waters. For example, some color realists have argued for the existence of colored objects on the grounds that bodies possess microstates that determine which light they reflect and absorb, and it is these states that constitute the reality of color. A color nihilist will reject this argument because microstates are

---

4   One might object that the evolutionary argument applies to primary as well as secondary qualities. Not so, since we cannot explain the utilities of objects without bringing in the primary qualities.

not observable features of objects, whereas colors are. In this case, the argument concerns not the existence of bodies or their microstates but how we should interpret our understanding of the concept of color or of the meaning of the word "color."

In reflecting upon the meanings of color terms as we have learned them in our earliest years prior to any acquaintance with scientific and philosophical thought, I find that our concept of color has the following content. First, colors are directly observable features of bodies *par excellence*. We can identify the colors of bodies just by looking at them; nothing more is required. Second, colors are objective features; the objects that appear to exemplify them would exemplify them even if no one was around to see them. In this respect, colors are on a par with the primary qualities, such as shape. Third, colors are occurrent or non-dispositional features of objects. Unlike, say, fragility or solubility, colors are not merely powers or potentialities of objects to react in certain ways under certain conditions, although, like all occurrent qualities, colors serve as the basis for certain powers. Fourth, colors are intrinsic, non-relational qualities of bodies. When we ascribe a color to a body, we do not imply that that body has any relation to anything else.

The Evidence of the Senses

Recall Peirce's formulation of Ockham's razor in which he said: "A hypothesis should be stripped of every feature which is in no wise called for to furnish an explanation of observed facts." Because colors furnish no explanations of observed facts, they should be expunged from our ontology, says the color nihilist. The realist replies, quite plausibly, that colored objects are among the observed facts, so that the razor provides no argument against realism. Consider, for example, Michael Dummett's appeal to the evidence of the senses:

> Any normally sighted person . . . can see at a glance that there are plenty of coloured material objects: the question is not whether the surfaces of objects have colour, but in what their having any given colour consists. . . . Modern physics does undoubtedly offer many affronts to common sense: but it does not appear that the denial that objects are coloured is one of them. (Dummett, 1996, pp. 389–90)

By saying that one "can see at a glance that there are plenty of colored material objects," by thus appealing to the evidence of the senses, Dummett appears to agree that our concept of color is a concept of an observable feature. The initial reply of the skeptic and nihilist to Dummett's dismissal of their view is that the evidence of the senses is not infallible, that our senses are capable of deceiving us, so that appeal to the senses on a contentious issue is not the last word. In our discussion of visual images, we also saw that theoretical and philosophical considerations are capable of outweighing the evidence of the senses. There is no room in any plausible ontology for the existence of colored visual images; they are mere appearances; in Galileo's words, they reside only in consciousness. So the fact that I am convinced that I see a yellow patch on the wall in front of me fails to establish that there is a yellow patch on the wall in front of me.

We are in a position, now, to understand that the very notion of an observed fact that Peirce deploys in his formulation of the razor is a contentious concept. The color nihilist concedes that things appear to be colored, so colors are observable in that sense; he also agrees that our concept of a colored object is the concept of an observable object. But he refuses to agree that there are colored objects; whether there are any such things is the point at issue, so he denies that the existence of colored objects is an observed fact. Arguments convince him that colors do no causal work and thus reside only in consciousness, so his notion of an observed fact allows theoretical considerations to outweigh the evidence of the senses.

Perspectival Relative Qualities

Dummett offers another consideration in favor of color realism by pointing out that the fact that some feature of objects is described in relational terms does not impugn its reality.

> The contrast is now not between the qualities that things appear to have and those different qualities that they really have: it is between a method of characterizing those qualities that they are agreed to have in terms of our own perceptual capacities and one that is independent of our modes of perception; it is therefore not a matter of discovering that they lack certain qualities that we wrongly suppose them to have. The attempt to say what things are like in themselves is an attempt to find a means of characterizing them that is independent, not only of the particular position of an individual observer, but also, more generally, of the situation of human beings, located on the surface of a certain planet at a particular stage in its history, being of a certain size, and having a particular range of sensory faculties. The making of such an attempt in no way involves us in thinking that a

description that is not independent of these things, but given in terms relative to or explained by reference to our own position and observational capacities is *incorrect* in any way: only that it does not accomplish what is achieved by a description that is independent of these contingent facts. (Dummett, 1996, pp. 388–9)

According to Dummett, when I say that lemons are yellow, I am correctly describing an objective or independent feature of lemons but using a description that makes reference to the human perceptual perspective. Thus, ascribing colors to bodies differs from ascribing, say, a particular chemical constitution to them, not because the colors are any the less independent than the chemical constitution but because the description of the colors alludes to the sensory capacity of the human constitution.

On Dummett's view, our observer-relative descriptions are not to be labeled as false just because they are observer-relative. If I say that a joke is funny, what I say may be true of the joke even though the concept that I use to characterize it has reference to my reaction to it (Dummett, 1996, p. 387). To say that something is funny is not to make a mistake. Similarly, to say that lemons are yellow is not to make a mistake:

Thus the distinction between "how things are in themselves" and "how they appear to us" bifurcates into two quite different, though related, distinctions: that between what is true of the world and what only appears to be, but is not actually true of it; and that between what may be called an absolute and what may be called a relative form of description. A description in relative terms may, in itself, be perfectly correct. . . . One of the things that a scientific theory aims to do is to attain an accurate description of things as they are in themselves, or as they really are, in this sense – that is, a description in absolute terms; and such a description need not invalidate, in the sense of showing to be incorrect, the form of description in relative terms that we employ in everyday life. (Dummett, 196, p. 389)

Our color descriptions pick out colors in relative rather than absolute terms. So our color descriptions are correct relative to the human perceptual perspective.

Goodbye Color; Hello Color*

Dummett's efforts to save our common sense judgments come at a significant cost, for his arguments are inconsistent with every one of the features of our common sense or naive concept of color that I have mentioned. Thus, on his view, colors are not intrinsic features because of the implicit reference to the human perspective. For the same reason, they are not objective features; in a world bereft of sentient creatures there would be no basis for color descriptions.

Moreover, Dummett is also compelled to deny that colors are non-dispositional occurrent qualities. The relativity of color to the human perspective suggests that the correct analysis of, say, "Lemons are yellow" is given by "Lemons appear yellow to most human observers under normal conditions of observation." Accordingly, Dummett asserts that "anyone accustomed to the use of observational predicates knows at least implicitly, and will recognize on reflection, that they stand for essentially dispositional properties, for a propensity to present a range of appearances under a variety of conditions" (Dummett, 1996, p. 398). But the claim that observational predicates are dispositional is paradoxical. On a dispositional view, to determine that lemons are yellow involves discovering that lemons possess a certain propensity, and this can be determined only by observing lemons in a variety of situations, finding out how they appear, and inferring that they are likely to continue to appear that way in the future. But we tend to contrast predicates that are observational from those whose application is inferential on the grounds that the applicability of an observational predicate can be determined by just looking, without any gathering of evidence or inductive extrapolation. Occasionally, when conditions are below par for the observational predicate in question, one must do more than just look, and sometimes an inference precedes judgment. But in the usual case, observable qualities are determined on the basis of how the object appears in a particular instance, something not possible in the case of dispositions.

The dispositional analysis also suffers from circularity. How else can we characterize the appearances of lemons except by saying that they appear yellow? Yet it was yellow as applied to bodies that the analysis was supposed to explain in the first place. Of course, those who favor the dispositional analysis might reply that "yellow" is ambiguous: when applied to physical objects it represents a disposition and when used to describe the appearances it represents an occurrent quality. But this ambiguity is not at all present in our naive concept of color. When I think that the lemon looks yellow, I may wonder whether it actually has the very color that it looks to have. What I am wondering about is whether there is an identity between the color it looks to have and the color it has. "Yellow" means the same whether applied to objects or appearances; there is no semantic duality in the concept as this effort to avoid circularity implies.

Moreover, the dispositional analysis fails to respect our common sense explanations of the appearances. Suppose that I look at a lemon in different lights and it presents a variety of appearances to me. Under the naive concept, I would explain these appearances by reference to the fact that the lemon is yellow and yellow objects tend to look in these ways under these conditions. That is, I would explain the propensity to appear in these ways by reference to the object's color, whereas on the dispositional analysis the propensity just is the object's color. Of course, the color nihilist would also reject the common sense form of explanation, but he, at least, is not committed to common sense so there is no incoherence in his criticism of it.

Dummett's defense of common sense realism leads him deny by implication at least the four essential features of colors that belong to the common sense view. The truth of our color predications can only be defended by modifying our concept, by replacing it with a different concept. But in that case, the concept of color has been replaced with a different though related concept, call it color*. And "yellow" is replaced by "yellow*." In fact it is not even correct to say that Dummett shows that "Lemons are yellow" is true; that judgment involves our naive concept of color and is simply false. What turns out to be true is the entirely different though verbally similar judgment "Lemons are yellow*."

Saving the Appearances

Because color nihilism is difficult if not impossible to believe, philosophers have adopted various positions intended to avoid nihilism, while simultaneously respecting the scientific facts. The dispositional account that goes back to Locke is one of them, but we have seen that it fails to respect our naive concept of color, which, after all, is the concept that defines the debate.

Another approach is to adopt an identity thesis. Most of those engaged in the philosophical debate about color are not challenging established scientific facts but are arguing about their implications; the identity approach says that color is to be identified with one among the variety of scientific facts whose existence is not in question, such as the microstates of bodies or waves of light or other relevant entities that are indispensable components of our explanations of why things appear to have the colors they do. The identity approach rejects the causal argument's claim that colors are causally inert and insists that references to colors do occur in explanations of why things look the way they do.

Berkeley discovered the main difficulty with the identity approach. Colors are "sensible qualities"; that is what "all mankind" thinks. Therefore, they cannot be identified with the "invisible . . . [qualities] of the philosophers" (Berkeley, 1713, p. 177). Nothing can be both observable and unobservable in the same respect, so the identification of colors with microstates or light waves or quanta or any other theoretical entities that physical theory may subsequently find it convenient to postulate for explanatory purposes must be mistaken. When we speak of colors, what we mean are certain easily observable visible qualities; identifying these with certain unobservable entities postulated in physical theory is merely changing the subject; that is, it brings into play a different concept, color*. Now for some purposes it may be perfectly legitimate to use the concept of color* rather than color, or even to replace color with color*, but the question about color to which realism and nihilism are answers cannot be answered by shifting the concept; nor does such a shift preserve the truth of statements formulated in terms of the naive concept.

Efforts have been made, however, to show that the identity approach does respect our naive concept. These appeal to the existence of theoretical identifications within science. We accept that water is a bunch of H_2O molecules even though water is something observable, so, it is argued, there should be no bar to saying that colors are microstates of bodies. However, the analogy with water is defective because water is not a quality as color is, but a substance or stuff. There is no conceptual barrier to thinking of a stuff as composed of entities that are too small to see. Thus, although this puddle of water is composed of molecules that are invisible to the naked eye when taken individually or in small numbers, the puddle itself is easily observed. So we can say that water is observable relative to one set of descriptions and unobservable relative to another. But colors are qualities, not stuffs. If we speak of the composition of colors at all, we have in mind other colors whose combinations produce some particular color, as the combination of the colors of the spectrum produce white. If we look at a white object, we can say that its color is composed of other colors, but in that case, it makes no sense to say that the items of which it is composed are too small to see. The composition of colors is quite unlike the composition of material stuffs and does not increase the plausibility of efforts to identify colors with unobservable features of bodies.

One type of identity approach takes the subjective turn and identifies colors with features of mental entities. Although, as we have seen, the subjective turn is not promising as far as colors are concerned, even if argument showed that colors could be truthfully predicated of mental entities, that would not save the truth of our common sense judgments that predicate colors of bodies. The subjective turn concedes the correctness of nihilism as far as bodies are concerned: no bodies are colored.

Science and Common Sense

Would the adoption of color nihilism imply some fundamental clash between science and common sense? There can be local conflicts, as Dummett has pointed out:

> Now, without doubt we may properly speak of views as forming, at a particular period and within a particular culture, a part of common sense. A common sense view is a conception on which most of those who belong to that culture at that time habitually rely in their everyday thinking. It is not required that they should actually hold it to be correct – they, or some of them, may know, or think otherwise: what matters is that their ordinary thinking proceeds *as if* it were correct. . . . Modern physical theory offers many affronts to common sense. It has often been remarked that common sense always lags behind scientific theory. (Dummett, 1996, pp. 390–1)

In some places I have spoken of common sense as if it consisted of those of our beliefs that preceded scientific and philosophical reflection. We might entitle that notion uninstructed common sense. Dummett's notion is slightly different since it allows the possibility that common sense is capable of incorporating the results of instruction by scientific and philosophical thought. Call this instructed common sense. "Perhaps the most striking example of this is the way in which our thought is permeated by the knowledge of the molecular structure of matter" (Dummett, 1996, p. 391).

According to Dummett, there is no inherent conflict between common sense and science. There can be local and temporary conflicts, and these are usually but not always resolved in favor of science. Sometimes common sense puts up a resistance; for example, although we have incorporated the notion of a Freudian slip into our everyday thinking, we have resisted incorporating Freud's notion of penis envy. Occasionally common sense turns out to be correct in resisting what science offers, for science itself is a fragmented series of enterprises of different epistemic worths and includes a fair amount of sheer speculation, some of which is later repudiated by scientists themselves.

Uninstructed common sense often receives instruction from other directions, such as religion. There were times when most people believed in God, so that belief in God deserved to be called a matter of common sense. Most people believed on the basis of observation that the sun revolves about the earth, and this was supported by biblical passages. These examples illustrate the point that conflicts between science and common sense sometimes occur when common sense incorporates instruction from non-scientific sources.

Avoiding Inconsistency

Our beliefs are involuntary in the sense that they are not directly subject to the will. I cannot, by sheer willing, make myself believe that $2 + 3 = 8$. However, if I find that the reasons I have in favor of believing a certain proposition are definitely and clearly outweighed by the reasons against, I automatically surrender my belief. Though I have reason to think that the sun revolves about the earth, I do not believe it because the weight of the astronomical evidence does not favor it.

I am convinced that the reasons I have given in favor of color nihilism outweigh the arguments for color realism. But, when I am searching in the market for a ripe tomato, I have no doubt that the tomato I purchase is red. It appears then that my system of beliefs contains a contradiction, one that is produced by my sympathy for color nihilism. In general, our beliefs about observable qualities, when formed under optimal conditions in the affairs of everyday life, are insensitive to countervailing abstract arguments. Although I think that color nihilism has the better of the argument, beliefs about colors are an exception to the rule that beliefs supported by weaker arguments give way to those supported by better arguments.

But this rule applies to practical contexts, so it does not prevent me from accepting color nihilism in my philosophical thinking. Here, then, is the inconsistency in my beliefs: I believe both that this tomato is red and that it isn't. One might think that the simplest and easiest way out is to jettison nihilism entirely and to yield to the irresistible force of common sense. And when I go to the market, that is exactly what I do. But, nevertheless, I cannot bring myself to believe in the correctness of my color judgments when I return to my study and take up philosophy again. I find myself in the same position with respect to color as did Hume with regard to the arguments for global skepticism.

A system of beliefs may be said to be inconsistent when a person assents to a proposition while, at the same time, being willing to assent to another proposition that implies the negation of the first. This reference to time is crucial, for if I believe P and later believe not-P, there is not necessarily any contradiction. I may have changed my mind. Even if I should still later resume my belief in P, there is no inconsistency provided that, at the time, I am not willing to assent to not-P. So as I move from the market to the study and back and forward again and again, I may avoid contradicting myself by being careful to avoid mixing up the thoughts solicited by practical life with the abstract though weighty pressures of philosophical argument. Thus I do not have to jettison color nihilism to avoid contradiction.

There is, however, this difficulty. Here I am in the market holding up a ripe tomato and saying to myself: "What a nice red one." At this very moment, I think of my philosophical arguments and the thought slips into my mind: "It is not really red." While I have asserted not-P, I have also been willing to assent to P. Here is an actual inconsistency in belief. My way out is to reflect upon my predicament. I take note of my inconsistent beliefs and realize that the results of my philosophical reflections have erupted into the stream of consciousness of everyday life. I accept the inevitability of an occasional clash between commonsensical and philosophical beliefs. But now I adopt a new position that stands above the conflict, recognizes its inevitability, and strongly affirms color nihilism while rejecting as false the color beliefs of the everyday self. In this way, I am able to find a consistent resting-place, at least for the moment.

3

Justification, Truth, and Realism

The Naive and the Philosophical Systems

The discussion of "the great deception of sense" in chapter 2 revealed a fundamental instability in human thought about the physical world. On the one hand, there is our naive system of belief, according to which the evidence of the senses reveals objects exemplifying both primary and secondary qualities. But, on the other hand, philosophical thought that applies various epistemic maxims, such as Ockham's razor and Ockham's guillotine, to our scientific knowledge of nature casts doubt upon the objectivity of the secondary qualities. We can never totally cast the naive system away, but the philosophical arguments against it are weighty and defensible and are capable of overpowering it in our philosophical moments. We move back and forth between the naive and the philosophical system. This instability itself can be a source of skeptical doubts about our ability to settle the question of the status of the qualitative aspects of nature.

Both the naive and the philosophical system appeal to the evidence of the senses. For the naive system, the senses directly testify to the objectivity of the secondary qualities. For the philosophical system, the senses provide evidence for the scientific theories about color that function as premises of arguments that overthrow the naive system. The naive system takes the beliefs that are directly and immediately triggered by the evidence of the senses for granted. The philosophical system, on the other hand, takes account of all empirically justified beliefs in order to use some of them to convict others of falsehood. According to the philosophical system, theories that the senses justify are employed to overthrow some beliefs that the senses justify. When we are thinking philosophically, we must examine our empirically justified beliefs not one by one but holistically, all things considered. My senses tell me directly that lemons are yellow, but when I bring into play everything that my senses justify me in believing, I can no longer believe that any color predication about anything is justified.

Both systems take for granted the truth of realism, according to which the senses reveal a world that exists independently of the senses and of thought. The philosophical system, however, refines our conception of nature by insisting that certain features immanent in sense experience are psychic additions that lack objective standing. According to the arguments for color nihilism, we can make use of our empirically justified knowledge to subtract the "noise" introduced by mental processing – the secondary qualities or, at least, some of them – from the intrinsic characteristics of nature. Contrary to Kant's transcendental idealism, our interpretation of nature is not restricted to the appearances because, by taking thought, we are able to break through the useful distortions produced by our sensory apparatus to the true character of things as they are in themselves.

Corresponding to the two systems are two versions of empirical knowledge. Naive empiricism accepts without question the basic accuracy of the representations of the senses. Philosophical empiricism, adopting a holistic approach instructed by scientific theory and philosophical argument, denies that the mind is a helpless prisoner of the data of sense and claims to be able to make use of theory to evaluate their accuracy and reliability.

Justification and Truth

Both systems, then, rely upon the senses, although the philosophical system is able to develop the basis of a thoroughgoing critique of the evidence of the senses. Both agree that the data of the senses contribute to justifying our beliefs about nature. To say that a belief is justified is not to say that it is true. A person uninstructed by philosophy and science may be perfectly justified in believing that lemons are yellow because that is how he and everyone else sees them. He is justified because he has reasons for his belief and no reasons against it. But the philosophical system says that his belief is not true. Justification is relative to the reasons that a person actually has for his beliefs. When those reasons offer greater support in favor of a belief than the reasons against it, he is justified even though the belief may not be true.

Although justification differs from truth, they are intimately related. For when a person asserts that he is justified in one of his beliefs, what he means is that he is justified in believing it to be *true*. Truth is what justification aims at. The reason is that truth is what belief aims at, for when I believe or accept a certain proposition, I believe or accept that it is *true*. Thus, although neither belief nor justification entail truth, they are internally and conceptually related to truth; it is inherent in the nature of inquiry that aims to fix belief by discovering reasons that justify belief to have truth as its aim.

Truth, Belief, and Propositions

What, then, does it mean to say that a certain belief is true? If we agree with realism that the aim of inquiry is to discover not just how things appear to us but how they are in themselves, then a belief is true if it tells how "the things that really are in the world without us" are in themselves.

But there is a certain imprecision in speaking of a belief as being true or false. When something is classified as a belief, it is being characterized as something that someone accepts as true or as likely to be true. It is always reasonable to ask of any belief: "Who believes it?" Moreover, when we say who it is that believes it, we are not confined to just one person; many can share the same belief. Therefore, we must distinguish the fact that this or that person has a certain belief from the thing he believes, the thing that can be shared by many. Let us call that thing a *proposition*. Thus all those who believe that lemons are yellow accept as true the proposition that lemons are yellow. That this person believes that lemons are yellow is a fact about him as well as about the proposition. That the proposition that lemons are yellow is true seems to be a fact about the proposition that has nothing to do with who believes it. Indeed, that it is believed by someone to be true seems inessential to its being true. According to our concept of truth, a proposition may be true even if no one believes it. This is implied by the fact that truth is something we can *discover*. When I discover something, I imply that it was so even before I discovered it; by discovering it, I do not cause a proposition to be true; rather I acknowledge it to be true.

Thus, when I ascribe truth to someone's belief, I am primarily saying that the proposition he believes is true, and I am secondarily asserting that, because the proposition is true, he is correct in believing it to be true. According to our ordinary conception of truth, for a person to believe something is for that person to enter into a relation to a proposition, a relation that we characterize as his believing it or accepting it or as his being of that opinion.

Propositions and Facts

According to realism, our inquiries aim at discovering truth in the sense of grasping the way the world is or the way that some aspect of some part of the world is constituted. On this view, it is quite natural to suppose that when a proposition is true, it corresponds to the facts. The phrase "it is true that P" is equivalent to "it is a fact that P." When we assert a proposition to be true, we represent the world as exemplifying some fact, and when our assertion is true, then that fact or state of affairs actually obtains. If it is true, it obtains whether or not we assert it as true. If it is false, it fails to obtain whether or not we assert it as false. From a realist perspective, it is natural to think of truth as a form of correspondence between our fact-stating representations, whether formulated in verbal or mental symbols, and existing facts or states of affairs. Our representations formulate various possible ways the world might be, and we encounter truth when the possibility represented actually obtains.

Philosophers have attempted to elucidate the nature of such a correspondence between thought and reality, and various disputes have broken out over the question of how our words and mental symbols relate to the world. I shall not here enter into the details of these disagreements, for they are not disagreements as to whether it is possible to formulate a plausible notion of correspondence but disagreements about which of the various plausible notions is correct. Philosophical disputes about the correct way of interpreting a concept do not of themselves cast doubt about its legitimacy provided it is coherent, has an entrenched and important role to play, and can be successfully defended against criticism.

One standard criticism of the correspondence theory of truth is that it unnecessarily bloats our ontology by positing the reality of facts or existing states of affairs as truth conditions of propositional representations. For example, consider these famous lines from the opening passages of Wittgenstein's *Tractatus*: "The world is the totality of facts, not of things. The world is determined by the facts, and by their being *all* the facts. . . . The world divides into facts" (Wittgenstein, 1921, 1.1, 1.11, 1.2). In criticism of this view, it has been claimed that facts are merely the shadows cast by verbal representations. Wittgenstein himself later echoed this criticism when he wrote: "We predicate of the thing what lies in the method of representing it" (Wittgenstein, 1953, para. 104). The ontology of facts illegitimately projects onto the world the patterns of our sentences.

There are ways of understanding correspondence that do not commit us to an ontology of facts (see Tarski, 1933). But, more to the point, if an ontology of facts is required as a factor in clarifying the notion of truth, then that itself is a good argument in its favor. Ockham's razor cannot be used against a claim of existence if that claim is part of the most plausible interpretation of an indispensable concept. The realist finds the idea that the patterns of our language are crafted to reflect the patterns of fact to be quite agreeable.

A second major criticism, one that stems from both the idealist and pragmatic traditions, is that facts are never given and that the best we can hope for is to formulate interpretations of experience justified in some way or other. Idealists then have been led to identify truth with coherence because the prime method of justification of a proposition is to find that it coheres with the body of our beliefs. Pragmatists identify truth with utility because finding an idea useful is the way we justify it. An idea is true if it works, says William James (1907, Lectures II and III).

As definitions of truth, neither idealism nor pragmatism are plausible. When we assert that a proposition is true, what we say is equivalent merely to asserting it. To cite Tarski's famous example, "Snow is white" is true if and only if snow is white. But neither of these definitions satisfy this formula. We cannot accept that "'Snow is white' coheres with our beliefs if and only if snow is white" because something may very well cohere with our beliefs and not be true. Similarly, a proposition may be useful to believe and not be true.

In the light of these difficulties, some critics of the correspondence account of truth have recommended that we replace the notion of truth with that of justification (see, for example, Dewey, 1938, pp. 9, 104, 138; Rorty, 1991, p. 120). Let us stop using the notion of truth because it causes too much trouble, and instead let us speak of an idea's being justified or possessing warranted assertability. Drop all talk of truth conditions and facts and confine ourselves to justification or assertability conditions.[1] After all, justification is the best we can ever have, and since it does not guarantee truth, the inference from justification to truth is invalid.

This criticism rests upon traditional skeptical arguments against the attainability of truth and will continue to be of interest in subsequent discussions. It is often presented as a way of avoiding skepticism but instead it seems to concede the soundness of its arguments. It is, to use a phrase of Hume's, a skeptical solution to the problems about human knowledge. In effect, it says that since realism is causing all the trouble and since realism presupposes or implies some version of the correspondence theory of truth, drop the theory as well as realism. This is a continuation and refinement of Kant's strategy for dealing with skepticism, his Copernican revolution in philosophy, which we discussed in chapter 1.

---

1 Kripke (1982, pp. 73–4) has argued that the later Wittgenstein adopted this view. According to Williams (1996, p. 21), a response like this "begins to look less like an all-out counter-attack than an exercise in damage control."

However, this strategy of the pragmatists is fundamentally in error because of the internal conceptual relation between justification and truth. We justify or warrant something *as being true*. Justifying a proposition is a way of trying to establish that it is true. So if we discard truth, we must discard justification as well. Of course, it is open to the pragmatists to say that they are introducing a different notion of justification, one not internally related to truth. Call it justification*. But if justification* makes use of all the standard and prevailing methods of justification as the pragmatists concede, then introducing justification* amounts just to an arbitrary relabeling of a familiar concept and fails to disconnect it from the notion of truth. Or if pragmatists simply stipulate that justification* is sundered from truth, then we can ask why we should believe the truth of a proposition that is justified*.

Since skepticism does not deny the internal relation of justification to truth, in casting doubt upon whether truth is knowable, it raises the question of whether justification is attainable. It is a more coherent response than pragmatism to the problem of knowledge. In our discussion of the great deception of sense, we have considered one example of local skepticism. Let us now turn to consider a version of the global variety.

4

Global Skepticism, Pyrrhonism, and the Criterion Argument

Pyrrho and Pyrrhonism

In this chapter, I shall discuss a central argument for global skepticism, the argument from the criterion. It appears in the thought of Pyrrho as recounted in Diogenes Laertius' *Lives of Eminent Philosophers*. Diogenes presents Pyrrho's skepticism as an extremely radical view, so radical that its coherence is threatened. For example, "he [Pyrrho] held that there is nothing really existent, but custom and convention govern human action; for no single thing is in itself any more this rather than that" (Diogenes Laertius, 1991, II, p. 475). On the surface, Pyrrho appears to contradict himself, since customs and conventions and actions are implied to be things really existent. But perhaps what he meant is that our beliefs about what exists are based upon custom and convention rather than the way the world is.

According to Diogenes, Pyrrho and his followers were well aware of the difficulty of formulating a coherent skeptical view:

> The Sceptics, then, were constantly engaged in overthrowing the dogmas of all schools, but enunciated none themselves; and though they would go so far as to bring forward and expound the dogmas of others, they themselves laid down nothing definitely, not even the laying down of nothing. So much so that they even refuted their laying down of nothing, saying for instance, "We determine nothing," since otherwise they would have been betrayed into determining. (Diogenes Laertius, 1991, II, p. 487)

The skeptics realized that if they refuted every assertion, then their own assertions would be refuted as well, so their position would have undermined itself. Their way out, apparently, was to make no assertions of their own, to determine nothing. But how then could they overturn the dogmas of the schools without asserting or presupposing that their own arguments against the schools are valid?

There are other passages, however, that appear to soften Pyrrho's scepticism enough so as to avoid outright incoherence. "For what we wish to ascertain is not whether things appear to be such and such, but whether they are so in their essence. . . . We merely object to accepting the unknown substance behind the phenomena" (Diogenes Laertius, 1991, II, pp. 503, 515). Here Pyrrho seems willing to concede that we have some knowledge, knowledge of the appearances, but not of things in themselves. On this interpretation, skepticism, unlike the other schools of philosophy, makes no claim to know "the things that really are in the world without us." It does not purport to be in possession of objective knowledge. It does not claim, however, that it is impossible to have knowledge of anything whatever; the notion of knowledge itself is not incoherent, but certain forms of belief concerning "the unknown substance behind the phenomena" fail to be substantiated.[1] If arguments are among the phenomena about which we can have knowledge, then it is open to the skeptic to put forward arguments whose validity he can ascertain.

Pyrrho and the Argument from the Criterion

Among the ideas that Diogenes attributes to Pyrrho is the most powerful general argument in support of global skepticism, the argument from the criterion. A criterion is something we can appeal to in order to justify a belief we are putting forward or to show that some proposition or other is true. Or, more broadly, a criterion is some feature of a belief or a relation of the belief to something else that establishes or tends to establish that it is true or that it is probably true. A criterion of truth is what helps us distinguish between true and false beliefs or between beliefs that are justified or reasonable to assert and those that are not.

Different schools of thought have put forward a variety of criteria. Thus empiricist schools identify the criterion of truth with sense experience and rationalists with what is evident to the intellect. Various methods of fixing belief – sense perception, memory, induction, proof, testimony,

---

1   "Pyrrhonism . . . is not directly concerned with knowledge at all, but only with justified belief" (Mates, 1996, p. 5). But if a belief fails to be justified, does it count as knowledge?

etc. – also qualify as criteria that we employ in the circumstances of everyday life.

For the skeptics, the very fact that the schools of philosophy disagree about the nature of the criterion and that the disagreements are longstanding and apparently irresolvable suggests that we cannot know what the true criterion amounts to and that truth is, therefore, unknowable (Diogenes Laertius, 1991, II, p. 507).[2] However, it is unnecessary for us to examine the particular criteria that the various schools have offered because it is impossible to establish any criterion, whatever it may be:

> The criterion has either been critically determined or not. If it has not, it is definitely untrustworthy, and in its purpose of distinguishing is not more true than false. If it has, it will belong to the class of particular judgments, so that one and the same thing determines and is determined, and the criterion which has determined will have to be determined by another, and that other by another, and so on *ad infinitum*. (Diogenes Laertius, 1991, II, p. 507)

The argument is in the form of a dilemma each horn of which entails an unacceptable consequence. If the condition put forward as a criterion has not been shown to be a reliable or certain mark of truth (i.e. if it has not been "critically determined"), then we have no good reason to accept it as a criterion. On the other hand, if we have put forward a reason for thinking that something is a reliable or certain mark of truth, then this has been accomplished by the application of a further criterion whose justification requires a still further criterion, and so on, without end. Since there is no end to the process, we have never succeeded in showing that the initial criterion is a mark of truth. But in the absence of a critically determined criterion, we have no knowledge of anything.

Sextus Empiricus and Pyrrhonism

The argument from the criterion was developed further by Sextus Empiricus in his *Outlines of Empiricism*; this book appears to have been composed as a

2   Ancient skeptics, observing the intellectual world, were struck by the fact of fundamental and intractable disagreement in the outcomes of inquiries fostered by the various philosophical schools. Today, despite continuing disagreement in religion, ethics, and politics, the method of science tends to generate agreements in the outcomes of inquiries into nature – a striking difference between our world and that of the ancients.

handbook or compilation of skeptical arguments; almost every argument developed or emphasized in later texts, such as Descartes' doubts about the senses and Hume's doubts about induction, are discussed or intimated in the *Outlines*. It is like a tourist guide to ancient skepticism, covering many topics and arguments but somewhat shallow in its analyses.

Sextus' account of the nature of Pyrrho's skepticism makes it clear that it is not merely a collection of philosophical arguments leading us to suspend judgment; it is, rather, a way of life aiming at tranquillity of mind, a rival to the ways of life proposed by Plato, Aristotle, Epicurus, and the Stoics. Skeptical doubts are a means to inner peace and harmony. The ways of life proposed by others are founded upon dogmatic beliefs that are easily undermined; once the intellectual debris is swept away by skeptical reasoning, the way is clear to a life free of the upsets produced by conflicts about the nature of things.

Here is a brief summary of the skeptic's position in Sextus' words:

> Skepticism is an ability, or mental attitude, which opposes appearances to judgments in any way whatever, with the result that, owing to the equipollence of the objects and reasons thus opposed, we are brought first to a state of mental suspense and next to a state of "unperturbedness" or quietude. . . . By "appearances" we now mean the objects of sense perception, whence we contrast them with the objects of thought or "judgments." . . . "Equipollence" we use of equality in respect of probability and improbability, to indicate that no one of the conflicting judgments takes precedence of any other as being more probable. "Suspense" is a state of mental rest owing to which we neither deny nor affirm anything. "Quietude" is an untroubled and tranquil condition of the soul. (Sextus Empiricus, 1955, I, 8–10)

This passage should not be interpreted to imply that the skeptic's state of mind involves the absence of all beliefs about anything whatever. The skeptic allows himself to form beliefs about the appearances (perceptual judgments) and about what is evident. He suspends his judgment only about the non-evident. "In his enunciation of these formulae he states what appears to himself and announces his own impression in an undogmatic way, without making any positive assertion about the external realities" (Sextus Empiricus, 1955, I, 15).

How shall we understand the connection between skeptical suspense of belief and judgment (*epoch ē*) and tranquillity of mind (*ataraxia*)? Sextus answers that the skeptics started out seeking tranquillity by trying to ascertain the truth about non-evident matters of fact. Since they found that truth was not to be had, the only reasonable outcome was to suspend or bracket all beliefs about the non-evident. It just so happened that tranquillity supervened. "They [the skeptics] found that quietude, as if by chance, followed upon their suspense, even as a shadow follows its substance" (Sextus Empiricus, 1955, I, 29). The connection between suspense of judgment and tranquillity of mind is not accidental, even though the discovery is:

> For the man who opines that anything is by nature good or bad is forever being disquieted: when he is without the things which he deems good he believes himself to be tormented by things naturally bad and he pursues after the things which are, as he thinks, good; which when he has obtained he keeps falling into still more perturbations because of his irrational and immoderate elation, and in his dread of a change of fortune he uses every endeavor to avoid losing the things he deems good. On the other hand, the man who determines nothing as to what is naturally good or bad neither shuns nor pursues anything eagerly; and in consequence, he is unperturbed. (Sextus Empiricus, 1955, I, 27–8)

Sextus concedes that uninterrupted tranquillity is not possible even if the skeptic succeeds completely in overcoming dogmatism. Some troubling things are unavoidable, such as the discomfort of cold and thirst.

> But even in these cases, whereas ordinary people are afflicted by two circumstances, – namely, by the affections themselves, and, in no less a degree, by the belief that these conditions are evil by nature, – the skeptic, by his rejection of the added belief in the natural badness of all these conditions, escapes here too with less discomfort. (Sextus Empiricus, 1955, I, 30)

The skeptic attempts, then, to live not according to the ways things really are, for these are unknown, but in accordance with the appearances. In practice, this means that he lives in accord with "the customs of the country and its laws and institutions" and with "our own instinctive feelings" (Sextus Empiricus, 1955, I, 17). "Adhering then to the appearances we live in accordance with the normal rules of life, undogmatically, seeing that we cannot remain wholly inactive" (Sextus Empiricus, 1955, I, 23).

The connection between living in accordance with the appearances and living in accordance with the customs of the country is not obvious. Their skeptical arguments probably convinced them that they had no better rules of life to offer than the customs of the country, and that challenging existing norms is more trouble than it is worth. The search for tranquillity in practice led the ancient skeptics to follow the path of least resistance. Not an admirable life, to be sure. Modern individualism tends to admire people who accept challenges and meet them successfully. But the skeptics, along with the Stoics and Epicureans, seemed to prefer avoiding problems instead.[3]

The Failure of Empiricism

Empiricism regards sense experience to be the criterion of truth about external realities. Sextus formulated a profound critique of the claims of our perceptual judgments to embody knowledge of reality:

> Nor, again, is it possible to assert that the soul apprehends external realities by means of the affections of sense owing to the similarity of the affections of the senses to the external real objects. For how is the intellect to know whether the affections of the senses are similar to the objects of sense when it has not itself encountered the external objects, and the senses do not inform it about their real nature but only about their own affections . . . ? For just as the man who does not know Socrates but has seen a picture of him does not know whether the picture is like Socrates, so also the intellect when it gazes upon the affections of the senses but does not behold the external objects will not so much as know whether the affections of the senses are similar to the external realities. So that not even on the ground of resemblance will he be able to judge these objects according to the presentation. (Sextus Empiricus, 1955, II, 74–5)

On Sextus' view, external realities are known only via the sense impressions that we take to represent them accurately. But, like the person who sees the picture of Socrates but has never seen Socrates himself, we have no way of ascertaining how accurate our sense representations are. In chapter 2, I argued that they are inaccurate as far as color is concerned. There the argument took for granted that we had some knowledge of external realities. Here Sextus is offering a general argument to the effect that we have no way whatsoever of determining their degree of either accuracy or inaccuracy. On the plausible assumption that our sense impressions constitute our only access to external realities, it follows that we have no knowledge of things as they are in themselves.

Moreover, not only does this argument tend to support the absence of

---

3   See Burnyeat (1983) for a discussion of whether it is even possible to live without belief.

knowledge of external realities, it also tends to support the idea that we have no probable belief about them either. Our ascriptions of probability are usually based upon judgments of frequency – it is, for example, highly probable that this object is red because in the past all or most objects that have looked this way have turned out to be red. Yet, like the man who has seen pictures of Socrates but not Socrates himself, we are in no position to verify such judgments. If knowledge and probability exhaust the domain of justified belief, then we have no justified belief about external realities.

Sextus also brings forward the fact of the relativity of sense impressions, a phenomenon that later generations of skeptics frequently appealed to. The same object is capable of appearing in many different ways. For example, "the same ship seems at a distance to be small and stationary, but from close at hand large and in motion; and the same tower from a distance appears round but from a near point quadrangular" (Sextus Empiricus, 1955, I, 118). We are in no better position to determine which of the many appearances most accurately portrays the external reality than is the man who has seen many different pictures of Socrates able to determine which resembles him best.

Another reason why we cannot overcome the relativity of the senses is that efforts to do so generate an infinite regress. Suppose we determine that appearance A is more accurate than appearance B because A possesses a certain feature F that B lacks. We think that it is F that makes A reliable or, at least, indicates its reliability. But then we can ask for a good reason or proof to suppose that the presence of F attests to the accuracy of A.

> If he asserts that the proof is true, he will be asked for a proof of its truth, and again for a proof of the latter proof, since it must also be true, and so on *ad infinitum*. But to produce proofs to infinity is impossible; so that neither by the use of proofs will he be able to prefer one sense impression to another. If, then, one cannot hope to pass judgment on the aforementioned impressions either with or without proof, the conclusion we are driven to is suspension; for while we can, no doubt, state the nature which each object appears to possess as viewed in a certain position or at a certain distance or in a certain place, what its real nature is we are, for the foregoing reasons, unable to declare. (Sextus Empiricus, 1955, I, 122–3)

Many centuries later, Kant will be motivated by these skeptical arguments to declare the need for a philosophical revolution in which transcendental realism is to be replaced by transcendental idealism. Sextus' solution is much simpler, namely to conclude that empiricism is mistaken and that we have no knowledge whatever of external realities.

The General Form of the Criterion Argument

We could brush aside these skeptical arguments if we were able to establish a criterion to distinguish those sense impressions that are accurate or veridical from those that are not. "Whether, then, one is to call all the appearances true, or some true and some false, or all false, it is impossible to say since we possess no agreed criterion whereby we shall judge the question we are proposing to decide" (Sextus Empiricus, 1955, II, 53). The various schools of dogmatic philosophers have proposed different and conflicting criteria of truth; "every criterion we may adopt is controverted and therefore discredited" (Sextus Empiricus, 1955, II, 178).

The fact that there is sharp disagreement among those who investigate the criterion of truth means that we need an argument, for any proposed criterion, that it is indeed the criterion. Suppose C is offered as the criterion. What reason do we have for thinking that any proposition that satisfies C is true or even likely to be true? Without a reason or argument in its favor, C has no plausibility, whatever it is. Even if C is well entrenched in our ordinary thinking, that merely shows that C is a well entrenched prejudice, not a reliable sign of truth.

Sextus offers a general argument to the effect that there can be no epistemically sound argument for a criterion and that, therefore, the only reasonable position is to bracket all our beliefs about external realities:

> This dispute, then, they [who have treated of the criterion] will declare to be either capable or incapable of decision; and if they shall say it is incapable of decision they will be granting on the spot the propriety of suspension of judgment, while if they say it admits of decision, let them tell us whereby it is to be decided, since we have no accepted criterion, and do not even know, but are still inquiring, whether any criterion exists. Besides, in order to decide the dispute which has arisen about the criterion, we must possess an accepted criterion by which we shall be able to judge the dispute; and in order to possess an accepted criterion, the dispute about the criterion must first be decided. And when the argument thus reduces itself to a form of circular reasoning, the discovery of the criterion becomes impracticable, since we do not allow them to adopt a criterion by assumption, while if the offer to judge the criterion by a criterion we force them to a regress *ad infinitum*. And furthermore, since demonstration requires a demonstrated criterion, while the criterion requires an approved demonstration, they are forced into circular reasoning. (Sextus Empiricus, 1955, II, 19–20)

Apparently, the friends of any particular criterion of truth whatever are faced with the alternatives of either putting it forward as an assumption that merely reflects their own prejudices and which no one else has any reason to accept or putting it forward on the basis of an argument. And if they put it forward on the basis of an argument, then the argument fails because it either is circular or generates an infinite regress. Not a happy condition for the dogmatists to be in, nor for us, because, with respect to a criterion, we are all dogmatists most of the time.

I think that this argument against the criterion is the most powerful argument in the skeptical tradition from ancient times to the present day. It requires a deep analysis, and for that we will move on to the next chapter.

5

The Argument Against the Criterion

Epistemically Sound Arguments

The argument against the criterion that Sextus Empiricus formulates implies that there can be no *epistemically sound argument* or *epistemically sound proof* that any condition whatever that is offered as a criterion of truth is indeed a valid criterion or mark of truth. Logicians speak of arguments and proofs that are deductively sound, by which they mean those that are deductively valid and have true premises. By a deductively valid argument is meant one whose conclusion follows necessarily from the premises: if the premises are true, then necessarily the conclusion is true. There is a weaker notion of validity, according to which the conclusion is supported or justified or confirmed or made likely or probable by the premises.

By an epistemically sound argument, I mean one that not only is valid and has true premises but can also be used to establish knowledge of the conclusion or to justify belief in the conclusion.

There can be deductively sound arguments that are not epistemically sound and hence do not constitute a *proof* of their conclusions. Consider any argument that satisfies the following conditions: the premise or premises are true, the conclusion follows deductively or necessarily from the premises, the conclusion is identical with one of the premises, and the premise that is identical with the conclusion is indispensable for deriving the conclusion. Let an argument that satisfies these conditions be of the following form: A, B, C, therefore A. The argument is deductively valid but is circular because A is used to prove itself.

The argument fails to constitute a proof of the truth of A even if A follows from the premises and the premises are true. That is, I cannot gain knowledge of the truth of A on the basis of this argument, assuming that I have no knowledge of A independently of this argument. For in order for me to gain knowledge of the truth of A on the basis of the premises A, B, and C, I would first have to know that each of these premises is true or, at least, that each of the indispensable ones is true. Thus, in order for me to gain knowledge of A on the basis of this argument, I would first have to know that A is true. But, by hypothesis, I do not already know that A is true. Thus although the argument is deductively valid and sound, it fails to be epistemically sound. In fact, no circular argument that satisfies these conditions is epistemically sound no matter how many premises it has. It is just not true that a vicious circle becomes virtuous by having a lengthy diameter.

In this discussion, I have used the notion of proof as it is used in ordinary discourse as a deductively sound argument that establishes knowledge of the conclusion; that is, that proves the truth of the conclusion. This notion must be distinguished from two others that are frequently used in technical discussions: a formal proof is a deductively valid argument whose validity can be determined from the logical form of the argument alone; a semantic proof is any argument whose conclusion follows necessarily from its premises in accordance with the semantic or meaning structure of the argument.

Let us suppose that someone doubts the truth of a proposition P. One way of convincing him of its truth is to present him with an epistemically sound proof with P as its conclusion and say to him: "Now surely you know that these premises are true, and you can see that P follows strictly from them; therefore, you have no basis on which to doubt the truth of P." But, according to Sextus, there is no such procedure available to remove anyone's doubts about any putative criterion of truth.

The Circularity of Arguments for the Criterion

Sextus stresses the fact that philosophers disagree about the criterion. If an advocate of any particular criterion admits that he has no way of resolving the disagreement in favor of his candidate, then we have no reason to either accept or reject the criterion he offers. But suppose he puts forward an argument in favor of his candidate that he claims is capable of ending the disagreement by providing a sufficient reason to accept his candidate. Such an argument will involve premises that he claims to know are true. But his claim to know them involves appealing to a criterion of truth, e.g. sense experience or self-evidence.

Now either this criterion is the same as the one whose validity he is attempting to prove or it is different. If it is the same, his argument is circular and fails to be epistemically sound. If it is different, we need a criterion to establish the validity of this one; that one will be either the same or different, and if it is the same, the argument will be circular and will fail to be sound. So the only hope for a sound argument is if the criterion is different at each stage in the regress.

Infinite Regress

Suppose the criterion is different at each stage of the regress. So at the completion of each stage, we can ask for a reason to accept the criterion used at that stage, and thus we are required to advance to a new stage if we are to come into possession of an epistemic proof. This process has no end. At each stage of this unending series of arguments, our knowledge of the reliability of the criterion being established depends upon our knowledge of the reliability of the criteria to be established at subsequent stages. Because there is no end to the sequence of subsequent stages, we fail to establish the reliability of the criterion we began with. Therefore, according to the skeptic, we have no option but to suspend judgment.

Humans live in a finite time and therefore are unable to complete the infinite regress that is generated by efforts to avoid circularity. So for us, the regress is vicious because it thwarts our efforts to establish any criterion. According to Sextus (1955, II, 78), "it is impossible to judge an infinite series." Could God, who knows everything, establish an epistemic proof in support of some criterion? The regress is endless, and thus has no last stage. In order to establish an epistemic proof, God would have to establish every one of the members of the unending series of stages. He would have to apprehend an infinite series. But in order to complete this regress, there would have to be a final step which brings the regress to an end; but there is no final step, since for any step there is always one more. So even the idea of an omniscient being proving a criterion seems incoherent. One might object by saying that God's apprehension is timeless, so that he can apprehend every step even though there is no temporally final step. But is the idea of a timeless apprehension of an actual infinite intelligible?

Is There No Criterion of Truth?

Sextus does not think that his arguments show that there is no criterion of truth. The fact that we cannot prove, for any suggested criterion C, that C is a reliable indicator of what is true does not itself prove that C is not a reliable indicator:

> But one should notice that we do not propose to assert that the criterion of truth is unreal (for that would be dogmatism); but since the dogmatists appear to have established plausibly that there really is a criterion of truth, we have set up counter-arguments which appear to be plausible; and though we do not positively affirm either that they are true or that they are more plausible than their opposites, yet because of the apparently equal plausibility of these arguments and of those propounded by the dogmatists we deduce suspension of judgment. (Sextus Empiricus, 1955, II, p. 79)

Even though there may very well be a reliable mark of truth, there is no chance that we will ever be in a position to establish that there is one or to determine what it is. There is no more reason to believe that there is a reliable mark of truth than to believe that there isn't. Therefore, suspension of judgment is the only acceptable alternative.

Chisholm's Objection

In his paper "The Problem of the Criterion," Roderick Chisholm challenges the main assumption of Sextus' argument, namely that knowledge of truth requires a criterion of truth. "To find out whether you know such a thing as that this is a hand, you don't have to apply any test or criterion. Spinoza has it right. 'In order to know,' he said, 'there is no need to know that we know, much less to know that we know that we know'" (Chisholm, 1982, p. 69). According to Chisholm, it is unnecessary to apply a criterion in order to acquire knowledge of the particular things we know. The existence of this knowledge does not depend upon our knowing a criterion. Whatever general rules we are able to arrive at to determine whether or not we have knowledge in any particular case are discovered through an examination of particular cases of knowledge that can be identified without applying a criterion. Our grasp of a criterion is, therefore, subsequent to our knowledge of particular truths; the latter does not depend upon the former.

Here is an example of a general rule concerning sense experience:

> But if nothing about this particular occasion leads you to suspect what the senses report on this particular occasion, then the wise thing is to take such a report at face value. In short the senses should be regarded as

innocent until there is some positive reason, on some particular occasion, for thinking they are guilty on that particular occasion. (Chisholm, 1982, p. 70)

For Chisholm, the way we arrive at such a rule or criterion (call it R) is by examining the circumstances in which we accept the testimony of the senses and those in which we do not. Those sensory reports that are innocent constitute knowledge and those that are guilty probably do not. So we are in a position to identify the innocence of sensory reports as a criterion of truth and the basis of knowledge of external realities, assuming, course, that we have correctly abstracted the rule exemplified in our practice.

Two Interpretations of the Argument Against the Criterion

There are two ways of looking at the argument from the criterion. Let us suppose a dogmatist proposes R as a criterion of truth. According to the first way, when R is satisfied, then, provided that R is a reliable indicator of truth, we actually have knowledge. Of course, we may be in ignorance as to whether R is satisfied, but even then, if it is satisfied we have knowledge. We also may be in ignorance as to whether R is reliable; that is, as to whether or not R does provide knowledge. That is why we search for further arguments to establish the reliability of R, namely in order to acquire knowledge as to whether or not R actually provides knowledge. But even if these arguments fail by turning out to be circular or by generating an infinite regress, if R is satisfied, then we have knowledge. Call this the *externalist interpretation*. It agrees with Spinoza that in order to know, one does not have to know that one knows. Sextus himself seems to be an externalist when he admits that his arguments do not show that there is no criterion of truth.

According to the second way (the *internalist interpretation*), we are to think of the criterion as a premise of an epistemic proof. In order for the argument to constitute an epistemic proof, it is necessary to know the premises. But in order to know them, one needs sufficient reason to think they are true. Thus one searches for additional premises or criteria to support these, for without them, we lack knowledge of the initial set of premises. But the search for additional criteria either ends in a circle or generates an unending regress, and the quest ends in failure; we never had an epistemic proof in the first place. One might understand this view to mean that in order to know, one must know that one knows.

According to the externalist interpretation, one may have good and suffi-cient reason for thinking that something is true without knowing what that reason is. One may have knowledge without knowing or understanding what having knowledge amounts to. In fact, one may have knowledge even when one thinks one does not have knowledge. According to internalism, on the other hand, in order to have knowledge, one must have access to an under-standing of the ground of that knowledge.

These interpretations generate different forms of skepticism. According to *externalist skepticism*, the skeptical arguments do not show that we lack knowledge; what they demonstrate is that we are never in a position to es-tablish that we do have knowledge. Thus we may very well be in possession of an epistemic proof without knowing it or without being in a position to establish that we are. According to *internalist skepticism*, the skeptical argu-ments show that we lack knowledge because our efforts to establish an epistemic proof end in either circularity or an infinite regress.

Difficulties with Chisholm's Way Out

Chisholm starts out with particular instances of knowledge: here is a hand; there is a pencil; the sun is shining, etc. The skeptic, obviously, will ask him to justify his claim that these are instances of knowledge rather than of mere opinion or even of false belief. Chisholm replies: "What few philosophers have had the courage to recognize is this: we can deal with the problem only by begging the question. It seems to me that, if we do recognize this fact, as we should, then it is unseemly for us to try to pretend that it isn't so" (Chisholm, 1982, p. 75). By "begging the question" here Chisholm seems to have in mind the fact that he is asserting without proof just what the skeptic would deny, namely that these actually are instances of knowledge. From the point of view of externalist skepticism, even if these are instances of knowledge, Chisholm has no basis for claiming that they are. From the internalist point of view, since Chisholm claims that these are instances of knowledge with-out being able to prove them to be true, then his claim is false. In either case, Chisholm turns out to be a dogmatist and should, according to Sextus, sus-pend his judgment. Therefore, when Chisholm identifies R as the rule com-mon to accepted sensory reports, even if R is indeed the common rule, we have no reason to think that it is a criterion of truth.

Chisholm claims that in order to determine a criterion one should start with particular cases and try to find their common basis. His method is in-ductive. Now R is either implicit in our practice or it is not. If it is implicit in our practice, then it functions to decide which particular cases constitute knowledge. The instances we select as cases of knowledge are selected because they satisfy R. Our abstraction of R from the individual cases is simply making explicit what was operative in our minds all along. So our method is not really inductive because we are selecting the particular cases just because they are instances of the general rule even though we might not have been conscious of the rule beforehand. So Chisholm's method again begs the question: instead of helping us discover a criterion of truth, it simply identifies a rule operative in our thought and dogmatically claims that it is a criterion of truth. Chisholm is not correct, on this alternative, when he says that "to find out whether you know any such thing as that this is a hand, you don't have to apply any test or criterion."

But perhaps R is not implicit in our practice so that in selecting instances of perceptual knowledge, Chisholm is not implicitly using R as the basis of selection and is not begging the question in that way. Now it would be surprising if we were not using some rule to generate our acceptances of perceptual reports because otherwise our acceptances would be random, and that would not be a satisfactory basis for defeating the skeptic's doubts. But whatever the operative rule amounts to, on this alternative, it is not R. R is not the rule we actually follow, but the rule we should follow if we are to obtain reliable reports about the external world. According to Chisholm, taking our sensory reports as innocent unless proven guilty is "the wise thing." R is here interpreted as a norm we should follow if we are to gain knowledge of the external world; it is not a procedural fact about the mind. It is a norm discovered by a consideration of instances of perceptual knowledge. Here the method is inductive because the instances are not generated by R but by some other procedure or, *per impossibile*, by no procedure at all.

But in order to have any reason to think that R is the norm, it is necessary first to identify that feature of the instances that is the guarantor of their reliability, that provides a reason to think that we are in possession of knowledge or even of justified belief. Suppose we think that the feature is F – innocent unless proven guilty – rather than any other common feature. Because these instances exemplify F, they are true or quite likely to be true, we think. The next step is to formulate a rule that incorporates F, and we end up with R.

The only thing that induction contributes here is the identification of the common features of our sample instances and their extrapolation to unexamined instances. Induction does not show us that F is reliable; moreover, on the alternative we are considering, where R is not actually operative in our thought, induction selects a feature F that is independent of what actually determines our beliefs. So what makes us think that F is a mark of truth? How can we tell that it is a mark of truth without first having determined a criterion? Do we have any access to truth independent of any mark or any criterion so that we are in a position to establish that these truths exemplify F and that F and nothing else guarantees their truth? It appears that only if we are entitled to answer "Yes" can we overcome the skepticism generated by the argument against the criterion. In subsequent chapters, we shall consider a point of view – reliabilism – that reveals the weakness of the skeptic's position.

6

Two Pyrrhonian Problems

The argument against the criterion assumes that rational assent to any proposition depends upon being in possession of a justified criterion. In this chapter, I shall not question this assumption, but simply consider two problems that arise for the Pyrrhonists, armed as they are with the argument against the criterion.

Suspension of Judgment

The Pyrrhonian skeptic recommends that, since the reasons used to support any judgment about external realities and non-evident objects in general are no better than the reasons used to support its negation, we should suspend judgment about them. On the basis of my visual experience, I judge that this is a hand. Because I cannot establish a criterion assuring me of the reliability of this judgment, I have no better reason to assent to it than to assent to its negation. But is it possible to withhold assent to our perceptual judgments? In chapter 2, we raised a similar issue as far as color nihilism was concerned. There the question was whether we could reject as false all propositions ascribing a color to an object. The difficulty was that many such propositions are so well entrenched that we cannot understand how we could bring ourselves to doubt the whole class. Here the question is whether we are able to bracket a much larger class of well entrenched judgments, where bracketing means not denial but suspending judgment about each affirmative member of the class as well as its negation.

There are two impediments to bracketing all our beliefs about external realities. The first is practical: such beliefs are guides to action; we could not move from here to there without accepting or assuming the evidence of the senses. The skeptical *epochē* or bracketing seems to be hostile to our continued existence.

The second is based on the fact that belief is involuntary. In H. H. Price's words, "we cannot assent to any proposition we please, just by an act of will here and now" (Price, 1969, p. 222). For the same reason, we cannot withhold assent to any proposition we please, just by an act of will here and now. Normally, the strength of our conviction is determined by our understanding of the strength of the relevant evidence. In the case of the hand, the relevant evidence consists of the appearances presented by the sense of sight, our visual sense impressions. The argument against the criterion appears to show that reason provides no basis for trusting them. In fact, the argument provides reasons for thinking that the evidence of the senses has no evidentiary weight at all. But even if we are convinced by the argument against the criterion, we cannot help ascribing the usual evidentiary weight to our sense impressions. The evidence of the senses seems impervious to philosophical criticism. Nothing we can say in philosophy can put it out of action. Reasons cannot be caused to cease being reasons by an act of will.

Price, however, does not think that that is the end of the story. For although our beliefs are not directly subject to the will, some of them, at least, may be indirectly controlled by the will over a period of time. "Belief can be voluntarily cultivated" (Price, 1969, p. 222), he argues.

> In other words, what we do is to direct our attention to the favourable evidence, the evidence for the proposition we were asked to believe, and avert our attention from the evidence against it. This is something which we can voluntarily do, if we try hard enough and go on trying. And as a result, we may be able in the end to assent to the proposition without any difficulty, though it was quite beyond our power to do so at the beginning. Thus assent may be voluntary in the long run, at least sometimes, even though in the short run it is quite beyond our voluntary control. (Price, 1969, p. 223)

Perhaps by attending for a time to the intractable and insoluble difficulties in establishing a criterion, by realizing that what I took to be the evidence for my judgment that here is a hand fails to support it, I can bring myself to bracket it.

Fideism

Let us suppose that we succeed in bracketing all beliefs founded upon the evidence of the senses. Then we die, for we cannot act. Let me suggest an explanation why, no matter what we do, it is impossible for us to bracket the whole class of judgments based upon the senses. Animals that do not trust their senses do not survive, and animals that do trust them are more likely to survive. So a general trust in the senses is likely to be part of our innate endowment, a part that cannot be put out of action by philosophical arguments. The global skepticism of Pyrrhonism cannot be implemented in practice. It is idle, as far as the structure of human action is concerned.

Of course, this does not show that there is anything wrong with the argument against the criterion. After all, the argument itself does not imply that we must suspend judgment. What it does say is that there is no non-circular sound argument for establishing a criterion. If sense impressions are nominated as a criterion of truth, then there is no non-circular sound argument for showing that they are reliable grounds of belief. To that extent, Pyrrhonian skepticism is correct. But nothing follows about what we should do next. That we ought to suspend judgment is a recommendation based upon the argument for the criterion, but it is not required by the argument. There is also the way of fideism, to have blind faith in our senses, or animal faith as Santayana (1923, p. 214) called it. That is another recommendation. Since suspension of judgment is impossible in practice and since fideism is consistent with practice, it looks as if fideism is the more reasonable recommendation.

But there is a third possibility, *qualified fideism*. It accepts that we have no alternative but to have a general faith in the senses, to trust our sense impressions except in those few instances when we have evidence, usually based upon the senses, that our senses have led us astray. But it also accepts the conclusion of the argument against the criterion that, when all is said and done, there is no non-circular ground to justify our reliance upon the evidence of the senses. Also, it claims that the evidence of the senses provides motives to accept the evidence of the senses – namely, the evidence of the senses shows that we have no alternative but to accept it. Finally, if we accept the evidence of the senses, we can explain, as we have, why the evidence of the senses is unshaken by skeptical arguments even if they cannot be rebutted.

Although qualified fideism does not require us to attempt to bracket our perceptual judgments, it does, in a way, qualify our assent to them. For, when we adopt a philosophical point of view and attempt to survey our putative knowledge of external realities, we come to realize that either we have no such knowledge or we cannot establish that we have it. That is, we do not suspend our judgments, but we offer a philosophical verdict about them, namely that they are, all things considered, groundless. Such a verdict is a kind of bracketing; although it has no direct application to practice, and it does not put our beliefs out of action, nevertheless it runs contrary to what we ordinarily think. Pyrrhonian skepticism overthrows any dogmatic convictions that our beliefs can be certified by reason to be reliable. I shall call a philosophical verdict of this kind *philosophical bracketing*, in contrast to practical bracketing, which is, after all, impossible to implement.

Problem of Dogmatism

A dogmatist is one who accepts certain beliefs unconditionally even though he has failed to establish their ultimate grounds. He claims to know the truth of the propositions he asserts. He is satisfied with too little in the way of evidence. This means that, in philosophy, each dogmatic system will encounter and oppose other dogmatic systems, and there will never be an end to this perpetual construction of dubious systems until there is a searching inquiry into the ultimate foundations of knowledge.

But when we undertake such an inquiry, we find that none of these systems has or can have any rational grounds, and the same holds for our common sense and religious beliefs as well. That is the verdict of Pyrrhonian skepticism. So dogmatism is mistaken if it takes itself to have a right to be certain, a right to claim knowledge of its claims.

But isn't the Pyrrhonian skeptic himself guilty of dogmatism? After all, he offers arguments which he claims to be sound and valid and to undermine the dogmatic theories that others have offered. But his arguments can be directed against his own claims to show that the verdict he directs against the views of others can also be reasonably directed against his own views. It seems that Pyrrhonian skepticism is incoherent: if it is correct, then, by its own arguments, it is incorrect. The very arguments it offers against dogmatism are instances of dogmatism.

Sextus' Solution

The Pyrrhonists were aware of this difficulty, and if they had not come upon it themselves, it would undoubtedly have been pointed out to them by their opponents. Here is how Sextus attempts to deal with it:

> So whenever the skeptic says "I determine nothing," what he means is "I am now in such a state of mind as neither to affirm dogmatically nor deny any of the matters now in question." And this he says simply by way of

announcing undogmatically what appears to himself regarding the matters presented, not making any confident declaration, but just explaining his own state of mind. (Sextus Empiricus, 1955, I, 197)

Sextus appears to be saying, on behalf of the Pyrrhonian skeptic, that the skeptic dogmatically affirms neither the truth of skepticism nor the soundness of the arguments for it, but that he is, nevertheless, sufficiently impressed by these arguments so as to be caused to adopt a skeptical state of mind.[1] Skepticism just seems to him the way to go. He is not asserting it with any confidence; he is not asserting it at all; he is simply describing his state of mind without recommending it to anyone else. He does not dogmatically assert a philosophical theory of knowledge. Since he does not claim to have arrived at knowledge of a philosophical truth, he does not mind if his critics point out that, by his own lights, he is in no position to claim such knowledge. He agrees with them. I shall label this way out *timid skepticism*.

This is not an effective solution to the problem of dogmatism and incoherence. First of all, by adopting this way out, the skeptic actually surrenders his position. Timid skepticism, not being an assertion, and the arguments for it, not being asserted to be sound, is not a philosophical view. It is just an attitude that occurs in his mind as a result of arguments that he notes but can give no credence to. Why should dogmatic philosophers pay any attention to what he says? He is in no better position than are those dogmatists who adopt a criterion while at the same time conceding that they can say nothing in its favor. He finds himself impressed by skeptical arguments, but refrains from asserting that they are sound because of the realization that if he does so, he will not only be dogmatic but also will contradict the very upshot of the arguments.

The Evident and the Non-evident

Some remarks of Sextus suggest another solution, one that I alluded to in chapter 1. He distinguishes between objects that are evident and objects that are non-evident, and claims that skepticism is concerned only with claims about non-evident external realities, such as material objects and Plato's

---

1   According to Benson Mates (1996, p. 5), Pyrrhonism does not speak of doubt. Its "characteristic attitude" is "one of *aporia*, of being at a loss, puzzled, stumped, stymied," arising from the equivalence of reasons for and against any assertion about the external world.

Forms. Suppose now we think that the constituents of arguments – propositions and concepts – are evident objects to which we have direct access and to some of whose properties we have direct access as well.

Consider the starting point of the argument against the criterion: either the dogmatist offers a proof or justification for the criterion he employs or he does not. Here is a proposition that is an instance of the logical law of the excluded middle, a law that one could plausibly affirm to be self-evident. Suppose now that the argument against the criterion could be so formulated so that each step in the argument consists either of a self-evident proposition or of a proposition deduced from self-evident propositions by steps each of which is self-evident. Making use of terminology introduced by the rationalist tradition in philosophy, we can say that we have intuitive knowledge of self-evident propositions and demonstrative knowledge of those deduced by self-evident steps from self-evident propositions. I shall use the term rational knowledge for knowledge that is either intuitive or demonstrative. This is knowledge because the truthfulness of the objects of rational knowledge and the validity of demonstrative arguments are evident. Such knowledge has been called *a priori* knowledge by the philosophical tradition.

According to some passages in Sextus, the skeptic not only accepts *a priori* knowledge (under the assumption that it is founded upon a grasp of evident objects) but, in addition, accepts that one is able to have knowledge of the appearances, of our sense impressions, even though one can and should doubt that one can have knowledge of external realities based upon them. I shall call such knowledge direct sensory knowledge, to distinguish it from the alleged inferential knowledge of bodies whose existence the skeptic doubts.

According to this interpretation, then, the Pyrrhonian skeptic allows himself two forms of knowledge – rational or *a priori* knowledge and direct sensory knowledge – because their objects are evident; he has direct, unmediated, and incorrigible access to them. The skeptic, on this interpretation, is a classical foundationalist of sorts, simply doubting whether we can go beyond the foundations to justify additional classes of belief. Even though he claims to have knowledge of a sort, he is not a dogmatist since his claim is justified. Those he calls dogmatists claim to have knowledge about non-evident objects that cannot be justified; at least that is what the argument against the criterion tells him.

A Priori Knowledge and the Argument Against the Criterion

Does this solution to the problem of dogmatism escape the argument against the criterion? The dogmatist could say to the Pyrrhonian skeptic: "Look, you too are employing a criterion. After all, self-evidence is a certain state of mind that you find within yourself upon contemplating certain propositions such as the law of excluded middle and its instances. Such a state of mind consists of a strong conviction of the truth of such propositions; so you are taking a strong conviction of truth based upon such contemplation as a criterion of truth. But do you have any arguments to show that such strong conviction is an infallible or even reliable indicator of truth? Either you have an argument or you do not. . . . And thus the skeptic is hoist with his own petard.

One response of the skeptic would be to deny that the sorts of knowledge he allows himself are based upon any criteria. We need criteria, he can say, when the objects are non-evident and our access is indirect. In that case, we cannot grasp the objects directly, and we need to rely upon reliable signs or marks of truth. Self-evidence, he continues, is not a sign or mark of truth; he is not inferring the truth of the propositions constitutive of his arguments merely from his being in the mental state of being strongly convinced of their truth. There is no inference involved at all because he has direct acquaintance with the objects of knowledge. A criterion only comes into operation with regard to propositions about non-evident objects.

This is a plausible response. The difficulty is that the epistemology of evident objects itself presupposes a questionable ontology. As far as rational knowledge is concerned, the skeptic is committed to the existence of propositions as objects to which one can have direct access. As far as direct sensory knowledge is concerned, this appears to imply the existence of sense-data, a commitment that we found in chapter 2 to be problematic. The problem is not that the skeptic is necessarily in error in making these commitments. Rather, the difficulty is that these commitments raise difficult and intractable problems that are centuries old. So he is in no position to claim that his views are justified, since they incorporate questionable presuppositions. In that respect, in developing his own theory of knowledge, the Pyrrhonian skeptic is just one more dogmatic philosopher.

Dogmatic Skepticism

Another solution suggests itself. Earlier I pointed out that no particular consequence with respect to the fixation of belief follows from the conclusion of the argument against the criterion. The Pyrrhonian skeptic insists upon suspension of judgment, but that, we found, is just impossible. Various forms of fideism are also possible, in which we simply accept as true those propositions that our prevailing methods of fixing belief establish.

So let the skeptic adopt a minimal dogmatism. "We have no knowledge," he asserts. The argument against the criterion inclines us in that direction. This assertion itself does not constitute knowledge. The argument against the criterion shows that as well. Even his claim that the argument against the criterion is sound does not constitute knowledge. He is willing to make the assertions that his reasoning faculties force upon him despite the fact that demands of consistency require him to doubt that they are things he knows or is justified in believing. He is not even sure that the demands for consistency are founded upon principles he knows to be true. He simply asserts them dogmatically.

Why, then, should the other dogmatic philosophers pay any attention to his views? Because once he has presented his arguments to them, their own reasoning faculties will similarly force upon them the view that they possess no knowledge either. They will realize that the systems of which they are so proud are nothing but conjectures or guesses which have no non-circular justification. They may continue to favor them, because they want or prefer the world to be what their systems represent it as being. They can assert whatever they want, but if they take the argument against the criterion really seriously and study it carefully, they will realize that they are dogmatists, not philosophers who know something that others do not know. So although the skeptic is a dogmatist as well, he no longer puts forward views about the way the world is as things he knows to be true or is even justified in thinking to be true. He recognizes his predicament, unlike those who continue their dogmatism in the face of overwhelming objections. In subsequent chapters, we shall consider whether there is any way to avoid the skeptical outcome of the argument against the criterion.

7

Descartes' Dream Argument

Descartes and Fideism

In his *Meditations on First Philosophy*, Descartes endeavored to face the Pyrrhonist arguments squarely and to show that we do have knowledge of the external world. In the First Meditation he attempts to give skepticism its due by formulating what he takes to be the most powerful skeptical arguments of all. He goes further than Sextus Empiricus by showing that even our beliefs about ostensibly evident objects are vulnerable to doubt. He attempts to formulate skepticism in its strongest, most radical version, so that his subsequent attempt to refute it will leave no platform on which the skeptic can stand.

When texts of ancient skepticism were rediscovered in the sixteenth century, their arguments were initially used to defend fideism, the view that faith, not reason, is the correct basis for religious belief. For defenders of the faith, the texts of the skeptics were useful in undermining the claims of reason to constitute the foundation of religious belief. Faith enters the picture to bridge the gap between what reason is capable of validating and what Christian belief requires.

Like the fideists, Descartes willingly made use of skepticism in order to advance his own system of the world. However, he did not embrace fideism because he was convinced that the fundamental truths of religion are demonstrable by reason; philosophy has no need of faith. So interesting and convincing were the skeptical arguments he deployed in the First Meditation that the task of refuting skepticism became one of the major items on the agenda of modern philosophy until Kant and even beyond Kant. It is no exaggeration to say that the philosophical topic that goes under the name of "epistemology," the effort to understand the nature and basis of human knowledge, has been propelled to a great extent by the loss of epistemic optimism caused by the skeptical revival.

Descartes and the Skeptics

In his writings, Descartes reveals a familiarity with the tradition of ancient skepticism and its modern followers. In his replies to Bourdin's objections, he writes:

> We should not suppose that sceptical philosophy is extinct. It is vigorously alive today, and almost all those who regard themselves as more intellectually gifted than others, and find nothing to satisfy them in philosophy as it is ordinarily practiced, take refuge in scepticism because they cannot see any alternative with greater claims to truth. (Descartes, 1985, II, p. 374)

Interestingly, he characterizes his skeptical contemporaries not just as fideists but as those who adhere to a philosophical position that could, plausibly, be true in its own right. In Descartes' eyes, skepticism appears to be a genuine alternative to the exhausted philosophical traditions that were then beginning to fade.

In a revealing passage, Descartes underlines the urgency of refuting skepticism:

> But it is wholly false that in laying down our foundations in philosophy there are corresponding limits which fall short of complete certainty, but which we can sensibly and safely accept without taking doubt any further. For since truth is essentially indivisible, it may happen that a claim which we do not recognize as possessing complete certainty may in fact be quite false, however probable it may appear. To make the foundations of all knowledge rest on a claim that we recognize as being possibly false would not be a sensible way to philosophize. If someone proceeds in this way, how can he answer the sceptics who go beyond all boundaries of doubt? How will he refute them? Will he regard them as desperate lost souls? Fine; but how will they regard him in the meantime? (Descartes, 1985, II, p. 374)

Here Descartes enunciates his famous quest for certainty. In philosophy, at least, we cannot be satisfied with probability or anything less than complete certainty. In explaining his point of view, he asserts a kind of epistemic holism: "Truth is essentially indivisible." If any part of the foundations should be less than certain, it would throw doubt upon all the other parts connected to it. Probability may be acceptable in practical life where certainty is unattainable, but even the slightest crack in the foundations would allow entry to skepticism. After all, to say that a proposition is probably true or that we have some justification in accepting it is quite compatible with its being false. Probability does not exclude falsehood. Moreover, probable or justified belief is not the same thing as knowledge, whereas the skeptic tries to show not that we lack some reason for our beliefs, but that our reasons fail to reach the level of certainty essential for knowledge.

Descartes considers himself to occupy a unique position in the history of philosophy as "the first philosopher ever to overturn the doubt of the skeptics" (Descartes, 1985, II, p. 376). The method of overturning these doubts is, surprisingly, to go along with them as far as possible, to see how far doubt can be made to extend, hoping that, when we have gone as far as possible, the road to absolute certainty will become clear:

> Now the best way of achieving a firm knowledge of reality is first to accus-
> tom ourselves to doubting all things, especially corporeal things. Although
> I had seen many ancient writings by the Academics and Sceptics on this
> subject, and was reluctant to reheat and serve this precooked material, I
> could not avoid devoting one whole Meditation to it. (Descartes, 1985, II,
> p. 94)

Descartes, however, underestimates the interest of the arguments of the First Meditation by describing them as "precooked material." Even if they are precooked, his use of them is "untrodden" and "remote from the normal way" (Descartes, 1985, II, p. 6).

Descartes' Project

It is not unusual to come upon reasons for doubting particular beliefs. New experiences and ideas overthrow existing opinions. Such changes in belief seldom involve a total revolution; most of our beliefs persist unchanged, while a few are modified or replaced. Piecemeal change rather than revolutionary upheaval is the typical pattern.

Descartes' philosophical project, on the other hand, is not limited to piece-meal change; it is potentially revolutionary. As Husserl (1960, p. 1) points out, "the aim of the Meditations is a complete reforming of philosophy into a science grounded on an absolute foundation." He intends to examine his system of beliefs as a whole, not just one at a time. His reason for undertak-ing this investigation is given at the outset of his *Meditations*:

> Some years ago I was struck by the large number of falsehoods that I had accepted as true in my childhood, and by the highly doubtful nature of the whole edifice that I had subsequently based on them. I realized that it was necessary, once in the course of my life, to demolish everything completely and start right again from the foundations if I wanted to establish anything at all in the sciences that was stable and likely to last. (Descartes, 1985, II, p. 6)

His project consists in surveying the totality of his beliefs in order to reduce the number of those that are false, to increase the number that are true, and to reduce the likelihood of acquiring false opinions in the future. His aim is not only to understand his epistemic condition but to improve it.

The explanation he offers in this passage makes it seem as if he was concerned with epistemic self-improvement in his own case alone. However, the autobiographical passages in the earlier *Discourse on Method* indicate that the negative verdict he applies to his own beliefs applies to the dominant intellectual tendencies in his culture. He was, he says, educated "at one of the most famous schools in Europe," and "there I had learned everything that the others were learning" (Descartes, 1985, I, p. 113). Philosophy, in particular, had been especially disappointing: even though "it has been cultivated for many centuries by the most excellent minds, . . . yet there is still no point in it which is not disputed and hence doubtful." Like the ancient Pyrrhonists, Descartes was struck by "how many diverse opinions learned men may maintain on a single question – even though it is impossible for more than one to be true" (Descartes, 1985, I, pp. 114–115). So the deficiencies in his own opinions merely reflect the defects in the opinions of the learned.

Nor did he think that the established methods of fixing belief would be of much help. Although the logic of Aristotle was heralded as the way to truth in scientific matters, Descartes recognized that "syllogisms and most of its other techniques are of less use for learning things than for explaining to others the things one already knows" (Descartes, 1985, I, p. 119). Formal logic is an art of arrangement rather than a method of discovery, and so it is of no help to one who wants to improve the content of his system of beliefs.

Because of these deep, systemic defects, only a searching examination of the totality of his beliefs would be able to reinstate his trust in methods of fixing belief. Although his existing opinions would continue to function as guides to action – there is no alternative to that – he would consider them merely as provisional, as preconceived beliefs on temporary duty until better ones could be found. But from the point of view of philosophical reflection –

when the exigencies of action are temporarily suspended – "I had to uproot from my mind all the wrong opinions I had previously accepted" (Descartes, 1985, I, p. 122).

The Nature of Knowledge and the Method of Doubt

Descartes wanted to assure his readers that, although he was presenting reasons to be skeptical about the body of his opinions, he "was not copying the sceptics, who doubt only for the sake of doubting and pretend to be always undecided; on the contrary, my whole aim was to reach certainty – to cast aside the loose earth and sand so as to come upon rock or clay" (Descartes, 1985, I, p. 125).

What, then, is certainty? Descartes identifies certainty with knowledge, and while he does not spend much time explaining how he understands the concept of knowledge, he provides several clues. Thus one has knowledge of something when one is "impelled to believe it by true reasons"; a belief derived from false principles falls short of certainty (Descartes, 1985, III, p. 27). What, then, is a true reason? "Knowledge is conviction based on a reason so strong that it can never be shaken by any stronger reason" (Descartes, 1985, III, p. 147). The reasons for the conviction must exclude any possibility of doubt. When that is achieved, one can be secure in one's conviction that one is in possession of the truth.

Descartes began the *Meditations* convinced that many of the things he was taught fail to conform to this conception of knowledge. If he intends to determine which of the things he thought he knew he really knew, it makes sense to survey the reasons on the basis of which he adopted them to see whether they are strong enough to exclude the possibility of doubt. If a reason for doubting a proposition he believes can be found upon reflection, it follows that his conviction may very well be false, even though he is convinced it is true. Beliefs that are doubtful he will bracket or put aside or even consider as false during the time that he is engaged on this reflective survey of all his opinions.

Descartes' project is not the same as a particular inquiry into a specific subject matter. Rather, he intends to survey all his opinions in a systematic manner, no matter what the subject matter is. Since they are too numerous to consider individually, he attempts to bracket large classes of them all at once by finding general though convincing reasons to doubt them. Here is the rationale he offers for this procedure:

Suppose [some person] had a basket full of apples and, being worried that some of the apples were rotten, wanted to take out the rotten ones to prevent the rot spreading. How would he proceed? Would he not begin by tipping the whole lot out of the basket? And would not the next step be to cast his eye over each apple in turn, and pick up and put back in the basket only those he saw to be sound, leaving the others? In just the same way, those who have never philosophized correctly have various opinions in their minds which they have begun to store up since childhood, and which they therefore have reason to believe may in many cases be false. They then attempt to separate the false beliefs from the others, so as to prevent their contaminating the rest and making the whole lot uncertain. Now the best way they can accomplish this is to reject all their beliefs together in one go, as if they were all uncertain and false. They can then go over each belief in turn and re-adopt only those which they recognize to be true and indubitable. Thus I was right to reject all my beliefs. (Descartes, 1985, II, p. 324)

Descartes' Pre-philosophical Understanding

Toward the beginning of the Sixth (and final) Meditation, Descartes undertakes to review what he believed about the knowledge he gained from his senses prior to initiating his inquiry. He provides an account of his pre-philosophical original understanding. He recalls his opinion that his senses informed him of a large number of qualities of the objects he apprehended through them:

Considering the ideas of all these qualities which presented themselves to my thought, although the ideas were, strictly speaking, the only immediate objects of my sensory awareness, it was not unreasonable for me to think that the items I was perceiving through the senses were things quite distinct from my thought, namely bodies which produced the ideas. (Descartes, 1985, II, p. 52)

By "ideas" Descartes refers, in this context, to the fact that when he perceives a feature of an object, both the object and its feature appear to him in some way. If he sees a red book, for example, the book will look red to him. Its appearing or looking red to him is what the idea of red consists of in that circumstance. The reason for describing this familiar fact using the terminology of ideas is to emphasize that the ways things appear to him are mental facts about him that represent the external world, that form the basis for his picture about what the world is like.

Not only does the idea or appearance represent the red book, but the book caused the occurrence of the idea, so there is, normally, a real connection between the object perceived and the idea of the object. Since cause and effect are distinct, the book is distinct from the way it appears. The way it appears is a mental fact, a thought, that inheres in the perceiver and that embodies information about the facts in the external world that produce it. Descartes' assertion that ideas are the "immediate objects" of sensory awareness means that our consciousness of external objects is derived from a prior consciousness of the ways they appear. Descartes seems to be incorporating the philosophical theory of epistemological dualism into the account of his pre-philosophical understanding, although some subsequent defenders of dualism have claimed that the most elementary philosophical reflections upon our original understanding establish that dualism is implied by what we all take for granted (see, for example, Lovejoy, 1929, chapter 1).

Descartes offers two reasons for his having thought, prior to the application of the method of doubt, that there is more to sensory consciousness than just the appearances. First, "these ideas came to me quite without my consent," so, unlike his other thoughts and the productions of the imagination, their occurrence seems caused by something outside his thought. Second, these ideas are "much more lively and vivid . . . than any of those which I deliberately formed," so "the only alternative was that they came from other things" (Descartes, 1985, II, p. 52). These are the reasons he has at the outset, if any reasons are needed, for thinking that his senses inform him of a physical world independent of his thought, independent because, while it is capable of causing him to have certain thoughts, his thoughts do not cause it to come into existence. Thinking does not make it so. Thus his pre-philosophical understanding incorporates the realism of common sense, although it is a realism tinctured by dualistic views according to which our access to the external world is mediated by mental representations.

The Problem of Representation

A critic of Locke's epistemology labeled his theory "the new way of ideas." It is clear that "the way of ideas" is more a discovery of Descartes than of Locke. The causal account of the origin of sensory ideas that Descartes found implied in his original understanding convinced him, prior to philosophical reflection, "that I had nothing at all in the intellect which I had not previously had in sensation" (Descartes, 1985, II, p. 52). The claim that all our ideas come from sense experience belongs to the versions of concept empiricism that can be found in Aquinas and, earlier, in Aristotle. Descartes will ultimately reject it on the grounds that we have ideas of things that, because they are not bodies – such as God and self – cannot be given in sensation. Instead, he will conclude that some of our ideas are innate. So the causal account of sensory ideas does not apply to all ideas.

Confining ourselves to sensory ideas for the moment, we can ask how they manage to represent and to carry information about the external world. Descartes' preliminary answer is that "since the sole source of my knowledge of these things was the ideas themselves, the supposition that the things resembled the ideas was bound to occur to me" (Descartes, 1985, II, p. 52). Later he will demonstrate via skeptical arguments that the source of our knowledge of the external world cannot consist just of sensory experiences. If all we have to go on are the ways things appear to the senses, then knowledge is impossible. Descartes' First Meditation constitutes an attack upon the empiricism implicit in our pre-philosophical understanding; instead, our knowledge is a cooperative effort depending upon reason as much as the senses. He denies not that our knowledge of particular bodies and their qualities depends essentially upon the senses, but only that sense perception alone will not do the job.

Let me call the supposition that "the things resembled the ideas" the *resemblance hypothesis* (RH). It seems to be a plausible answer to the question as to how the appearances which are events in the mind produced by the actions of bodies upon the sense organs manage to convey information about bodies. The reason why the book's looking in a certain way to me informs me of its color is that the idea presented to the mind in virtue of its looking that way resembles and, therefore, represents the color.

In the Sixth Meditation, Descartes will qualify the resemblance hypothesis. He thinks that the ideas of the secondary qualities fail to resemble the qualities of the bodies we take them to represent; there is nothing in bodies exactly like these ideas. To this extent, Descartes endorses "the great deception of sense" that we explored in chapter 2.

In his objections to Descartes' philosophical system, Gassendi pointed out a fundamental difficulty with RH: "For how, may I ask, do you think that you, an unextended subject, could receive the semblance or idea of a body that is extended?" (Descartes, 1985, II, p. 234). Perhaps Gassendi is thinking of the Aristotelian doctrine that in perception the mind literally receives a form or semblance of the object, and is wondering how that can be squared with Descartes' view that the self or mind is an unextended substance.

Descartes, however, has repudiated this Aristotelian account of sense perception (Descartes, 1985, II, p. 174). He concedes that Gassendi is correct:

"Nor does it [the mind] understand extension by means of an extended semblance which is present within it (although it does imagine extension by turning to a corporeal semblance [in the brain] which is extended)" (Descartes, 1985, II, p. 266). But even if the brain event has spatial as well as temporal features, there is no reason to suppose that when I imagine a red book, there is something literally red going on in the brain.

Another problem with the resemblance hypothesis is that from the fact that one thing resembles another, it does not follow that either represents the other. This red book does not represent that one, although both are red. Clearly, resemblance is not sufficient for representation.

There is, however, a way to understand RH that is compatible with Descartes' view of the mind and with the relevant facts about the brain. To return again to our example, when the book looks red to me, a thought occurs in my mind, the thought that the book is red, caused by a brain event that itself is ultimately caused by the light reflected from the book falling upon my sense organs. This thought cannot literally resemble the red color of the book; nor, for that matter, can it literally resemble any of the book's primary or secondary qualities. But in having that thought, I am vividly representing the book as having that color. The mental aspect of that thought is the activity of the mind in representing the book as having that color. If the book has the color it is represented as having, then its sensory appearance is accurate or veridical; in that case the color represented resembles, indeed, is, the same color as the color exemplified by the object.

On this interpretation, RH is an account not of representation as such but of accurate or truthful representation. And the resemblance involved is exact resemblance or identity, the identity of the character represented with the character exemplified by the object. Nothing in this account implies that the mind itself exemplifies the character it represents, and thus Gassendi's objection can be circumvented. However, one can no longer appeal to resemblance to explain how the mind is able to represent an object's possessing a character, whether the representation is true or false. Perhaps Descartes' system is in no position to explain representation or intentionality in more fundamental terms. After all, the mind or self is, according to his definition, a thinking thing; that is, a thing that has thoughts and is thus capable of representing the world to itself. There is no reason to suppose in Descartes' system that we can analyze this basic fact about the mind in more fundamental terms than we can analyze the essence of body, namely that it is extended. That there are these two sorts of substances with these essential natures is the way God willed the world to be, and there is nothing more to be said about it.

The Question of the Reliability of the Senses

According to Descartes' original pre-philosophical understanding of the matter, the information delivered by the senses constitutes the foundation of our knowledge of the external world. But it is also part of the original understanding that the senses are not infallible: "The senses occasionally deceive us with respect to objects that are very small or in the distance" (Descartes, 1985, II, p. 17). In addition, we are occasionally confronted with contrary appearances; something that looks one way from a distance looks quite different close up. The thought thus engendered may be mistaken due to such inaccuracies of representation. Descartes quite correctly concludes from these common observations that our senses should not be trusted completely; they are not perfectly reliable.

It seems, however, that there are some sense experiences that it would be mad to doubt because we are in the best possible position for getting the facts. The example Descartes employs is: "I am here, sitting by the fire, wearing a winter dressing-gown, holding this piece of paper in my hands" (Descartes, 1985, II, p. 13). This is an example of a privileged perceptual judgment, privileged because the conditions under which it is made are optimal as far as its accuracy is concerned. There is nothing that Descartes could do to improve the conditions under which he has come to believe that he is holding a piece of paper in his hands, nothing. Or if there is something he can do – looking closer, asking someone's opinion, and so forth – let him do it and then there is nothing more he can do. It seems that there is no longer any possibility of error. So it looks as if he has arrived at an indubitable proposition, at which point skepticism is defeated.

Dreams

It turns out that even privileged perceptual judgments are open to doubt. For there is a difference between doing everything one possibly can to insure against error within the framework of our pre-philosophical understanding and doing everything one possibly can within the corrected framework introduced by philosophical reflection. There may be things that are left to be done that our pre-philosophical understanding fails to recognize.

The instrument that Descartes uses to advance into skepticism is the fact that he dreams. The use of dreams to argue for skepticism was no novelty even in Descartes' time. Sextus Empiricus relied upon dreams for one of his numerous arguments in favor of skepticism (Sextus Empiricus, 1955, I, 104). Montaigne (1533–92), whose writings Descartes was familiar with, also appealed to dreams to support skeptical conclusions:

> Those who have compared our life to a dream were perhaps more right than they thought. When we dream, our soul lives, acts, exercises all her faculties, neither more nor less than when she is awake. . . . Since our reason and our soul accept the fancies and opinions which arise in it while sleeping, and authorize the actions of our dreams with the same approbation as they do those of the day, why do we not consider the possibility that our thinking, our acting, may be another sort of dreaming, and our waking another kind of sleep? (Montaigne, 1965, p. 451)

But instead of wrestling with skepticism and trying to conquer it, Montaigne was content to allow himself to be subdued by it because it was part of a fideist picture of man as a helpless being in the hands of God, depending upon the grace of God even as far as knowledge of the world is concerned.

As I pointed out earlier, Descartes did not take the fideist road since he claimed that reason was sufficient to establish the existence and nature of God; faith, for Descartes, only comes into the picture as the basis for a few tenets of Catholic theology that cannot be established by argument.

Like Montaigne and Sextus, Descartes appeals to dreams for a skeptical argument. Although, as he admits, the reference to dreams did not originate with him but was part of the stock in trade of the skeptical tradition, his formulation was sharper and deeper than any of the other texts in the tradition. Here is the argument of the First Meditation:

> How often, asleep at night, am I convinced of just such familiar events – that I am here in my dressing gown, sitting by the fire – when in fact I am lying undressed in bed! Yet at the moment my eyes are certainly wide awake when I look at this piece of paper; I shake my head and it is not asleep; as I stretch out and feel my hand I do so deliberately, and I know what I am doing. All this would not happen with such distinctness to someone asleep. Indeed! As if I did not remember other occasions when I have been tricked by exactly similar thoughts while asleep! As I think about this more carefully, I see plainly that there are never any sure signs by means of which being awake can be distinguished from being asleep. The result is that I begin to feel dazed, and this very feeling only reinforces the notion that I may be asleep. (Descartes, 1985, II, p. 13)

Let us be clear about the features of dream life that propel this argument. In the first place, Descartes supposes that while he dreams, he entertains thoughts similar to the thoughts that occur to him while he is awake. For example, that he is holding a piece of paper in his hands may occur to him while asleep as well as when he is awake and looking at the paper.

Second, the reason why he entertains similar thoughts is that "the visions which come in sleep are like paintings, which must have been fashioned in the likeness of things that are real" (Descartes, 1985, II, p. 13). Thus the experience he is having when he dreams that he is holding a piece of paper in his hands is formed of the same general constituents – images of colors and shapes, for example – that form his waking perceptual experiences. Just as perceptual experiences trigger certain beliefs, the visions that occur in dreams trigger similar thoughts.

Third, the thoughts that occur in dreams are capable of tricking him. That is, he accepts them as true even though they are actually false. Dreams are a form of hallucinatory experiences leading to false beliefs. I do not mean to suggest, and nor does Descartes, that a thought that occurs while asleep must be false. One may dream, for example, that a bell is ringing at the very moment that a bell is really ringing. The point is that dream visions are not usually controlled and caused by events in the external world, so that the thoughts that occur are usually mistaken. That is why one can be tricked.

In the fourth place, when one is dreaming, one does not usually believe that one is dreaming. Moreover, when one is awake, one usually does not believe that one is dreaming. So if one is engaged in a project such as Descartes' to improve one's system of beliefs by expunging those that are false, it is reasonable to try to identify some sign or mark or criterion by which dreams can be distinguished from waking life so that the false dream thoughts can be identified.

Fifth, one form that a sign can assume is if I act in a way that I could only be doing when awake, such as shaking my head or extending my hand. But the experiences in which I seem to be engaged in such actions and which seem to verify the thought that I am awake are of a sort that also occur in dreams and would then also trigger the same thought. So the fact that I am having an experience that triggers the thought that I am awake is not itself a sure sign of being awake.

Sixth, since the only items available to the pre-philosophical understanding for distinguishing dreams from waking life are the experiences and thoughts that occur in each, and since any experience and thought that can occur in the one can also occur in the other, Descartes concludes that "there are never any sure signs by means of which being awake can be distinguished from being asleep." The evidence of the senses, considered by itself, does not make it any more likely that I am awake than that I am dreaming.

Finally, on the basis of these reflections, Descartes also feels justified in concluding "I may be asleep." Since it is possible that he is asleep, and since the thoughts that occur while asleep are usually false or at least have no rational basis, it follows that it is possible that any such thought is mistaken. Thus, it is possible that any of our beliefs about the external world is mistaken. Thus no such belief is certain. Thus no such belief is known to be true. Therefore, skepticism about our alleged knowledge of the external world is justified up to this point.

Dreams and the Criterion Argument

One of the reasons why Descartes' dream argument appears so powerful and convincing is that it is based upon premises that almost everyone would, upon reflection, find acceptable: we have dreams; in our dreams we have experiences and thoughts; these thoughts are almost always mistaken; while dreaming we usually think we are awake; anything we try to do to prove to ourselves that we are awake is something we could also dream we are doing. There does not seem anything particularly contentious about any of these claims. If the argument is valid, it appears to show that, starting with unexceptional premises, it reaches the extraordinary conclusion that we have no knowledge, absolutely no knowledge at all, about things in the external world. Hobbes' notion of the great deception of sense is extended beyond its original application to secondary qualities to encompass all perceptually given qualities and bodies.

In trying to place the dream argument within the skeptical tradition, we can see that it illustrates Pyrrhonist doubts about criteria of truth. It applies not to all knowledge as the general form of the argument against the criterion does, but to a large class of beliefs concerning objects in the external world. (For the moment we shall put aside Descartes' other arguments concerning *a priori* knowledge and self-knowledge; these will be considered in subsequent chapters.) It shows that we lack a criterion or sure sign or mark for distinguishing between true and false perceptual judgments. Unlike the general form of the argument, it appeals to a particular feature of our perceptual judgments, namely that they occur in dreams as well as in waking life.

The dream argument in particular overturns both of the reasons in Descartes' pre-philosophical understanding for thinking that his perceptual judgments embody information about the external world. The first was that these judgments and the experiences that trigger them "came to me quite without my consent." But dream experiences and thoughts are similarly exempt from control by the will. The second was that these experiences are "much more lively and vivid . . . than any of those which I deliberately formed." But dream experiences can also be quite lively and vivid and, in that respect at least, are indistinguishable from waking experiences.

Representational Experience

Although the argument appeals to facts about dreams, the reference to dreams is actually quite incidental. In order to see this, let me introduce the notion of a representational experience. A representational experience is one in which something appears to us in a certain way or, more cautiously, in which it is just as if our sense experience is presenting us with some object or quality or fact in the external world and we take it to be the object or quality or fact that it seems to be. If, for example, it appears to me that I am seeing a red book, and if I take it that I am seeing a red book, then that is a representational experience. Thus a representational experience includes both a sensory appearance and a judgment that accepts that experience as revealing an aspect of the external world. The judgment may be true or it may be false; its truth value is not entailed by the notion of a representational experience.

Dreams are introduced by Descartes as memorable examples of representational experiences whose constituent judgments are mostly mistaken. Moreover, with respect to the example that Descartes introduced – "I am here, sitting by the fire, wearing a winter dressing gown, holding this piece of paper in my hands" – dreams incorporate privileged perceptual judgments; we cannot do better than these as far as capturing the truth is concerned.

The Indeterminacy of Sense Experience

Let me now examine the basis of Descartes' conclusion that no perceptual judgments, not even the privileged ones, are cases of knowledge. Consider some representational experience R. Let R include a privilege perceptual judgment J together with a triggering experience E. There is nothing intrinsic to the nature of E that entails the truth of J or even its probability. That is, if E were considered in isolation and its features described independently of its causal connections to anything else and of any inductively based conjectures, the description by itself would not prove that J is true or even probably true. That is, there is nothing extractable from E taken by itself that would satisfy a criterion on the basis of which we would be justified in thinking that J is true. Thus there is no intrinsic feature of my present experience that excludes the possibility that I am dreaming. I shall characterize this fact about E and about perceptual experiences generally as *the indeterminacy of sense experience* (see Hill, 1999, p. 117 for a similar formulation).

In our original pre-philosophical understanding, we would not hesitate to endorse the truth of any privileged perceptual judgment. Our original framework provides ways and means, in the form of prevailing modes of verification, for convincing ourselves of the truth of J. For example, let J be "There is a red book on that table" and E be an experience that I would describe as its appearing to me that there is a red book on the table. If I were asked to provide reasons why the occurrence of E was an excellent reason for thinking that J is true, I could say, for example, that the judgments incorporated in the representational experiences of things I had examined closely in the past invariably turned out to be true, and that in no case in the past has any experience just like E turned out to be just a dream. But these reasons appeal to extrinsic features of E as well as to memory and past perceptions whose veracity has yet to be tested. Descartes' project, remember, is intended to examine all at once all our cognitive faculties and their propositional claims, so we are not able to rely upon them without begging the question. The reason we have no knowledge of J is that no intrinsic feature of the experience on which J is based taken in isolation makes it likely that J is true and that we are not entitled to appeal to any other of our prevailing modes of justification, in which appeal is made to extrinsic features.

Two Assumptions about Knowledge

Implicit in this argument is an assumption about the nature of knowledge. Remember that, for Descartes, in order to know that a certain proposition is true, our conviction must be based upon unshakable, indubitable reasons. This means that in order to know that J is true I must have access to such reasons, I must have, at some time or other, consciously entertained such reasons, I must have based my conviction on such reasons, and I must have assured myself that these indeed are unshakable reasons. In order to have knowledge about anything, I must be in a position to prove to myself that I have knowledge; that is, in order to know, I must know that I know. Such a conception of knowledge will be labeled *strong cognitive internalism*.

There is a related assumption about knowledge that is concealed within Descartes' argument. In order for Descartes' project to be intelligible, it must rely upon the concept of knowledge incorporated in our original pre-philosophical understanding. At the end of the First Meditation, he is telling us that he does not know any of the things he thought he knew prior to his reflections upon the human cognitive condition. The question he is raising is whether any of the things he thought he knew can be shown to be things that he actually does know, whether his ignorance can be transformed into knowledge. This question depends upon his employing an unambiguous conception of knowledge. The concealed assumption is that strong cognitive internalism constitutes this unambiguous conception of knowledge that stays the same from beginning to end.[1]

One initial difficulty with strong cognitive internalism is that it implies a vicious infinite regress. For if the conditions of knowledge are such that in order to know anything at all, I must know that I know, it follows that in order to know that I know, I must also know that I know that I know, *ad infinitum*. The reason why the regress is vicious is that in order to have any knowledge at all, I must have completed the impossible task of traversing an infinite number of arguments, each one showing that I have knowledge of the knowledge I have claimed to have at the previous level.

One might attempt to avoid this consequence by interpreting Descartes as claiming that strong cognitive internalism applies not to all knowledge but just to knowledge of the external world. Therefore, the regress can be terminated at the second level. My knowledge that I know the existence of things in the external world is not strongly internalist and thus does not require any further knowledge. However, this interpretation would not be correct, since Descartes does not introduce a multiplicity of conceptions of knowledge. Moreover, if there is another conception of knowledge lurking behind the scenes, then it could be applied to our knowledge of the external world at the outset and skepticism might be avoided. I consider this issue further in subsequent chapters.

One might attempt to weaken strong cognitive internalism. For example, one might say that although one's reasons for a belief must exclude the possibility of all doubt, one need not know this. Let us label this view *weak cognitive internalism*. It is an internalist position for it claims that one must have reasons, know what these reasons are, and base one's belief upon them.

---

1   One reader has pointed out that Descartes may also be criticizing our pre-theoretical concept of knowledge, so that the concept he ends up with may not be the same as the concept he starts with. I have been unable to discover any evidence of this within the *Meditations* itself.

However, although, for Descartes, these reasons must be unshakable, this does not require that one be able to prove them. However, this weaker view cannot be Descartes', since his project involves showing how one can ultimately obtain unshakable reasons and show they are unshakable. Only then is skepticism refuted. His very idea of what it takes to refute skepticism commits him to the strong view.

Perceptual Experience and Sense Data

I have interpreted Descartes as claiming that dreams involve two constituents: perceptual experiences and thoughts or judgments. In chapter 2 I rejected one of the dominant accounts of perceptual experience, the sense datum theory. Sense data are supposed to be objects of direct and immediate awareness that exemplify the sensory qualities that bodies appear to exemplify, such as color and shape. We found good reason to doubt the sense datum theory but did not subscribe to any alternative theory. It is important to note here that Descartes' dream argument does not depend upon the sense datum theory. In fact, it does not depend upon any particular contentious theory of the nature of sense experience (see Curley, 1978, p. 53). Since Descartes is operating within the framework of his original understanding, it is sufficient for his argument if we interpret sense experience in the noncommittal pre-theoretical terms of the original understanding as simply the ways things appear: the ways they look, feel, sound, taste, and smell. Even though he speaks of "the visions which come in sleep" he does not explicitly adopt a sense datum approach. In fact, in the face of Gassendi's objections, Descartes must see that sense data are incompatible with his conception of the nature of mind. Sensations and ideas are modes of the mind for Descartes, and there is reason against supposing that they exemplify the qualities that they represent.

Empiricism

If we ignore questions of logical and mathematical knowledge and focus simply upon our knowledge of bodies in the external world, it is common to suppose that empiricism is the correct account of that sort of knowledge. Yet Descartes' dream argument shows serious problems with empiricism. By *simple empiricism* I mean the claim that the occurrence of the relevant sense experiences is sufficient to confirm and lend credibility to perceptual judgments.

On this view, the occurrence of the experience that I describe in the words "It seems to me as if I am seeing that there is a red book lying upon a table" is sufficient to lend some credibility to the proposition that there is as red book lying upon the table. Yet according to the dream argument, this claim is not true. There is nothing about the experience, considered in isolation from everything else we know or believe, that tends to show in the slightest that the proposition is true or is likely to be true. After all, the existence of the red book on the table is only one of various possibilities to explain the occurrence of the experience; another possibility, of course, is that it is just a dream. Descartes considers still a third:

> And yet firmly rooted in my mind is the long-standing opinion that there is an omnipotent God who made me the kind of creature that I am. How do I know that he has not brought it about that there is no earth, no sky, no extended thing, no shape, no size, no place, while at the same time ensuring that all these things appear to me to exist just as they do now? (Descartes, 1985, II, p. 14)

George Berkeley will later adapt this idea to his own empiricist philosophy: God directly produces our ideas of the external world; our sense experiences are direct communications from God. As the First Meditation comes to an end, Descartes mentions even a further possibility, namely that "some malicious demon of the utmost power and cunning has employed all his energies in order to deceive me" (Descartes, 1985, II, p. 15). The demon argument will be considered in a later chapter.

It is clear that, for Descartes, in order for me to know that there is a red book on the table on the basis of my experience, I must be in a position to exclude all other explanations of the occurrence of that experience. But there is nothing in the experience itself that tells me which possibility is the true cause. Thus when Descartes concludes the dream argument with "I may be asleep," the sort of possibility expressed by the verb "may be" is that of an unexcluded alternative explanation. My current experience fails to establish in the slightest degree that none of the alternatives to the existence of the red book on the table is true. My current experience is completely indeterminate with respect to all possible explanations of its occurrence.

To avoid this difficulty, an empiricist may suggest a more complex epistemology that I shall call *framework empiricism*. According to framework empiricism, the various possibilities are to be excluded by interpreting the present experience in the light of one's existing background knowledge. Thus, it is a valid inductive generalization that experiences of this kind are probable signs of the existence of a red book on the table. Since I employ my memory of these experiences to arrive at this generalization, I can call upon a further inductive generalization of my past exercises of memory to tell me that my memory is reliable.

In order for framework empiricism to be plausible, the only elements of the background knowledge that are admitted into the framework are those consistent with empiricism. Assuming that an empiricist can provide an account of our logical and mathematical knowledge, then truths of logic and mathematics are eligible candidates for the framework. So are inductive generalizations, since these are based upon past experience. So are our past perceptual judgments on the basis of which these generalizations are confirmed. Using this background knowledge, I am in a position to exclude all possibilities to explain my experience other than the existence of the red book on the table. So, from the standpoint of framework empiricism, it is just not true that "I may be asleep."

Solipsism

But it is easy to see that framework empiricism is no better than simple empiricism at overcoming the skepticism engendered by the dream argument. The elements of the framework are entitled to be employed in eliminating the unwanted possibilities only if they themselves constitute knowledge, or at least justified or probable belief. But the dream argument applies to our past perceptual judgments as well as to those of the present, so we have no more right to consider past experiences to be veridical than we have to consider the present ones veridical.

Moreover, the basic structure of the dream argument applies to memory as well. The mere occurrence of a memory belief does not prove that it is true. There are explanations of the occurrence memory beliefs other than that the event recollected really happened: for example, to adapt Descartes' example, God could have created me with just these memories even though none of them are true.

In a later chapter, we shall consider Hume's inductive skepticism, according to which inductive generalizations are founded upon custom, not reason, and fail to count as knowledge or credible belief. Assuming Hume's arguments to be correct, inductive generalizations are not allowed in the framework.

Because the dream argument justifies doubting the existence of bodies, it also provides reason for doubting the existence of other persons as well, since our beliefs about others are founded upon observations of their bodies and behavior. Not only are beliefs about other persons not admissible into the framework, neither are any beliefs communicated to us by others, since we have reason to doubt the existence of these others, and such communications reach us in the form of various perceptual experiences whose veridicality is in question.

What is left? Since others are in doubt, I must shift into the first person and speak only to myself. Perhaps that is why Descartes entitled his great work *Meditations*, since after the First Meditation he could not assume the existence of an audience. I am left with myself, my ideas, and my experiences. Moreover, the ideas and the experiences that I am left with are those that exist now, at this very moment, since, as we saw, both memory of the past and inductive extrapolation into the future are victims of skeptical arguments.

George Santayana has called this view *solipsism of the present moment*. It is a consequence of the failure of framework empiricism to salvage our knowledge of the external world. Here is Santayana's view of the framework itself: "The postulates on which empirical knowledge and inductive science are based – namely, that there has been a past, that it was such as it is now thought to be, that there will be a future and that it must, for some inconceivable reason, resemble the past and obey the same laws – these are all gratuitous dogmas" (Santayana, 1923, p. 14). Framework empiricism as a theory of human knowledge seems hopeless in the face of Descartes' skeptical onslaught. From the skeptical standpoint, the elements of the framework are "gratuitous dogmas." Of course, Descartes himself hoped to refute skepticism, and did not intend to end as a solipsist of the present moment. He agreed with framework empiricism to this extent, that our present experiences can be the basis of our knowledge of the external world only if they are interpreted on the basis of a framework. However, the elements of the framework cannot be the same as those the empiricist admits, for skeptical arguments exclude them entirely. Only those elements are admissible that can be certified by an *a priori* argument. But before we go any further with Descartes' account of human knowledge, we shall examine an attempt to refute skepticism about the external world that will lead us to a totally different conception of what it means to know something.

8

Skepticism and Common Sense

Common Sense

Some things are just a matter of common sense, and it appears absurd to deny things that common sense affirms. Skepticism in general and Descartes' skepticism about the external world in particular defy common sense and seem absurd on the face of it. But what is common sense anyhow? For Kant, common sense consists, as we saw in chapter 1, of "an appeal to the opinion of the multitude, of whose applause the philosopher is ashamed." Is common sense just what most people think? If so, it is a matter of common sense that one or more gods exist, since most people have believed that. But atheism, whether right or wrong, is not absurd on the face of it.

So we cannot identify common sense with what most people think if common sense is supposed to have some epistemic weight. Moreover, what most people think at any given time sometimes changes. There was a time when most people believed that the Earth was at the center of the universe, an opinion that no longer has any support. Kant is right that the philosopher should be ashamed to appeal to the opinion of the multitude as the sole reason for accepting a philosophical view.

P. F. Strawson introduces a more useful concept of common sense:

> For there is a massive core of human thinking which has no history – or none recorded in histories of thought; there are categories and concepts which, in their most fundamental character, change not at all. Obviously these are not the specialties of the most refined thinking. They are the commonplaces of the least refined thinking; and are yet the indispensable core of the conceptual equipment of the most sophisticated human beings. (Strawson, 1959, p. 10)

Let us call these unchanging concepts and categories of our least refined thinking our *common sense conceptual scheme*. It incorporates the basic concepts by means of which the multitude expresses many of its opinions, and it implicitly includes an ontology because the use of this scheme commits the user to the existence of instances of the basic concepts.

Strawson characterizes these concepts as "indispensable." By that he means, I think, first, that no matter what changes occur in human thought about the world, they will still remain entrenched in our efforts to describe, understand, and interpret our experience. Second, because they will remain entrenched, we will always think of the world as containing actual instances of them. The discussion of color in chapter 2, however, challenges their indispensability. The concepts of color and the other secondary qualities certainly belong to this core of human thinking. But it was a conclusion of the arguments of chapter 2 about "the great deception of sense" that we should surrender our ontological commitments to the existence of colored objects. I pointed out there that, as long as humans possess the visual equipment that allows them to make color discriminations and as long as color appearances reflect useful and important features of bodies, people will still employ color concepts and act as if there are colored things. In that sense the concept of color is indispensable and will remain a commonplace of the least refined thought. But it should no longer be part of the core of the most sophisticated thought. We find in the history of sophisticated thought – in the writings of Galileo, Hobbes, Locke, Descartes, and many others – that the ontology of colored objects is seen as a problem and is frequently rejected.

Common Sense and Philosophy

As we saw in chapter 7, Santayana thinks that the ontology of common sense consists of "gratuitous dogmas." The project that Descartes introduced in the First Meditation subjects common sense to a plausible challenge. So, if the appeal to common sense is to be persuasive in refuting philosophical opinions that challenge the common sense conceptual scheme, it must be accomplished in a manner that does not seem to us to be merely dogmatic. As we saw in chapter 1, Kant pointed out that dogmatism must be tested by the fires of skepticism and that a return to dogmatism as if skepticism provided no plausible challenge is impossible. After Kant, any legitimate appeal to common sense must reflect the overcoming of dogmatism.

Let us consider two examples drawn from the history of philosophical thought to see how the appeal to common sense has worked. In his *Lives of the Philosophers*, Diogenes Laertius provides many amusing anecdotes about

Diogenes the Cynic. According to one of them, "when somebody declared that there is no such thing as motion, he [Diogenes] got up and walked about" (Diogenes Laertius, 1991, II, p. 41). Over two millennia later, Boswell reported that after he and his friend Samuel Johnson had left church,

> we stood talking for some time together of Bishop Berkeley's ingenious sophistry to prove the non-existence of matter, and that every thing in the universe is merely ideal. I observed, that though we are satisfied his doctrine is not true, it is impossible to refute it. I never shall forget the alacrity with which Johnson answered, striking his foot with a mighty force against a large stone, till he rebounded from it, – "I refute it *thus*." (Boswell, 1791, p. 285)

By walking about, Diogenes the Cynic defended the commonplace idea that things sometimes move. By kicking the stone, Johnson was defending the concept of matter. Both of these arguments exemplify the same pattern: in reply to a philosopher who denies or appears to deny some common sense fact such as the existence of motion or of matter, the defender of common sense simply produces an actual example of the concept being challenged. In this way, he hopes to reinstate the ontology that has been denied.

G. E. Moore's Appeal to Common Sense

From almost the very beginning of his philosophical career (in 1910–11), G. E. Moore displayed an admiration for this type of argument, and he was quite willing to apply it not merely to some of the more salient categories of our conceptual scheme, such as motion and matter, but also against skepticism in general. Skeptical claims can consist not only of theories about human knowledge (*epistemological skepticism*) but also of ontological assertions about the existence or non-existence of instances of basic concepts (*ontological skepticism*) or of both together. The concept of knowledge belongs to our common sense conceptual scheme, and the global skeptic asserts that this concept is quite empty. There are no actual instances of it, so his views possess both ontological and epistemological import.

Here is how Moore assessed this pattern of argumentation when applied to skepticism about the external world: "If the object is to prove *in general* that we do know of the existence of material objects, no argument which is really stronger can, I think, be brought forward to prove this than particular instances in which we do in fact know of the existence of such an object" (Moore, 1953, p. 143). Moore here claims that this pattern of argument is the strongest one available to refute skepticism of the senses. It is not the only one, but it is the most powerful. Here is his explanation:

> I admit, however, that other arguments may be more convincing; and perhaps some of you may be able to supply me with one that is. But, however much more *convincing* it may be, it is, I think, sure to depend upon some premiss which is, in fact, less certain than the premiss that I do know of the existence of this pencil; and so, too, in the case of any arguments which can be brought forward to prove that we do not know of the existence of any material object. (Moore, 1953, p. 143)

Moore here points out that one argument may be more convincing than another even though the premise of the latter is more certain than the premise of the former. Being convincing is how an argument strikes one; a proposition's degree of certainty, however, is not a fact about the mentality of the person who believes or entertains it, but a fact about its epistemic value or worth. The reason why there is no stronger argument against the skeptic is that the certainty of the existence of an actual instance of our knowledge such as "I know that here is a pencil" is greater than the certainty of any other premise that one might put forward in a philosophical argument against the skeptic, as well as any premise the skeptic might offer. As far as disputes about philosophical skepticism are concerned, the appeal to common sense has greater epistemic value than any other form of argument. In fact, for Moore, it is conclusive.

Common Sense as a Body of Truisms

In 1925, Moore published his famous paper "A Defence of Common Sense." It begins with what he calls a list of "obvious truisms" which he says "I *know*, with certainty, to be true" (Moore, 1970, p. 32). Here is a brief selection from this list:

> There exists at present a living human body, which is *my* body. This body was born at a certain time in the past, and has existed continuously ever since, though not without undergoing changes. . . . I am a human being . . . I have often perceived both my own body and other things which formed part of its environment, including other human bodies; I have not only perceived things of this kind but have also observed facts about them, such as, for instance, the fact which I am now observing, that that mantelpiece is at present nearer to my body than that bookcase. (Moore, 1970, p. 33)

Although Moore intends these to be truisms, the reader may very well be startled by one of them: "This body was born. . . ." It would have been unexceptionable for Moore to have said "I was born" but it strikes the ear as peculiar to speak of a certain body being born. Perhaps it is not as easy to establish certain propositions as being truisms as Moore believes. He then goes on to assert that many other human beings have known similar things about themselves, their bodies, and objects in their environment. These claims about the knowledge that he and others possess he calls *the Common Sense view of the world*, about which he says:

> I am one of those philosophers who have held that the "Common Sense view of the world" is, in certain fundamental features, *wholly* true. But it must be remembered that, according to me, *all* philosophers, without exception, have agreed with me in holding this: and that the real difference, which is commonly expressed in this way, is only a difference between those philosophers, who have *also* held views inconsistent with these features in "the Common Sense view of the world," and those who have not. (Moore, 1970, p. 44)

Of course, the philosophical skeptic denies that he himself knows these things to be true. A solipsist of the present moment would not bother denying that Moore knows these things for he does not even know of the existence of Moore. But the fact that the skeptic denies that he himself has this knowledge does not prove that he does not have this knowledge; just as one can fail to know something that one thinks one knows, so also one can know something that one thinks that one does not know. "The strange thing is that philosophers should have been able to hold sincerely, as part of their philosophical creed, propositions inconsistent with what they themselves *knew* to be true; and yet, so far as I can make out, this has really frequently happened" (Moore, 1970, p. 41). Philosophers are not only capable of logical inconsistency – that is, believing both a proposition and one logically incompatible with it – but they are also capable of epistemic inconsistency – that is, believing a proposition inconsistent with a proposition they know to be true.

It is interesting to note that no proposition ascribing a color or any other secondary quality to an object is included in the list of truisms that Moore puts forward. Perhaps that was just an oversight on his part, but another explanation is that he was not sure that such propositions are actually true. Or perhaps he wanted his list of truisms to include propositions that everyone other than the global skeptic would find acceptable, and he knew that many thinkers who are not global skeptics believe in "the great deception of sense." So Moore's claim that this list of truisms is known by him to be true and that a comparable list is known by many others to be true is consistent with color nihilism.

Moore's Dogmatism

Can anything be said in favor of Moore's claim that he knows these things to be true? He is aware that the skeptic would not be impressed by his claim to know them, but he is not sure that he has anything better to offer:

> But do I really *know* all the propositions in (1) [the list of truisms] to be true? Isn't it possible that I merely believe them? Or know them to be highly probable? In answer to this question, I think I have nothing better to say than that it seems to me that I *do* know them, with certainty. It is, indeed, obvious that, in the case of most of them, I do not know them *directly*: that is to say, I only know them because, in the past, I have known to be true *other* propositions which were evidence for them. If, for instance, I do know that the earth had existed for many years before I was born, I certainly only know this because I have known other things in the past which were evidence for it. And I certainly do not know exactly what the evidence was. Yet all this seems no good reason for doubting that I do know it. We are all, I think, in this strange position that we do *know* many things, with regard to which we *know* further that we must have had evidence for them, and yet we do not know *how* we know them, i.e. we do not know what the evidence was. (Moore, 1970, p. 44)

This passage includes a number of interesting points about human knowledge. First, Moore distinguishes without comment between knowing something with certainty and knowing something to be probable. Second, he distinguishes between direct knowledge and knowledge that is based upon evidence. Third, he implies that it is possible to know something with certainty even though our knowledge of it is based upon evidence. And fourth, he claims that we may know something with certainty that is based upon evidence even though we do not remember what the evidence consists of.

None of these interesting points is developed in this paper. But the most striking fact of all is how feeble the argument actually is. When asked whether he really knows these things, all he offers in reply in this paper is to reiterate that he does know them. Moore's claim to know each of these truisms is, to use Santayana's expression, a gratuitous dogma.

We are now in a position to discern the problem with the strategy adopted by Diogenes the Cynic, Samuel Johnson, and Moore that attempts to refute an apparently absurd philosophical claim by producing an actual instance of the concept whose emptiness is asserted. The claim that we have an actual instance is, as it stands, dogmatic. It is no better founded than the claim it rejects. When Diogenes the Cynic walks about, the philosopher who denies the existence of motion can merely say or think that he seems to walk about but his seeming to walk about has no tendency to show that he is actually walking about.

Is there any way of developing this strategy so that it incorporates some argument or consideration that removes the taint of dogmatism? Is there a better argument against skepticism than simply countering the apparent absurdity of the skeptic's denial of knowledge with a dogmatic counter-assertion? In the next chapter we shall consider Moore's attempt to provide a proof of the existence of the external world.

9

Moore's Proof of an External World

Moore's Proof Stated

Moore returned to the problem of skepticism in his 1939 paper "Proof of an External World." Here is the proof in his own words:

> It seems to me that, so far from its being true, as Kant declares to be his opinion, that there is only one possible proof of the existence of things outside us, namely the one which he has given, I can now give a number of different proofs each of which is a perfectly rigorous proof; and that at many other times I have been in a position to give many others. I can prove now, for instance, that two human hands exist. How? By holding up my two hands, and saying, as I make a gesture with the right hand, "Here is one hand," and adding, as I make a certain gesture with the left, "and here is another." And if, by doing this, I have proved ipso facto the existence of external things, you will all see that I can also do it now in numbers of other ways: there is no need to multiply examples. (Moore, 1970, pp. 145–6)

If this is a proof, one should be able to express it in the form of a proof by indicating a premise or premises as well as the conclusion. There is textual evidence (Moore, 1970, pp. 145–6) that Moore understands the proof to consist of a single premise with two distinct conclusions. Here is the formulation that I shall follow throughout this chapter:

The Proof (P):
Premise: Here is one hand and here is another.
First Conclusion: Two hands exist at this moment.
Second Conclusion: At least two external objects exist at this moment.

It is obvious that the premise entails the first conclusion. It is not obvious that the first conclusion entails the second, and Moore devotes most of the paper to explaining how to obtain the latter from the former.

Briefly, Moore explains that among the items that he intends to classify as external things or objects are physical things that are public, perceivable, and that exist independently of being perceived. In contrast, visual after-images would not count as external things, since they are neither public nor do they have independent existence. Moore takes his hands (as he points out, he could have taken many other things) as paradigm cases of external physical objects; this means that from the fact that his hands exist, it follows that there exist objects that are public, perceivable, and independent; therefore, his hands count, for the purposes of the argument as external objects. The reason why they count is that if someone thought he saw a hand, but it turned out that what he saw or thought he saw did not exist independently of the perception of it and that no one else could perceive it, it would follow that he did not actually see a hand but was undergoing a hallucination. Whatever he saw wouldn't be hands if they could not pass this test. So the fact that they are capable of passing this test follows from the fact that they are hands. And the fact that they are external things follows from the fact that they are capable of passing this test.

Moore's Proof and Idealism

We can see that P bears some similarity to the argument we considered in chapter 8, in which Moore argues against the skeptic by producing what he takes to be an actual instance of our knowledge of external objects. However, the premise of P produces not an instance of our knowledge of external objects but an instance of external objects themselves. This raises the question of whether Moore's proof is directed against epistemic skepticism at all.

Moore opened his paper with a quotation from Kant's *Critique of Pure Reason*: "It still remains a scandal to philosophy . . . that the existence of things outside of us . . . must be accepted merely on faith, and that, if anyone thinks good to doubt their existence, we are unable to counter his doubts by any satisfactory proof" (Kant, 1781, p. Bxxxix). Although Kant attempted to remove the scandal to philosophy by offering a proof of his own, Moore thinks that "it is by no means certain that Kant's proof is satisfactory." He thinks that the question of whether a satisfactory proof can be given "still deserves discussion." He thinks that this is "a matter of some importance" (Moore, 1970, pp. 128, 129, 127).

Kant asserts in this passage that, in the absence of proof, we must accept the existence of things outside us on faith. It would appear that, for Kant, the point of a proof of the external world is to show that we do not have to accept its existence on faith, that we actually know that it exists. When we turn to the proof that Kant offers in the section called "The Refutation of Idealism," we find that the point of view that he is attempting to refute is one that he calls "material idealism," which "declares the existence of objects in space outside us either to be merely doubtful and indemonstrable or to be false or impossible" (Kant, 1781, B274). It appears that Kant's proof is directed against both epistemic skepticism, which says that nobody knows of the existence of external objects ("objects in space outside us"), and ontological skepticism, which says that there are no external objects. Epistemic skepticism is clearly one of the views against which Kant's proof is directed.

It is quite a surprise to realize that the issue of epistemic skepticism is never mentioned in Moore's paper. In his "A Reply to My Critics," which was first published in 1942, he writes: "this [remark of Alice Ambrose] assumes that my refutation was intended to be a refutation of 'Nobody knows that there are external objects,' whereas it was only intended to be a refutation of 'There are no external objects'" (Moore, 1968, pp. 673–4). So it looks as if skepticism with regard to the senses is not one of the targets of Moore's paper even though it is one of the targets of Kant's "Refutation of Idealism." It is, then, puzzling why Moore introduced his discussion with a quotation from Kant in which the scandal to philosophy that Kant mentions consists in the failure by philosophers to have refuted epistemic skepticism.

Kant calls the epistemic disjunct of material idealism "problematic idealism" and ascribes it to Descartes. The ontological disjunct he calls "dogmatic idealism" and ascribes to Berkeley, who, according to Kant, "maintains that space, with all the things of which it is an inseparable condition, is something which is in itself impossible; and he therefore regards the things in space as merely imaginary entities" (Kant, 1781, B274). These characterizations of Descartes and Berkeley seem to me to be misinterpretations: as we saw, Descartes did not endorse skepticism but merely used skeptical arguments to arrive at non-skeptical conclusions; and Berkeley did not deny the truth of our common sense statements about the spatial locations of material objects, although he was a critic of Newton's assertion of the existence of absolute space, time, and motion.

Moore's response to Ambrose indicates that the prime philosophical target of his proof is Berkeley's alleged dogmatic idealism. In *Some Main Problems of Philosophy*, Moore offered a subtle defense of Kant's misinterpretation of Berkeley:

> He [Berkeley] says that he is not denying the existence of matter, but only explaining what matter is. But he is commonly held to have denied the existence of matter, and I think quite rightly. For he held that these Appearances do not exist except at the moment when we see them; and anything of which this is true can certainly not be said to be a material object: what we mean to assert, when we assert the existence of material objects, is certainly the existence of something which continues to exist even when we are not conscious of it. . . . I think that it may fairly be said that Berkeley denies the existence of any material objects, in the sense in which Common Sense asserts their existence. (Moore, 1953, pp. 34–5)

According to Moore, although Berkeley did not intend to be a dogmatic idealist, his theory of matter actually entails dogmatic idealism because a material thing, construed according to common sense (and Berkeley wished to construe material things according to common sense), exists independently of the perception of it, something Berkeley denies. Berkeley's error consists in misunderstanding the common sense concept of matter, which incorporates independent existence as a necessary condition. Moore maintained the same view when, almost thirty years later, his proof of an external world incorporated independent existence into the concept of matter.

Thomas Baldwin takes Moore's statement of his intentions in his "A Reply to My Critics" as the last word on the issue: "Moore's proof is not a refutation of skepticism, nor was it intended to be. It was intended to be a refutation of idealism; as such it is a total failure" (Baldwin, 1990, p. 295). The reason the proof fails, according to Baldwin, is that the idealist is able to provide an analysis of the notion of a material object according to which there are material objects in space and time. That is exactly what Berkeley thought he was doing. Where the idealist disagrees with the realist is not on the question of the external world but on what it means for there to be one.

However, in the passage from *Some Main Problems of Philosophy* that is echoed in "Proof of an External World," Moore points out that despite the intentions of Berkeley's idealism to conform to our common sense conception of the nature of matter, the analysis that the idealist provides of our common sense concept is simply mistaken because it leaves independent existence out of the concept.[1] And Moore is correct on this score; the failure of subsequent efforts to capture our common sense concept of a material object mak-

---

1   Berkeley might reply that he allows material objects to exist independently of perception by humans although none exist independently of God's perception.

ing use only of appearances or ideas in the mind is proof of that. So if Moore's proof of an external world should turn out to be sound, given what he means by an external world, he would have succeeded in refuting dogmatic idealism and establishing the truth of common sense realism.

Moore's Proof and Epistemic Skepticism

Even though skepticism of the senses was not Moore's directly intended target in his proof, nevertheless, the issue of epistemic skepticism is inextricably woven into the fabric of his argument. When Moore speaks of a proof, he clearly does not mean merely a formal proof in the logician's sense, in which a conclusion follows from the premises in accordance with the rules of formal logic. In his paper, P is intended to be a sequence of statements that possesses epistemic import. An epistemic proof can be used to show that its conclusion is true. It can be used to remove doubts about its conclusion and to convince someone of its truth.

Another reason why P is not a formal proof is that the entailments that hold between the premise and the first conclusion and the first conclusion and the second are not formal implications but depend upon the meanings of their constituent terms.

Among the conditions that Moore mentions that are necessary for P to constitute a proof of this kind is that "the premiss which I adduced was something which I knew to be the case and not merely something which I believed but which was by no means certain, or something which, though in fact true, I did not know to be so" (Moore, 1970, p. 146). So P would not count as a proof in the intended sense unless Moore actually knows that its premise is true. But if he does know it to be true, then skepticism with regard to the senses is mistaken, and it is simply false that "nobody knows there are external objects." So even if epistemic skepticism is not Moore's direct target, it would suffer refutation if the proof succeeded in refuting idealism.

Knowledge of the Premise

Does Moore actually know the truth of the premise of P as he says he does? To anyone who doubts that he knows it he responds by saying: "How absurd it would be to suggest that I did not know it, but only believed it, and that perhaps it was not the case! You might as well suggest that I do not know that I am now standing up and talking – that perhaps after all I'm not, and that it's not quite certain that I am" (Moore, 1970, pp. 146–7). The reason why it would be absurd to deny that he knows the premise is that he is standing before an audience, holding his hands up in plain view so that everyone can see them. It appears absurd to deny the existence of things that are in plain view. How can anyone fail to see them?

Wittgenstein points out, however, that it is also absurd to assert the premise and claim that one knows it to be true. "I am sitting with a philosopher in the garden; he says again and again 'I know that that's a tree,' pointing to a tree that is near us. Someone else arrives and hears this, and I tell him: 'This fellow isn't insane. We are only doing philosophy'" (Wittgenstein, 1969, para. 467). Why the appearance of insanity? Well, the tree is in plain view, and no one doubts that it is a tree, so it seems pointless to utter those words. The purpose of the use of "I know" in our language games is to remove doubt or to provide assurance to someone who is in doubt that the proposition is true. In the garden, no one requires such assurance so the conditions under which "I know" is properly used fail to be satisfied.

It is characteristic of Wittgenstein's thinking about these matters to identify the meaning of a word with its use in the appropriate language game, so that the failure of a condition of proper use destroys the intelligibility of the utterances in which it occurs. However, that way of thinking is not suitable to our concept of knowledge since our use of the concept is not restricted to circumstances in which one aims at removing doubt. One may just happen to discover something and add it to the stock of things one knows to be true without attempting to remove anyone else's doubt or even one's own. Even though doubt is a spur to inquiry and the absence of doubt may occasionally make it pointless to assert that one has knowledge, it does not follow that the presence of doubt is a necessary condition for the proposition that one has knowledge to be intelligible or to be true. A pointless communication may nevertheless be true (see Stroud, 1987, chapter 2) So the absurd and comical character of Moore's uttering both the premise of P and that he knows it to be true in the circumstances in which his hands are in plain view to everyone does not defeat the assertion that the things he said are true. Moreover, since the context in which he spoke of his knowledge of his hands was one in which he was trying to rebut a philosophical thesis which denied what he was asserting, there was then a point to his claim. Even Wittgenstein recognizes that once the philosophical context is known, it can be seen that the participants are not insane. Wittgenstein might reply that the philosophical context is not a legitimate language game; it is a language game in which the rules for correct use are seldom if ever satisfied, but this is not the place to discuss Wittgenstein's view of philosophy.

But is it really absurd to claim that Moore does not know the premise of P? Wallace Matson tells this story:

> G. E. Moore was delivering the Howison Lecture in Wheeler Auditorium [in Berkeley in 1941], which had a handsome coffered ceiling inset with glass panels. Giving a local angle to his defense of common sense, Moore declared that among the things he knew there and then was that light from the sun was streaming through the roof. Most of the audience were aware, however, that the glass panels were diffusers for electrical illumination; the roof of the building was solid and opaque. Someone had the temerity to point this out to Moore in the question period. He responded "Oh dear me!" and went on to the next question.

One of the lessons that Matson claims can be learned from this incident is that "saying that you know, even emphatically and when you are eminent, does not add anything to the validity of your utterance" (Matson, 1991, p. 7).

Does this incident provide a reason for thinking that Moore did not know the premise of P? I do not think so. After all, the fact that Moore is capable of error does not prove that he made an error in the case of his hands. We can explain why he erred during the Howison Lecture: the glass panels looked like windows; the light streaming from them looked like sunlight; he could not see the roof beyond them; that the roof was opaque was not in view, and so forth. But the circumstances in which he uttered the premise of P did not contain any such potential sources of error. There was nothing there that he could have mistaken for his own hands. One can imagine a possible world which contains things that look like hands and feel like hands but are not really hands, and in which someone might be convinced of an analogue of the premise of P and just be mistaken. If such a counterfactual situation is imaginable, then in one sense of "possible," it is possible that Moore was mistaken about the premise. It is logically possible that Moore's claim to know it to be true is false; there is no logical contradiction in that supposition. But the logical possibility of error is not something that defeats his claim to know it in the circumstances in which he uttered it in the actual world. So his embarrassment during his delivery of the Howison Lecture fails to provide a reason for thinking that there was a similar opportunity for error when he delivered his "Proof of an External World."

One might object that if there is a logically possible world in which the circumstances in which he utters the premise of P are perceptually indistinguishable from this world but in which the premise is false for reason R, then Moore does not actually know that it is true. The reason for this failure of knowledge is that his perceptual evidence for the premise of P is compatible with its falsity, and he has asserted it without excluding the possibility that R, which explains how P could be false under such circumstances, is true. This objection raises the issue of how knowledge is possible when various possibilities have not been excluded. It is, after all, quite similar in structure to Descartes' dream argument. I shall consider a reply to this objection in the two following chapters, which will attempt to establish that Moore's proof, if understood in a certain light, does indeed prove the skeptic mistaken.

The Question of Proving the Premise

Moore recognizes that people will not be satisfied with his proof, and he surmises that their dissatisfaction will be based upon the fact that he has not offered a proof of the premise of P. They would want, he thinks, "a general statement as to how any propositions of this sort may be proved." Some of these doubters will assert that if the premise is not proved, then Moore does not know it to be true. He supposes, then, that the basic challenge to his proof will be directed at his claim that he has knowledge of its premise (Moore, 1970, pp. 148–9).

Moore agrees that he has not provided a proof of the premise, and he does not believe that he can prove it.

> How am I to prove now that "Here is one hand, and here's another"? I do not believe I can do it. In order to do it, I should need to prove for one thing, as Descartes pointed out, that I am not now dreaming. But how can I prove that I am not? I have, no doubt, conclusive reasons for asserting that I am not now dreaming; I have conclusive evidence that I am awake: but that is a very different thing from being able to prove it. I could not tell you what all my evidence is; and I should require to do this at least in order to give you a proof. (Moore, 1970, p. 149)

Moore here seems to agree that if he does not know that he is not dreaming, then he does not know the premise of P. But he claims that he does know that he is not dreaming even if he cannot prove it. Both "I am not dreaming" and "Here is one hand and here is another" can be known to be true without any proof whatsoever.[2]

---

2   If Moore has conclusive evidence that he is awake, then perhaps there is a proof that he is not dreaming even though he does not know what it is. Moreover, Moore

Moore does not think his proof, or any proof for that matter, is defective just because he has not provided a proof of the premise. He asserts:

> I can know things, which I cannot prove; and among things which I certainly did know, even if (as I think) I could not prove them, were the premises of my . . . proofs. I should say, therefore, that those, if any, who are dissatisfied with these proofs merely on the ground that I did not know their premises, have no good reason for their dissatisfaction. (Moore, 1970, p. 150)

With these words, his paper comes to an end.

There is an ancient and convincing argument to the effect that if we know anything by means of a proof, then there must, on pain of avoiding an infinite regress or blatant circularity, be things that we know without a proof. In fact, Moore accepts this argument (Moore, 1953, p. 139). To accept this argument together with the claim that we do know some things without proof is to imply that the argument against the criterion of Sextus Empiricus is unsound. For that argument was intended to show that any claim to knowledge required the application of a criterion, and this meant that any claim to knowledge required a proof or backing from a premise from which it could be inferred. Therefore, no claim to knowledge could be true because any claim to knowledge required an impossible infinite regress or was guilty of the fallacy of circular argument.

When Moore asserts "I can know things, which I cannot prove," he is speaking dogmatically. His paper has offered no reason whatsoever for thinking that he knows anything without proof. Moreover, even if he should know some things without proof, Moore has not shown that the premise of P is or could be one of those things. Wittgenstein concluded that Moore failed: "Moore's mistake lies in this – countering the assertion that one cannot know that, by saying 'I do know it'" (Wittgenstein, 1969, para. 521).[3]

One might respond on Moore's behalf by asking what else he could do. Let

here assumes that if he knows the premise of P, then he knows that he is not dreaming. But that assumption is an instance of the controversial closure principle, according to which if a person knows A and knows that A entails B, then he knows B. See Nozick (1981, pp. 204–11).

3   In a similar vein, H. P. Grice remarks: "A quite common reaction to Moore's way with paradoxes has, I think, been to feel that it can't be as easy as that, that Moore counters philosophical theses with what amounts to a blunt denial and that his 'disproofs' fail therefore to carry conviction" (Grice, 1989, pp. 156–7).

us suppose that he does know the premise of P without proof and that skepticism is mistaken. What else could he say to the skeptic and idealist except to assert that he knows it?

But there are certain things that can be said. Moore ended his paper too soon. He could have explained how he knows those things that he knows without proof. And once that has been done, it is possible to develop a convincing argument against skepticism of the senses. I shall develop this line of inquiry in the next two chapters.

10

Defending Moore's Proof

How Moore Knows the Truth of the Premise

Moore ended his paper too soon; he should have explained how he knows that the premise of P is true. It would have been easy enough for him to have done so. Consider any of the things he might have chosen to hold up before the members of the audience in his lecture: his hands, a pencil, a book, or anything visible that he can wave before their eyes while saying, "Here is one hand and here is another," or "Here is a pencil," or "Here is a book." How does he and the members of the audience know that each of these is true? Simple. They can all see the objects in question. "By seeing them" is one pretty good answer to the question: "How do you know the premise of P to be true?"

Avrum Stroll, however, argues that Moore had a good reason for refusing to offer this obvious answer. It was part of his strategy for defeating skepticism. According to Stroll,

> The sceptic can move in for the kill once his dogmatic opponent proffers a criterion for supporting what he has asserted. The kill consists in making it plain that there is a logical gap between the criterion he has given and the claim that the criterion supposedly supports. . . . So the appeal to any sort of experience, such as seeing or hearing something, does not guarantee that one cannot be mistaken. Thus one might have the experience of seeing a door in a place where in reality there is none. . . . Moore met this set of maneuvers by refusing to play the sceptic's game. He did this by refusing to explain *how* he knows what he claimed to know. That refusal blocked the sceptical regress at its source; it made it impossible for the sceptic's pattern of moves to get off the ground. (Stroll, 1994, pp. 51–2)

This is a feeble strategy for Moore to pursue if indeed Stroll is correct in think-ing that this is what was on Moore's mind. The skeptic need merely point out that Moore is being dogmatic and that one need not pay any attention to his claim to know when he refuses to explain how he manages it.

In addition, Stroll is mistaken when he says that "the appeal to any sort of experience, such as seeing or hearing something, does not guarantee that one cannot be mistaken." There are several problems here. First, when one explains how one knows of the existence of something by saying that one sees it, one is not appealing just to an experience. Of course, when a person sees something, he is having a visual experience; something appears to him in a certain way. But more than an experience is involved in seeing it; there is the thing seen as well. One is not, then, appealing just to the experience but to the very presence of the thing that is in plain view. The experience is the vehicle by means of which the thing is in plain view. There is no logical gap between "I see X" and "X exists." The former entails the latter.

Second, the way Moore and the members of the audience know of the ex-istence of the hands is that they see them. Clearly, there is a difference be-tween seeing them and saying that one sees them. One can see them without saying that one sees them. Saying that one sees them is not how they know the truth of the premise of P. There *is* a logical gap between uttering a sen-tence and that sentence's expressing a truth. When Moore sees them, he in a position to know that the premise is true no matter what he says or does not say.

Has Moore Proved the Premise?

There is another explanation as to why Moore failed to explain how he knows the premise of P to be true. Remember that Moore asserted that he could not prove it to be true and that he knows it to be true without proof. That is, he knows it to be true without inferring it from any other statements. However, at one time Moore accepted an account of what is involved in seeing a physi-cal object, according to which it involves a propositional claim: "The seeing of sense-data consists in directly apprehending them. But the seeing of a material object does *not* consist in directly apprehending *it*. It consists partly in directly apprehending certain sense-data, but partly also in *knowing, be-sides and at the same time*, that there exists *something* other than these sense-data" (Moore, 1953, p. 66). According to this account, then, in seeing his hands, Moore knows a proposition that is used in justifying the premise of P. Years later, when he wrote "Proof of an External World," he might have recollected his earlier thoughts and realized that explaining how he knows the premise to be true contradicted his claim that he knows it without proof. Moreover, the absence of any analysis in this paper of what it means to see something suggests that Moore thought that his proof of an external world did not depend upon any controversial philosophical claim about the nature of visual perception. Although these motives are not entirely consistent among themselves, perhaps both together convinced him to bring his argument to an end without entering the contentious field of the philosophy of perception.

In any case, it might be objected that if Moore had *appealed* to his seeing his hands, then he would have been in the position of attempting to prove the premise. And that is true: after all, the statement "I see that here is one hand and here is another" does entail "Here is one hand and here is another." But in my effort to extend the argument beyond the termination of his lecture, the explanation I have given of how he knows the premise to be true does not consist of his *saying* that he sees his hands, but of his seeing them. Since his seeing them is not itself a further premise and is not a statement or proposition at all, then the fact that he knows the premise to be true by seeing his hands does not constitute a proof of it. He does not need a proof of it in order for him to know it to be true in the way indicated.

But what about Moore's earlier view that seeing something does involve a propositional claim? As we move beyond his own formulation to my amended and expanded version, a few words need to be said about the nature of visual perception.

Seeing Things

The verb "see" is used to express several different concepts, and this ambiguity has infected various theories of visual perception, including Moore's, according to which seeing something involves knowing the truth of a certain proposition, namely that something corresponds to our sense-data. We can approach the problem by reflecting upon the following example. Suppose Jones sees a certain automobile passing by, and that the automobile is a Honda Civic. So it is true that (1) Jones saw a Honda Civic. Let us suppose, however, that at the time he saw the Honda Civic, he failed to identify it as a Honda Civic; perhaps he was paying no attention to what kind of car it was, or perhaps he did not know what a Honda Civic looked like. So it is also true that (2) Jones did not see that it was a Honda Civic. What this example shows is that there is a distinction between simply seeing something and seeing that something is so. You can have the former without having the latter. Now suppose that Jones not only saw the Honda Civic, he also saw what kind of car it was. In that case, it is true that (3) Jones saw that it was a Honda Civic. (1) tells us what Jones saw without telling us how he understood what it was that he saw or what he learned from what he saw. On the other hand, (3) tells us that Jones learned from what he saw that it was a Honda Civic that was passing by. (3) expresses a judgment based upon a visual perception, whereas (1) reports the perception itself.

Statements such as (3) need not be based upon a visual perception. Let us say that Smith is describing to Jones some of the features of his new car, and Jones, who knows lots about cars, says that (4) I see that your new car is a Honda Civic. Here (4) tells us not what Jones learned from seeing the car (perhaps he never saw it) but what he inferred from Smith's description. The most frequent use of "I see that" is to report what one has come to know or what one thinks one knows, but it does not tell us how one has acquired that information. The meaning of "He sees that" is not inherently connected to "He sees". Whereas "He sees that" is followed by a proposition and reports what someone came to know or find out, "He sees" reports a visual perception that involves no proposition or judgment whatsoever. In fact, contrary to Moore's analysis, (1) may be true even if Jones does not know or even believe that anything corresponded to his sense experience. Suppose Jones thought he was hallucinating at the very moment that the Honda Civic passed by. He might then believe that nothing corresponded to his sense experience, but since something did, he in fact saw a Honda Civic even if he did not believe he did or even if he believed he didn't. In short, it is necessary to distinguish between a case of seeing something and the interpretations made about what is seen. The phrase "I see that" sometimes introduces an interpretation of a visual perception. But the propositional content belongs to the interpretation and not to the perception. It is important not to confuse the item interpreted with the act of interpretation. (See Landesman, 1989, chapter 6 for further discussion.)

Appearance and the Object that Appears

In visual perception, an object is presented to a subject. When Jones sees the Honda Civic, the car is presented to Jones, it appears to him; he is made aware of it, no matter how he interprets or understands it. If (1) is true, then any other correct description of the Honda Civic may replace "Honda Civic" without making it false, whereas that does not hold for (3). If the Honda Civic was stolen from Smith, the statement that (4) Jones sees that it was a car stolen from Smith does not follow from (3).

When Jones sees the car, the car appears in some way to Jones; he is having a particular visual experience. That is a fact about him. In addition, there is the car that is seen that "corresponds" in some way to the experience. Can we say anything more about this correspondence?

According to *the causal theory of visual perception*, correspondence is explained in terms of causality. To say that Jones sees a Honda Civic means that Jones is having a certain visual experience that is caused to occur by the presence of the car. Our concept of seeing something is a causal concept. How the causation works is to be explained by the sciences concerned with visual perception; its exact working is not included in the concept. The virtue of the causal theory is that it is consistent with the idea just defended that our concept of seeing something does not incorporate any reference to propositional or interpretive content.

H. P. Grice attempts to defend the causal theory by constructing the following example:

> It might be that it looked to me as if there were a certain sort of pillar in a certain direction at a certain distance, and there might actually be a pillar in that place; but if, unknown to me, there were a mirror interposed between myself and the pillar, which reflected a numerically different though similar pillar, it would certainly be incorrect to say that I saw the first pillar, and correct to say that I saw the second; and it is extremely tempting to explain this linguistic fact by saying that the first pillar was, and the second was not, causally irrelevant to the way things looked to me. (Grice, 1989, p. 238)

Now it is true that the first pillar played no causal role in the way things looked to him, but does it follow that our concept of seeing something incorporates a reference to the causal role of the object seen? I do not think so because another more plausible explanation of the linguistic fact is available, namely that the reason why he failed to see the first pillar was that the mirror was in the way and that the reason why he saw the second was that he saw its reflection in the mirror. Causality comes into the picture not from our concept of seeing something but from attempts to go beyond our everyday explanation for further understanding of what went on. So the reason why the mirror's getting in the way prevented him from seeing the pillar is that it blocked the light rays from reaching his eyes, and the reason why his seeing the reflection in the mirror enabled him to see the second pillar is that the reflection was caused by rays of light coming from the pillar.

If the conceptual relation between a visual experience and an object seen is not causal, what, then, is it? When we see something, it follows that the object seen appears to us in some way or looks in some way to us. Let me use the term *visually appearing* to denote this relation. This and nothing else is the conceptually implied relation between the experience and the object. When Jones sees the Honda Civic, it appears to him in some way. That is all that is involved in his seeing it. Of course, from a scientific standpoint, we want a deeper understanding of what goes on. Using the theories drawn from the sciences concerned with vision, we can say that in order for the car to appear to Jones, light reflected from it must enter his eyes, thus causing various chemical changes in his retina which cause a signal to go from his optic nerve to his brain, which finally terminates in the occurrence of a visual experience or sensation. This level of explanation is a product not of conceptual analysis but of scientific inquiry. In any case, neither the conceptual nor the scientific analysis of visual perception requires us to bring propositional content or interpretation or thought into the picture. Experience precedes thought and provides matter for interpretation.

Grounded Belief

Some of the things we know are inferred from other things we know. If knowledge is possible and an infinite regress or circularity is to be avoided, then some things we know cannot be inferred from other things we know; they must be known non-inferentially. The premise of P is an example. Moore knows it not because he has inferred it from anything else but because of what he sees; his seeing his hands is not a proposition from which anything is inferred. So the knowledge of the premise that he and the members of his audience have acquired is not based upon anything else he knows (see Chisholm, 1963).

But Moore's belief in the premise of P is based or founded upon something, namely upon the fact that he sees his hands. It does not just come out of the blue. When something comes to be believed non-inferentially, I shall call it, following established practice, a *basic belief*. When a basic belief is justified by something outside of itself, such as in Moore's knowledge of the premise of P, I shall label it *a grounded belief*. When the ground consists of the person's seeing or hearing or, in general, perceiving something, I shall call it *a perceptually grounded belief*. Not all basic beliefs are grounded; for example, that white is not black is known just by reflecting upon what is said; when one understands what is said, one is in a position to realize that it is true. Such knowledge deserves the name of self-evident knowledge because in order to gain such knowledge one does not have to go outside the proposition being considered; one merely has to clarify one's understanding of it, to transform one's understanding into, in Descartes' phrase, a clear and distinct perception. Beliefs that are self-evident are basic but ungrounded.[1]

What exactly is the relation between a belief or judgment such as Moore's belief in the premise of P and the visual perception that grounds it? Two relations are frequently involved. One is a form of causation: the perception triggers the belief or judgment; with the aid of contributing factors, most of which are unknown, it brings it about that the agent comes to have that belief or, if he already had it, to entertain it once again.[2] Thus, by seeing Moore's hands, the members of the audience at his lecture were caused to believe "There is one hand and there is another." In addition, the grounding perception justifies the judgment. It is because Moore and the members of his audience saw his hands that each of them acquired a good reason to believe the premise of P. And the reason was good enough that each not merely believes it but also knows it.

According to our common understanding, there is a connection between the causal and justificatory roles of visual perception. When Moore sees his hands, part of the reason why this perception gives rise to this belief is that the fact in which he is interested is right there before his very eyes; one might say that he is aware of this very fact. So in judging that here is one hand and here is another, Moore is just recording the information that perception delivers. It is because this fact is visually detectable that Moore comes to believe it and that his belief is fully justified.

Grounded Belief, Justification, and Knowledge

Not all beliefs that are triggered by seeing something are grounded. For example, suppose someone looks at a transparent jar full of pennies and guesses that there are 4,673 pennies in it. Suppose he guesses right, so that his belief

---

1   One might object that even self-evident knowledge is grounded. In realizing that white is not black, do I not have to consider the colors themselves, and are not these colors things outside the judgment? To consider this issue here would take us well beyond the issue under discussion.

2   This should not be confused with the causal theory of perception, which concerns the relation between a perception and the thing perceived. Here we are concerned with the relations between a perception and the belief it triggers.

is true; it contains just 4,673 pennies, no more and no fewer (see Stroud, 1987, pp. 237–8, for a similar example). But since this was a lucky guess, his seeing the jar with 4,673 pennies in it fails to justify his judgment that it contained just this number of pennies. His judgment, being a guess, was not justified at all and certainly did not count as something he knew.

In order for some state of affairs to ground a person's belief, it must trigger it in such a way that the fact that the belief is true is non-accidental. He must acquire his belief in a way that explains why he was in a position to capture the truth. In the case of the jar, he could only guess because the fact that it contained just 4,673 pennies was not visually detectable just by looking at it; it was not a fact that was in plain view. That it was a jar and that there were pennies in it are things that are visually detectable. But there is no visual experience that could be described as its looking like there were exactly 4,673 pennies in the jar.

Now suppose a member of Moore's audience saw Moore's bare hands in a good light, suppose he knew what hands are and what they look like, suppose his vision was normal and undisturbed, and suppose his looking at them triggered the belief "There is one hand and there is another." In that case, not only was his belief true, but it was grounded and, hence, justified. Not only was it justified, but he knew it to be true. Why was it justified? Because the way he acquired the belief and the conditions under which he acquired it were such that his acquiring it in that way and under those conditions guaranteed that the belief he acquired is true. He did not merely guess or conjecture that they were hands. That they were hands there was something that was visually detectable; it was in plain view. The way in which he acquired it and the conditions under which he acquired it are of a type that generally produce beliefs that are true. That way and those conditions represent an example of a process that is reliable in the sense that it can be counted upon to be productive of truth more often than not.[3]

Not only was his belief grounded and hence justified, it also counts as knowledge. The reason is that the process under which he acquired it was of a type that was not merely reliable, but *super-reliable*; it never or hardly ever misleads. Some reliable processes are not super-reliable. Let us suppose that someone is told that in a bag containing 100 marbles, there are 70 red and 30 green marbles, and he is asked to predict the color of the next marble

---

3   In subsequent chapters this reliabilist approach will be elaborated and defended. In recent years, versions of reliabilism have become quite prominent in epistemological discussions. Two influential papers are Goldman (1979) and Sosa (1991).

drawn from the bag. If, every time he predicts, he says that it will be red, he will obtain truth more often than not. So this is an instance of a reliable, but not super-reliable, method of fixing belief. This method of making predictions is truth-tending. The fact that he obtains truth more often than not is not accidental or a lucky coincidence. Such a method justifies the beliefs it fixes because the point of justification, as we saw in chapter 3, is to provide a reason for thinking that what is believed is *true*. The aim of the practice of rational justification is to arrive at truth, so a method of fixing belief that can be counted upon to provide truth more often than not succeeds in providing a justification, a reason for thinking that what is believed is true.

Thus far, it seems reasonable to say this: Moore has attempted to provide a proof of the external world whose premise is true and whose conclusions follow strictly from the premise. So the proof is logically sound. Moreover, Moore as well as the members of his audience know that the premise is true. So the proof is epistemically sound. Since Moore and the members of his audience are capable of deducing the conclusions from the premise, they also know that they are true as well. So all of them know that at least two external objects exist. It looks as if Moore has succeeded in proving the existence of an external world. Let us see how the skeptic might respond to this argument.

11

The Problem of the Shaky Inference

How Moore's Proof Refutes Skepticism

In this chapter, we shall examine some problems and difficulties with Moore's proof that are connected with attempts to provide an inferential justification of Moore's premise "Here is one hand and here is another." Before we engage these issues, it is necessary to become clear about how Moore's proof refutes or purports to refute skepticism. What exactly is its force? In chapter 10, I explained how Moore can reasonably claim to know the premise of his proof. If the conditions put forward for his having this knowledge are satisfied, then the premise is true, he knows it to be true, and his proof is sound not only logically but epistemically. These conditions are, briefly, that Moore sees his hands, that his hands are in plain view, and that his belief in the premise is triggered by and based upon his seeing his hands. Of course, it is also necessary for Moore to be in possession of the requisite concepts involved in the formulation of the steps of the proof. A process that satisfies conditions of this sort is super-reliable and generates true beliefs that deserve the honorific "knowledge."

Skepticism is challenged because the skeptic's arguments insist upon additional conditions that are not really necessary. Therefore, the arguments of the skeptic fail to show that Moore does not know the premise of P. To see this, consider two of the arguments that have been thought to be most convincing: the argument against the criterion of Sextus Empiricus and Descartes' dream argument. The criterion argument says that in order to have knowledge, one must apply a criterion, or, more broadly, one must be able to defend one's claims to know by formulating a good and sufficient reason for them. But in order to apply a criterion or to provide a reason, one either falls into an infinite regress or engages in circular reasoning. But Moore could know the premise of P even if he does not apply a criterion or offer a reason justifying the premise. There is nothing in the explanation of how Moore knows it that requires him to formulate any justification at all. The reliability of a process of fixing belief does not depend upon being able to prove its reliability or even to know or believe that it is reliable.[1]

Similar considerations apply to the dream argument. It says that in order for Moore to know the premise of P, he must be able to prove that he is not dreaming by discovering a mark of veridicality within his experiences. It is not enough that he is not dreaming and that he sees his hands; he must prove it by applying a criterion. But this requirement was not included among the conditions sufficient for Moore to know it to be true.

In order to clarify the force of Moore's proof, it is useful to distinguish three claims incorporated in skepticism about the senses:

(A)   *The force of skeptical arguments.* There are, the skeptic claims, epistemically sound arguments that prove that no one has knowledge of the external world.
(B)   *Skepticism with regard to the senses.* No one does have knowledge of the external world.
(C)   *Skepticism with regard to the possibility of knowledge.* Knowledge of the external world is not possible.

If Moore's proof of an external world is epistemically sound, then (B) is false, since Moore among others does have knowledge of an external world. (C) is false as well, since the most convincing way of proving that something is possible is to come up with an actual instance of it. Since (B) is false so is (A) because there can't be a sound proof of the truth of something that isn't true.

Grounding and Justification

Moore's belief in the premise of P is grounded and is thereby justified. The thing that grounds it, his seeing his hands, can be considered to be a reason, even a conclusive reason, in favor of the premise, so that Moore is fully justified in accepting it. Of course, in my amplified account of his proof, Moore hasn't offered his seeing his hands as a reason or justification (although he

---

1   Further discussion of the worth and limits of this reliabilist approach will appear in chapter 15.

could have) because formulating the reason or expressing the reason is not necessary for his knowing it to be true.

Donald Davidson rejects this way of thinking about justification. In defending a coherence theory of knowledge, he asserts: "What distinguishes a coherence theory is simply the claim that nothing can count as a reason for holding a belief except another belief. Its partisan rejects as unintelligible the request for a ground or source of justification of another ilk" (Davidson, 1986, p. 310). If that is what is characteristic of a coherence theory, then it appears that any coherence theory must lapse into either an infinite regress or circular reasoning if justification is to be possible. That is a difficult situation for any philosophical view to be in if it is presented as one that does not entail skepticism.

However, it is difficult to understand what is so unintelligible about the claim that Moore's seeing his hands is his reason for thinking that here is one hand and here is another. From the standpoint of our everyday discourse in which we offer justifications, we frequently mention the fact that we have seen or heard or otherwise perceived something to explain the reasons we have for believing in its existence. Moreover, what does the justifying is not our mentioning this fact, but the fact that is mentioned, not the saying we see but the very seeing itself. Seeing something often goes without saying. We need not conceptualize or interpret our perceptions or express them in words (although we are not forbidden from doing so) in order for them to have the epistemic power to ground our beliefs.

Davidson might have adopted this view of justification because he thinks that seeing something incorporates belief. He asserts that if a justification depends upon being aware of a sensation, then this awareness "is just another belief" (Davidson, 1986, p. 311). If by a sensation he means just the fact that something appears to a subject, then the claim is that the ways things appear consist of beliefs.

There are uses of "appear"and related verbs that do express tentatively held beliefs or even inclinations to believe. If you ask me at night what animal I am seeing I might reply: "I'm not sure but it looks to me to be a wolf." Here I can be interpreted to be using "looks" to express an opinion. But that is not its only usage. If, in response, you ask what inclines me to be of the opinion that it is a wolf, I could then say "It sure looks like one," in which case I am describing how something appears in the non-propositional sense to justify how it appears in the inclination to believe propositional sense. So we need to distinguish between a non-propositional phenomenological use of appears talk and a propositional use; the former describes our perceptions without a commitment to their veridicality, whereas the latter expresses a weak commitment to the truth of a proposition.

In any case, we saw in chapter 10 that we need to distinguish Moore's seeing his hands from the quite different fact of his seeing that these things are hands. The latter is propositional and implies both belief and knowledge, whereas simple seeing is non-propositional and implies no belief at all. Simple seeing is not a propositional attitude. That they are distinct was established by the fact that one can see something without knowing what it is that one sees. Moore's seeing an electric light during the Howison lecture is a handy example; he saw the electric light but failed to see that it was an electric light.

One may wonder what leads philosophers to adopt such an implausible view as the coherence theory of knowledge given that a system of beliefs may be internally coherent yet include many false beliefs that fail to correspond to the way the world is. It looks like the coherence theory is just one more unsuccessful way of grappling with skepticism. Perhaps it just is skepticism in disguise.

What underlies Davidson's adoption of the coherence approach is the idea that if what justifies our beliefs about the world were not just other beliefs but non-propositional states of affairs, then it should be possible to compare or confront our beliefs, or some of them anyway, with the states of affairs they purport to represent, and, in this way, to determine whether or not they are true. But, says the coherentist, we can't do that. "No such confrontation makes sense," says Davidson, "for of course we can't get out of our skins to find out what is causing the internal happenings of which we are aware" (Davidson, 1986, p. 312).

So if we could "get out of our skins," then we need not rely upon coherence alone in matters of justification. I suppose that the metaphor of getting out of our skins means getting into epistemic contact with the world, gaining access to the world via the senses so that we may acquire knowledge about it. But, according to my expanded version of Moore's proof, we can get out of our skins by seeing things. In seeing things, we do not just come upon additional beliefs but we become aware of things and facts that our cognitive apparatus is subsequently capable of representing in propositional form. If a doubt arises whether a proposition is true, then, in some cases, we can compare what it says with what we see and verify it directly.

Evidence and Visual Perception

In chapter 2, I distinguished two accounts of the human epistemic condition. One is the original or common sense understanding according to which our senses provide us with a direct access to objects, events, and states of affairs that exist independently of our perception of them. This view is frequently called *naive realism*, naive because it is the view we have prior to any input from philosophy or science. The other is the philosophically instructed understanding, "the way of ideas," according to which, when a person sees something, he is aware of his inner sensations or ideas that he takes as signs or representations of things without. This view is usually called *representative realism* because it denies that the senses provide direct acquaintance with independent objects; our access to external things is indirect, mediated by the inner traces in our brains and minds of the impact of energies impinging upon our sense organs. As we saw, the representative approach leads us to speak of "the great deception of sense," according to which these inner traces provide as much misinformation as correct information about the qualities that bodies exemplify. On this view, there is no direct confrontation between our beliefs and external facts. If there is any direct confrontation at all, it is between our beliefs about our inner experiences and the experiences themselves.

On the representational view, inner experiences furnish evidence for our beliefs about material objects, and these beliefs, then, are analogous to theories or hypotheses that are to be accepted or justified on the strength of the evidence. It is appropriate to think of our sense organs as instruments for extracting information from impinging energies and the mind as an organ for developing hypotheses about the real nature of the objects that are the ultimate sources of the information transmitted.

When Moore looks at his hands, that here is one hand and here is another appears to be a matter of fact that he can just read off from what he sees. But for the representative realist, this immediacy is an illusion produced, as Hume noticed, by the mind's tendency to project qualities that inner experience presents upon objects; such qualities seem to us to be predicates of independently existing entities, but they are not; they are presentations of inner experience, appearances merely, that function as clues to the true character of things in themselves. Just as our sense organs are instruments capable of transmitting such clues to that part of the mind that engages in reasoning, so our faculty for making perceptual judgments aims at inferring the nature of things as they are in themselves using these clues in combination with other information available to it. Such inferences are shaky and liable to error, as "the great deception of sense" establishes.

It looks as if there is an opening here for the skeptic, since it is easy enough for him to raise doubts about whether or not we ever have a good reason to think that such inferences deliver the truth about external matters of fact.

However, the skeptic is not entitled to assert the truth of our scientifically instructed understanding of perception and its objects. The scientifically instructed understanding determines its conclusions about what lies beyond immediate experience by forming hypotheses about the best explanation of the character of immediate experience. It identifies facts about the constitution of material things in order to explain such facts as that this looks red and that looks square, and so forth. But the main arguments of the skeptics raise doubts about whether such inferences to the best explanation are capable of providing knowledge or even justified belief. Moreover, as both Descartes and Berkeley pointed out, the existence of matter is not the only explanation for the course of our experience; both believed that God could cause perceptions directly in the absence of matter, and Berkeley, who called his system *immaterialism*, claimed that that is what God actually does.

It is characteristic of skepticism to think of sense perception as involving a contrast between inner experience and outer objects, the latter supposedly inferred from the former. Since the inference is shaky it does not provide knowledge of the external world. So Moore is not entitled to his claim that he knows the premise of P. He doesn't know it, because there is no way to infer validly the existence of his hands from his present experience.

Sense Experience as Evidence

In my development of Moore's proof, I argued that his belief in the premise of P was grounded upon his seeing his hands. For the skeptic, his seeing his hands could not be the real ground for his asserting the premise because his access to his hands is derived from his access to his sense experience. The skeptic will claim that it is experience that does the grounding if, indeed, the premise is grounded at all. Since it is experience that does the grounding, it is up to Moore to show how he can plausibly arrive at the premise on the basis of the evidence available to him. Since he fails to do that, he is not justified in claiming to know the premise of P. He says he knows the premise without proof, but the premise, based as it is upon an inference, is something that requires proof in order to be justified.

Now, as we saw, the skeptic is not entitled to think of this evidence as sensory traces caused by the impingement of energies from the external world upon his sense organs, for that story is based upon a scientific construction that, for him, must be open to doubt. The skeptic is committed to occupying the common sense framework in the course of showing that it is not capable of delivering the goods (Williams, 1996, p. 17). Starting with our well entrenched pre-scientific and pre-philosophical belief system, the skeptic attempts to show that its constituent beliefs are neither justified nor cases of knowledge; in fact he claims that knowledge is impossible. None of Descartes' skeptical arguments in the First Meditation appealed to science or philosophy; they were formulated in terms of our common sense conceptual scheme.

The only items in that scheme that could plausibly function as evidence for our perceptual judgments are the ways things appear to us: how they look, sound, feel, taste, or smell. That something looks red is our evidence that it is red; that something sounds like Placido Domingo singing is our evidence that it is Placido Domingo singing. For Moore, that something looks like hands is his evidence that here is one hand and here is another. It is the appearances that count as inner experience as far as skepticism is concerned. The skeptic, now, needs only to appeal to the familiar arguments: that something looks in a certain way does not entail that it is that way; since we cannot find within the appearances a criterion for distinguishing dreams from reality, we have no way of telling whether it is even probable that something that looks that way really is that way. The inference from appearance to reality is too shaky to be the basis for knowledge or justified belief; there are alternative explanations of the character of the ways things appear and we have no way, outside of appealing to mere prejudice, of determining which is the best in the sense of most likely to be true; there is no way of checking up on the reliability of our inferences to external things since we have access to the facts reported in the premises only, never to those represented by the conclusions.

The Problem of the Shaky Inference

Bertrand Russell formulated the problem in this way: "We must . . . if possible, find, in our own purely private experiences, characteristics which show, or tend to show, that there are in the world things other than ourselves and our private experiences" (Russell, 1912, p. 22). Given the plausible conclusion of Descartes' dream argument that there are no marks of objectivity internal to experience, it is doubtful that there is any solution. And Berkeley showed why the idea of inferring the existence of material objects that exist independently of our experience is hopeless:

> Either we must know it [the external world] by sense or by reason. As for our senses, by them we have knowledge only of our sensations, ideas, or those things that are immediately perceived by sense, call them what you

will: but they do not inform us that things exist without the mind, or unperceived, like to those which are perceived. . . . It remains therefore that if we have any knowledge at all of external things, it must be by reason, inferring their existence from what is immediately perceived by sense. But what reason can induce us to believe the existence of bodies without the mind, from what we perceive, since the very patrons of matter themselves do not pretend, there is any necessary connection betwixt them and our ideas? I say it is granted on all hands (and what happens in dreams, phrensies, and the like, puts it beyond dispute) that it is possible we might be affected with all the ideas we have now, although no bodies existed without, resembling them. (Berkeley, 1710, para. 18)

Berkeley here points out an additional implication of Descartes' dream argument: the existence of dreams proves that there isn't the right connection between ideas and bodies to justify inferring the latter from the former.
 Russell concedes that

In one sense it must be admitted that we can never *prove* the existence of things other than ourselves and our experiences. No logical absurdity results from the hypothesis that the world consists of myself and my thoughts and feelings and sensations, and that everything else is mere fancy. . . . There is no logical impossibility in the supposition that the whole life is a dream, in which we ourselves create all the objects that come before us. (Russell, 1912, p. 22)

What Russell wants from a proof is different from what Moore offered. Moore merely showed that the existence of external objects followed from certain things he knew. But for Russell, a proof of the external world consists in deducing a contradiction or a necessary falsehood from the solipsistic hypothesis. Russell thinks it can't be done. The best that can be done is to rely upon "our instinctive belief that there *are* objects *corresponding* to our sense-data."

Since this belief does not lead to any difficulties but on the contrary tends to simplify and systematize our account of our experiences, there seems no good reason for rejecting it. We may therefore admit – though with a slight doubt derived from dreams – that the external world does really exist, and is not wholly dependent for its existence upon our continuing to perceive it. (Russell, 1912, pp. 24–5)

Russell claims that our belief system is, on the whole, simpler and more systematic if we accept our instinctive belief in an external world. This is the sort of argument one would expect from the standpoint of a coherence theory of knowledge: the hypothesis of an external world produces greater overall coherence in one's beliefs than solipsism. But it is hard to understand how coherence in the form of simplicity and systematicity guarantees truth about things as they are in themselves. How does one argue from coherence to correspondence with fact? Of course, the coherence theorist may deny a realist or correspondence theory of truth, but such a denial would be more a product of skepticism than a refutation of it.

In any case, Russell did not find characteristics in his "purely private experiences" that are sufficient to establish the existence of an external world. He found it necessary to appeal to the extrinsic idea of "a harmonious system" to refute solipsism. The hypothesis of the external world is the best way, Russell thinks, to introduce order into the chaos of our individual streams of consciousness. But the skeptic will find this to be a feeble argument. He will want a reason for thinking that the external world must obey our instinctive need for harmony, for simplicity, for system. Russell's way out is just another instance of dogmatism, no more persuasive than positing the existence of an external world directly.

Descartes' Way Out

Although Descartes did not offer a proof in Russell's sense showing that solipsism is logically absurd, he claimed to be able to refute it on the basis of certain self-evident necessary truths, together with other truths that are contingent though indubitable. He believed that he could provide an epistemic proof of the existence of the external world. Starting out only with the contents of his own mind, which, he claimed, he was sure of, Descartes came across the idea he had of a perfect being, of God. He claimed to be able to deduce the existence of God from the fact that he was in possession of this idea (together with some assumptions that he asserted are self-evidently true). From the fact that God is perfect, it follows that he is not deceptive and that the capacities for knowledge with which he endows us are designed not to lead us astray. God is no evil demon devoting himself to misleading us, but a benevolent creator who furnished us with the best possible cognitive abilities given our finite and imperfect nature. Therefore, we are entitled to trust our instinctive beliefs, and, since these are incompatible with solipsism, solipsism must be false. Although the proof that Descartes offers is much more complex and extended than Moore's, the two proofs offer similar responses to skepticism: in both, the existence of the external world is deduced from premises which both Descartes and Moore claim to know to be true.

At the very beginning of his *Meditations*, Descartes said: "From time to time I have found that the senses deceive" (Descartes, 1985, II, p. 12). Nothing in his subsequent argument led him to withdraw this obvious truism.

As the *Meditations* came to a close, he pointed out that "notwithstanding the immense goodness of God, the nature of man as a combination of mind and body is such that it is bound to mislead him from time to time." And at the very end of the *Meditations*, Descartes returned to the dream argument and concluded that he no longer needed to fear the skepticism that it engendered in the First Meditation.

> The exaggerated doubts of the last few days should be dismissed as laughable. This applies especially to the principal reason for doubt, namely my inability to distinguish between being asleep and being awake. For I now notice that there is a vast difference between the two, in that dreams are never linked by memory with all the other actions of life as waking experiences are. . . . But when I distinctly see where things come from and where and when they come to me, and when I can connect my perceptions of them with the whole of the rest of my life without a break, then I am quite certain that when I encounter these things I am not asleep but awake. And I ought not to have even the slightest doubt of their reality if, after calling upon all the senses as well as my memory and my intellect in order to check them, I receive no conflicting reports from any of these sources. (Descartes, 1985, II, pp. 61–2)

Speaking of dreams in the First Meditation, Descartes claimed that "there never are any sure signs by means of which being awake can be distinguished from being asleep" (Descartes, 1985, II, p. 13). Now he is in a position to identify a "sure sign." What convinces one of the veridality of one's sense experience is its connectedness or coherence, as distinct from the chaos and disorder of dream experience, illusions, and hallucinations.

He illustrates what he means with this example: "If, while I am awake, anyone were suddenly to appear to me and then disappear immediately, as happens in sleep, so that I could not see where he had come from or where he had gone to, it would not be unreasonable for me to judge that he was a ghost, or a vision created in my brain, rather than a real man" (Descartes, 1985, II, pp. 61–2). Real things do not manifest themselves in such a disconnected manner. The external world is relatively stable and change occurs in an orderly and predictable way, so that a corresponding order and predictability in sense experience testifies to the truth of our everyday beliefs.

Russell's appeal to coherence as an answer to skepticism was not very convincing, but Descartes thinks that his argument goes so far as to establish the certainty of some of our privileged perceptual judgments, such as "I am here, sitting by the fire, wearing a winter dressing gown, holding this piece of paper in my hands." For Descartes, we are instinctively inclined to take coherence as a mark of veridicality, and we are justified in doing so because God is not a deceiver.

> For from the fact that God is not a deceiver it follows that in cases like these I am completely free from error. But since the pressure of things to be done does not always allow us to stop and make such a meticulous check, it must be admitted that in this human life we are often liable to make mistakes about particular things, and we must acknowledge the weakness of our nature. (Descartes, 1985, II, p. 62)

God guarantees the truth and certainty of those of our perceptual judgments formulated in the light of the criterion of coherence and corroborated with a "meticulous check." Under these conditions, our perceptual beliefs can be proved to be super-reliable, but, when a "meticulous check" is not possible because of "the pressure of things," they are merely reliable and occasionally mistaken.

Why Descartes' Way Out Is Superfluous

If Descartes had known of Moore's proof of an external world, he might have agreed with the standard criticism of it that in order for it to be convincing, Moore should have provided a proof of the premise. For Descartes, Moore's premise would have counted as a privilege perceptual judgment whose truth and certainty is guaranteed by the criterion of coherence, which is itself guaranteed by the existence of God. Unlike Moore, Descartes would have thought that *he* could have provided a proof of the premise of P that would have shown that Moore really did know it as he claimed.

The reason why Descartes would have agreed with the skeptical critics of Moore's proof on this point is that he is, as we saw in chapter 7, a strong cognitive internalist who thinks that in order to have knowledge, one must be in a position to establish that one has knowledge by offering a proof of or criterion for what one claims to know.

According to Descartes' system, Moore could have knowledge that here is one hand and here is another because Moore's sense experience that triggers his belief in the premise fits in with his other experiences, his belief coheres with his other beliefs, and he has made a meticulous check to make sure he is not being deceived. All that remains is for Moore to accept, on the basis of Descartes' own conclusive proofs, that God exists and is not a deceiver.

Suppose that Descartes is right about God but that Moore is an atheist who refuses to accept that God exists. So Moore would not (and he did not) apply Descartes' criterion to prove the premise of P. Even though Moore does not believe it, God guarantees the truth of the premise as well as the general reliability of Moore's perceptual judgments. It seems quite consistent with our concept of knowledge to assert that under these conditions Moore does know that here is one hand and here is another. He cannot be mistaken, and his belief is properly grounded. If that is so, then Descartes' version of strong cognitive internalism is in error. In order to have knowledge, one's beliefs must be assured of truth, they must be produced by a super-reliable procedure whether or not one can establish that the procedure is super-reliable. It is not even necessary to believe that it is super-reliable or even to consider the issue in order to be in possession of knowledge. The cogency of Moore's proof depends upon an externalist conception of knowledge, according to which one's beliefs count as knowledge to the extent to which they are fixed by super-reliable processes and they count as justified to the extent that they are fixed by reliable processes. So no proof or any criterion whatsoever is necessary for Moore to know the truth of the premise.

Why Descartes' Way Out Is Impossible

Not only is Descartes' refutation of solipsistic skepticism unnecessary, his approach has been thought by many commentators to be mistaken in principle. Hume has offered several devastating criticisms:

> It [Descartes' skepticism] recommends an universal doubt, not only of all our former opinions and principles, but also of our very faculties; of whose veracity . . . we must assure ourselves, by a chain of reasoning, deduced from some original principle, which cannot possibly be fallacious or deceitful. But neither is there any such original principle, which has a prerogative above others, that are self-evident and convincing: or if there were, could we advance a step beyond it, but by the use of those very faculties, of which we are supposed to be already diffident. The Cartesian doubt, therefore, were it ever possible to be attained by any human creature (as it plainly is not) would be entirely incurable; and no reasoning could ever bring us to a state of assurance and conviction upon any subject. (Hume, 1748, pp. 149–50)

Hume does not find the principles Descartes depends upon to prove God's existence to be self-evident; nor does he find Descartes' project of attempting universal doubt to be humanly possible. Hume also discovers a circle in Descartes' argument. The effort to doubt as much as possible has the result of impugning human cognitive faculties: simply put, we have no reason to trust them at least until God's existence has been proved. But in order to prove it, Descartes must rely upon those very faculties (of grasping self-evident propositions or, in his terms, clear and distinct perceptions and of reasoning, using them as premises) which he has thrown into question. Thus, in order to prove God's existence, Descartes must assume the reliability of his faculties, which reliability he has no right to count on (in his own terms) until he has succeeded in producing a proof.

The existence of a circle invalidating Descartes' proof of an external world was noted even by his contemporaries. For example, in a conversation with Descartes, Burman insists: "It seems there is a circle. For in the Third Meditation the author uses axioms to prove the existence of God, even though he is not yet certain of not being deceived about these" (Descartes, 1976, pp. 5–6). Descartes, of course, denies that he is guilty of such an obvious and enormous error. Burman reports his reply as follows:

> He [Descartes] does use such axioms in the proof, but he knows that he is not deceived with regard to them, since he is actually paying attention to them. And for as long as he does pay attention to them, he is certain that he is not being deceived, and he is compelled to give his assent to them . . . we are able to grasp the proof of God's existence in its entirety. As long as we are engaged in this process, we are certain that we are not being deceived, and every difficulty is thus removed. (Descartes, 1976, pp. 6–7)

In this response to Burman's criticism, Descartes claims we can achieve certainty and overcome all doubt about self-evident propositions provided that, in our effort to penetrate into their meaning in order to achieve a clear and distinct perception of them, we are actually paying attention to them. An attentive consideration leaves no room for error.

The problem with Descartes' way out is that it fails to appreciate the force of his own internalist standpoint. The problem of the circle begins to emerge in the First Meditation when, after having shown by the use of the dream argument that we have reason to doubt all those beliefs based upon our sense perceptions, Descartes turns his attention to the simple and general truths of arithmetic and geometry that "contain something certain and indubitable." "For whether I am awake or asleep, two and three added together are five, and a square has no more than four sides. It seems impossible that such transparent truths should incur any suspicion of being false" (Descartes, 1985, II, p. 14). He finds that the dream argument fails to generate doubts about these propositions because our knowledge of them is not founded upon the course of sense experience. Experience cannot falsify or confirm these *a priori* propositions; they are transparent to the mind, and their verification depends upon their own internal evidence.

But Descartes realizes that the mere conviction that he knows them to be true is not sufficient to establish that, even here, there is no room for error. "Since I sometimes believe that others go astray in cases where they think they have the most perfect knowledge, may I not similarly go wrong every time I add two and three or count the sides of a square, or in some even simpler matter, if that is imaginable?" (Descartes, 1985, II, p. 14). The thought comes to him that he is ignorant of the original cause of his existence, so that he is in no position to trust his cognitive capacities even in such simple matters. Perhaps he was created by a perfect God who would not deceive him. But he is in no position to assert God's existence in the midst of all his doubts. Also, he finds that he must do something to prevent those habitual opinions of his that he has already succeeded in doubting from returning. In order to keep up the pretense that these opinions could be false,

> I will suppose, therefore, that not God, who is supremely good and the source of truth, but rather some malicious demon of the utmost power and cunning has employed all his energies in order to deceive me. I shall think that the sky, the air, the earth, colours, shapes, sounds and all external things are merely the delusions of dreams which he has devised to ensnare my judgement. (Descartes, 1985, II, p. 15)

The idea of the malicious demon is a supposition which performs several functions in the course of Descartes' argument. In addition to helping him resist the return of his habitual beliefs, it explains how he might be deceived by dreams. The very possibility that his experiences are under the demon's control makes it plausible for him to think that he might be dreaming and that none of his perceptual judgments are true. The dream argument becomes a special case of the malicious demon supposition. Moreover, the possibility of the evil demon has, as a reason for doubt, greater generality than the dream argument since it allows him to doubt propositions of arithmetic and geometry whose verification is independent of sense experience. Their very transparency might be an illusion.

The evil demon supposition supplies Descartes with a "slight reason for doubt" that can only be dispelled if he can prove that there is a God who is not a deceiver. "For if I do not know this, it seems that I can never be quite certain about anything else" (Descartes, 1985, II, p. 25). Because he is a strong internalist, Descartes insists that he cannot attain his goal of absolute certainty about anything until he can prove that it is impossible for him to go wrong about even the most transparent propositions. Therefore, he has boxed himself into an impossible situation; he cannot know anything with certainty until he has established a sound epistemic proof that God exists and is not a deceiver. But he cannot succeed in constructing such a proof unless he knows its premises with certainty, something he cannot do prior to arriving at the proof. His reply to Burman avoids the issue and conceals the difficulty, perhaps even from himself. His only way out would be to drop his internalist assumption. But if he did that, then Moore's simple proof would be sufficient to refute skepticism of the senses, and Hume's remark that "to have recourse to the veracity of the supreme Being, in order to prove the veracity of our senses, is surely making a very unexpected circuit" (Hume, 1748, p. 153) would bring home to us how unnecessary is Descartes' complex line of reasoning for solving the problem of knowledge.

Perceptual Judgments and Their Grounds

The question of the shaky inference comes down to the issue of whether an inference is necessary for knowledge at all. What actually grounds our perceptual judgments? Is it the perception itself – e.g. Moore's seeing his hands – or its experiential constituent – e.g. its looking to Moore as if here is one hand and here is another?

What counts in favor of its being the experiential constituent is the idea that what has grounding force is something to which we have direct access, something with which we are directly acquainted, to use Russell's term. It is the appearances and only the appearances that constitute the evidence and the only evidence for the existence of external objects. This argument guarantees the triumph of the skeptic who points out how shaky is the inference from the appearances to the objects that appear, so we should be hesitant about adopting it if we think that we have knowledge of the external world.

What reply can one make on Moore's behalf? I think, from the outset, that it can be denied that the sensory appearances constitute the first object of knowledge in our quest for certainty about the external world. Many things must occur in the external world and in the human body and nervous system in order for experience to occur and knowledge to be possible. Most of the events that occur to and within the human body belong to the subconscious subpersonal level; we are not normally aware of them and usually know nothing about them. When we see something, we have no awareness or knowledge (unless we are experts on the eye) of the changes our retinas undergo when affected by rays of light. In a similar way, we seldom note the exact character of the ways things appear, since we are more usually interested in the ways they actually are. Our tendency is to pass through the appearances on the way to the objects. So I might very well know that it is a ripe yellow lemon that I am seeing even though I cannot identify the precise shade of color or the exact shape that experience presents to me.

Therefore, even though sense experience is causally and temporally prior to my beliefs about objects, it is not epistemically prior. With effort, I can attend to the appearances and temporarily lay aside my interest in objects, but this is not the normal condition of perception. The appearances do not characteristically function as evidence – that is, as something we explicitly take account of in arriving at judgments about objects – although how things appear does, in a causal sense, guide and correct our judgments. Usually, there is no movement of conscious thought or explicit inference from the character of the appearances to the character of the object, any more than there is an inference from the retinal image to the object. Certainly the brain and nervous system and perhaps the mind itself process the material produced by sensory stimulation. But this processing occurs below the threshold of consciousness and plays a causal rather than an epistemic role in the production of belief and knowledge.

As we have seen, in sense perception the object appears in a certain way; that is what perception amounts to and no inference is involved. Thus *what* we see and hear and otherwise apprehend in sense perception are the things we mention when pressed to explain how we know something. We appeal to the appearances only in those few cases when we are not sure what we have perceived; in such cases the appearances, by becoming objects of attention, can acquire evidential status, but that is not their usual role. Even if the appearances are the first items in consciousness, they are not usually the first objects of knowledge.

Russell frequently spoke of *knowledge* by acquaintance. There is a more attenuated non-epistemic use of "acquaintance" in which it refers to things that occur in consciousness whether or not we are paying attention to them or using them as evidence of something or other. In this attenuated sense, I might be said to be acquainted with my toothache even when I am not paying attention to it or thinking about the tooth decay that causes it. Acquaintance in this sense does not entail knowledge of the object of acquaintance.

12

Inference and Interpretation

Perceptual Consciousness and Sensory Consciousness

In chapter 11, I argued that, as far as our knowledge of the external world is concerned, the problem of the shaky inference can be overcome by denying that our knowledge depends on it. "Here is one hand and here is another" is grounded by Moore's seeing his hands, and such grounding does not essentially incorporate an inference. Simple seeing is not a discursive process; it consists merely of the fact that an object appears in some way to a subject. There is, however, a problem that remains to be clarified and that is illustrated in the way that Kant deals with knowledge of objects.

Kant undertakes to refute the skepticism of Descartes' First Meditation in the section of the *Critique of Pure Reason* that he calls "Refutation of Idealism." He calls this skepticism by various names: sometimes he uses "dogmatic idealism," sometimes "skeptical idealism," and sometimes simply "idealism." What he rejects under these names should not be confused with the transcendental idealism that he accepts, according to which "appearances are to be regarded as being, one and all, representations only, not things in themselves." He rejects transcendental realism "which interprets outer appearances . . . as things-in-themselves, which exist independently of us and of our sensibility" (Kant, 1781, A369).

In Kant's discussion of these issues, we find a tension caused by a certain understanding of the role that inference plays in our knowledge of the external world. The mistake of skeptical idealism, according to Kant, is to suppose that an inference is necessary:

> [Skeptical or dogmatic] idealism assumed that the only immediate experience is inner experience, and that from it we can only *infer* outer things – and this, moreover, only in an untrustworthy manner, as in all cases where

we are inferring from given effects to determinate causes. In this particular case, the cause of the representations, which we ascribe, perhaps falsely to outer things, may lie in ourselves. But in the above proof ["Refutation of Idealism"] it has been shown that outer experience is really immediate. (Kant, 1781, B276–7)

Kant's view, then, agrees with the conclusion of chapter 11 that seeing something is immediate or non-inferential.

In accordance with this conclusion, it is necessary to distinguish two forms of immediate consciousness involved in our ability to gain knowledge of objects. The one is *perceptual consciousness,* of which simple seeing is an example. The other is *sensory consciousness,* which consists of the fact that outer objects appear to us, and, as the case of dreams and hallucinations demonstrates, appearances may occur even in the absence of objects. So sensory consciousness can exist without perceptual consciousness. Sensory consciousness is a necessary condition of perceptual consciousness; this is an analytical claim because perceptual consciousness just consists in an object's appearing to a subject. Neither form of consciousness involves inference or propositional content; both are immediate. Propositional content as well as knowledge of the external world only come into the picture once we have formed judgments about objects and their characteristics. Knowledge about the appearances is not essential for the perceptual apprehension of objects; that is why perceptual consciousness is immediate or non-inferential. This account is quite consistent with transcendental realism, according to which our knowledge of objects is knowledge of things as they are in themselves, objective knowledge in other words.

For Kant, however, transcendental realism inescapably leads to skepticism:

For if we regard outer appearances as representations produced in us by their objects, and if these objects be things existing in themselves outside us, it is indeed impossible to see how we can come to know the existence of the objects otherwise than by inference from the effect to the cause; and this being so, it must always remain doubtful whether the cause in question be in us or outside us. (Kant, 1781, A372)

Kant's solution – the shift in point of view discussed in chapter 1 – is to reject realism in favor of transcendental idealism, according to which objects are to be identified with the appearances rather than with things in themselves. The transcendental idealist "considers this matter and even its inner possibility to be appearance merely; appearance, if separated from our sensibility, is nothing. . . . External objects (bodies) . . . are mere appearances" (Kant,

1781, A370). For Kant, perceptual consciousness is just a form, a special case, of sensory consciousness, whereas for the realist the objects of the former, but not the latter, exist independently of consciousness. Skepticism, according to Kant, is the inescapable result of sundering objects from our sensory representation of objects. If sensory consciousness gives us only representations, then we have no way to acquire a consciousness of the objects themselves other than by an inference that is too unreliable to constitute the basis of knowledge of the external world.

According to my discussion of Moore's proof, however, Kant has simply misunderstood the relation between the two forms of consciousness. He has supposed that if perceptual consciousness consists of an awareness of things as they are in themselves and if sensory consciousness consists simply of traces in consciousness caused by the things in themselves as they interact with our sense organs, then the only way to get from the traces to things in themselves is by a shaky inference. But we have seen that our access to things in themselves is via perception that involves no inference at all. So there is no need to abandon the realism of common sense for transcendental idealism.

However, the feeling that something remains to be settled persists. If the trace is one thing and the object an entirely distinct thing, and if our knowledge of the latter depends in some way upon the former, how can our awareness of objects be immediate and non-inferential?

Inference and Interpretation

In this discussion, the term *inference* has been used to refer to a movement of thought or discourse from one proposition to another, an unfolding of and an examination of the implication relation among propositions. Inferring is a phase in the search for truth. If I accept certain propositions as true, by investigating what they imply, I can discover the truth of other propositions (as in Moore's proof). Or, in attempting to determine whether or not a proposition is true, I can unfold its implications to see whether they are acceptable.

There is, however, another movement of thought, not exclusively propositional, that resembles inference. If, for example, I hear a sound overhead and think to myself that an airplane is passing by, I have derived the proposition that an airplane is passing by from my hearing the sound. This is not an inference, for this proposition emerges in thought from the experience (which, as we saw, is not propositional), not from another proposition. I shall use the term *interpretation* to include such cases.

An interpretation of an item, whatever it is, consists of a judgment about what that item is or what it signifies or represents or implies or means or portends, where all these terms are to be understood broadly, not in a narrow technical sense. Thus when I think, on the basis of hearing the sound, that there is a plane overhead, I am taking the sound to signify the presence of a plane. When, on the basis of sounds that come from your mouth, I decide that you are a follower of Kant's philosophy, my judgment is an interpretation of your speech. Inference is a species of interpretation; it is a way of exploring the implications and hence the meaning and representational significance of propositions. What Locke calls *the doctrine of signs*, "the business whereof, is to consider the Nature of Signs, the Mind makes use of for the understanding of Things, or conveying its Knowledge to others" (Locke, 1690, IV, pp. xxi, 4), is the theory of interpretation. Interpretation is the use of signs for "the understanding of Things." In inference, the signs we use are propositions whose implications and presuppositions we explore. But the class of things made use of is not limited to items with propositional content: that is why we need the broader notion of interpretation. Note that while the interpretive judgment tells us about the signification of the sign, it need not say anything about the sign. When I think that there is a plane overhead, my thought is about the plane, not about the sound it makes, but it is the sound that it being interpreted; what it signifies is represented in the judgment. In Locke's terms the sign itself is something used, but it need not itself be something known in the propositional sense; one can pass directly from it to what it signifies without formulating a judgment about it. We know almost nothing about the mechanism within the mind/brain system that makes this possible.

The Shaky Interpretation

Return now to Moore as he says "Here is one hand and here is another." The members of the audience see his hands and thus verify the truth of what he says. What he says, the premise of his proof of an external world, is not inferred from his seeing his hands, although it is based upon it. We are now in a position to say that the premise is an interpretation of what he sees; it tells us what these things are that he sees. It is selective, as are interpretations generally; he could have reported other facts within his field of vision. Interpretations are motivated by the interests of the speaker.

For Locke, the main principle of the doctrine of signs is formulated in this way: "For since the Things, the Mind contemplates, are none of them, besides itself, present to the Understanding, 'tis necessary that something else, a Sign or Representation of the thing it considers, should be present to it: And these are *Ideas*" (Locke, 1690, IV, pp. xxi, 4). When a member of Moore's audience sees his hands, he has an idea of it. Earlier I interpreted this to mean that, in the perceptual case, the hands appear to him in some way. The appearances play the role of ideas in the mind. Whereas the hands themselves are not present to the understanding (they are remote, external objects), the appearances are present and thus function as representations of the hands. On this view, when he says, speaking of Moore's hands, "There is one hand and there is another," the appearance of the hands is a sign of the hands. Now, his seeing Moore's hands is not itself an interpretation because that is non-propositional. But his judgment "There is one hand and there is another," as well as Moore's corresponding premise, should be understood as interpretations of the appearances as well. The premise is an interpretation of two things: the things seen – it tells us what they are – and the appearances – it tells what they signify.

There is a sound reason in favor of Locke's view that our interpretations of perceived objects must be based upon things present to the mind. After all, these interpretations express information about remote objects, information that is made available to the perceiver via the appearances and only the appearances. It is because the things Moore is holding up look like hands that anyone observing them has reason to think that they are hands. What is distinctive about sense perception is that information is made available to the perceiver via items in consciousness. So even though Moore sees his hands and that is the basis of his knowledge of the premise of P, it is not the hands themselves that make the information that these are hands available to Moore; it is the way they appear; it is the sensuous constituent of the perception that is doing all the work here as far as the delivery of information is concerned. So we can say that Moore's knowledge of the premise is both based upon and grounded upon his seeing his hands and also based upon and grounded upon their appearing to him in the way they do. Even if the premise of P is not based upon a shaky inference, it is, so the skeptic will argue, based upon a shaky interpretation. So shaky is it that it is insufficient to provide knowledge of the external world.

How Shaky Is the Interpretation?

In chapter 11 we saw Berkeley use the examples of dreams and frenzies to conclude that "the supposition of external bodies is not necessary for producing our ideas." It would seem, then, that there is no rational basis for the interpretation "Here is one hand and here is another" in Moore's experience. Moore could be having just these sensory experiences even if there were no hands there at all. The skeptic will then wish to conclude that Moore does not know the premise of P because it is possible that it is false. The skeptic's argument here has the following form: given E (an experience of A), it is not necessary that O (an object allegedly corresponding to the experience) exists; therefore, given E, it is possible that O does not exist; therefore, assuming that E is A's only access to what lies beyond his experience, he does not know of the existence of O.

On the other hand, if we bring into the picture what we have learned of the relation between appearances and the objects of which they are appearances on the basis of both everyday experience and science, we can see that Berkeley has exaggerated the looseness of the connection. The connection between objects and their appearances is quite regular. We can predict with a high degree of accuracy how things will look when objects are presented to the senses under various circumstances. This is not surprising, since both ordinary experience and evolutionary considerations confirm that the survival of the species depends upon a regular connection between outer objects and inner experience. We are so designed by nature that how things appear generally depends upon how they are. Dreams and frenzies are the exceptions rather than the rule, and we are beginning to understand the conditions on which they depend as well. In fact, that a round object will look round to most normal observers under a large variety of circumstances is itself a law of nature, a regularity reporting a substantial degree of dependence of the inner appearance upon the outer object. Like many or most natural laws, it is subject to the condition that other things are equal, and the exceptions such as occur in dreams and frenzies themselves depend in a lawlike way upon certain conditions. So the interpretations we make of the appearances are not so shaky after all. They are sufficiently regular to justify our perceptual judgments; our knowledge of how perception works gives us excellent reason to think that perception is quite reliable and that, in some circumstances, it is so reliable that perceptual interpretations qualify as knowledge.

Of course, the skeptic will insist that, in constructing a response to his critique of human knowledge, we are not entitled to make use of our prior understanding of how perception works based upon everyday experience and scientific inquiry. That would simply beg the question, for it assumes that this understanding is sufficiently reliable to serve as a datum in explaining how knowledge takes place.

However, one of the skeptic's arguments is that, given E, it is physically possible that O does not exist. So he has assumed that, in the circumstances in which Moore uttered his premise, the sensory experience that he and his audience underwent did not depend in a law-like way upon the fact reported by "Here is one hand and here is another." For if there is a law-like dependence in those circumstances, then it is not true that given E, it is possible that O does not exist, since, given E, it is necessary, according to a law of nature, that O does exist. Although Moore is not entitled, in replying to skepticism, to suppose that there is a lawful dependence, the skeptic is not entitled to suppose that there isn't. Since the fact of dreams and frenzies does not refute the existence of lawful regularity, the skeptic is not entitled to conclude that Moore does not know the truth of the premise of P. Once again the skeptic's arguments fail to show that Moore does not have knowledge.

Does Moore Beg the Question?

This is a good place to introduce Barry Stroud's criticism of Moore's proof in his *The Significance of Philosophical Scepticism*. Stroud objects in principle to Moore's introduction of the premise of P in his attempt to prove the existence of an external world:

> If we have the feeling that Moore nevertheless fails to answer the philosophical question about our knowledge of external things, as we do, it is because we understand that question as requiring a certain withdrawal or detachment from the whole body of our knowledge of the world. We recognize that when I ask in that detached philosophical way whether I know that there are external things, I am not supposed to be allowed to appeal to other things I think I know about external things in order to help me settle the question. *All* of my knowledge of the external world is supposed to have been brought into question at one fell swoop; no particular piece of it is to be available as unquestioned knowledge to help me decide whether or not another particular candidate is true. . . . The sceptical philosopher holds that what Moore says is no refutation of philosophical scepticism. I think the sceptical philosopher is right on this point. (Stroud, 1987, pp. 117–18, 126)

One way of seeing the force of this criticism is to reflect upon Moore's insistence that he is appealing to ordinary and trite empirical claims in refuting both skepticism and idealism. The thesis that he was directly refuting – that there are no external objects – as well as his counter-thesis – that there are external objects – qualify as empirical assertions. "The proposition I make, when I say now 'I know that I am sitting in a chair,' is, I think, certainly an empirical one; and any philosopher who says, 'Nobody knows that there are external objects' is I think certainly saying something incompatible with this proposition of mine, and therefore something empirical" (Moore, 1968, pp. 673–4).

By using as the premise of his proof "Here is one hand and here is another," Moore is refusing to adopt the detached position that Stroud thinks is required in order to refute philosophical skepticism. Moore thinks it is perfectly acceptable to appeal to everyday empirical truths, whereas Stroud, with the force of Descartes' First Meditation behind him, claims that such an appeal violates the conditions of the debate between the skeptic and anti-skeptic by making use of the very beliefs that are in question. If the question is whether you know the truth of this or that, you cannot just answer the question by asserting the truth of this or that. To appeal to propositions grounded upon the evidence of the senses merely begs the question against skepticism; such an appeal takes as acceptable the very mode of verification that philosophical skepticism brings into question.

Stroud's argument against Moore makes us wonder what the issue is between the skeptic and the anti-skeptic. For Stroud, there is a "philosophical question about our knowledge of external things." A bit later he speaks of "whether I know that there are external things." The skeptic says there is no such knowledge and the anti-skeptic says there is.

In chapter 11, I distinguished three skeptical claims and came to the conclusion that the main skeptical arguments failed to show that any of them are true. So when the skeptic says that there is no knowledge of the external world, my verdict is: not proven.

But the skeptic may now challenge the anti-skeptic such as Moore to prove that there is knowledge of the external world. He can say to Moore: "You claim that you know that the premise of P is true. If you know it, perhaps that is because of evidence of the senses. You say you see your hands. But in order to convince me, you must show me that you really do see them. After all, you said you saw sunlight come through the roof during the Howison Lecture, and you were mistaken in that. So, infallible you are not."[1] Moore could reply by making the familiar move with his hands in front of the skeptic

---

1   It is interesting that in a paper written many years before "Proof of an External World," Moore claimed that a "proof" of the sort given in that paper begs the question at issue (Moore, 1909, pp. 159–60).

and saying "Here is one hand and here is another." But this reply bumps up against Stroud's detachment condition. On his view, Moore is not entitled to appeal to what he knows about external things because all such knowledge has been called into question. If he has such knowledge, Moore must demonstrate it without appealing to any instance of it. After all, if the anti-skeptic cannot appeal to any obvious instance of knowledge of the external world, then all that remains for him to rely upon is knowledge of the contents of his own mind, together with insight into evident conceptual and logical connections. That is what Descartes tried to do, but no one today thinks that he was successful.

Although my commentary on Moore's proof has not demonstrated that Moore actually does know the premise of P, it does show how such knowledge is possible. It gives an account of a number of conditions, such that if they were satisfied, then Moore knows the premise of P. And since the joint satisfaction of those conditions is possible, it follows that the skeptical claim that knowledge of the external world is impossible is not merely not proven but mistaken.

We have arrived at an interesting impasse. Under Stroud's detachment requirement, it is probably impossible to prove that there is knowledge of an external world. On the other hand, if the detachment requirement is rejected and one appeals, as does Moore, to instances of knowledge of external objects, one begs the question against the skeptic who has questioned the epistemic worth of *all* such putative instances.[2]

The anti-skeptic or philosophical realist should reject the detachment requirement, for it dooms his efforts at the very outset. To accept it is, in effect, to accept conditions which set up anti-skepticism for defeat. It immediately transports the anti-skeptic to enemy territory. It accepts, in addition, a certain condition of entitlement: unless one can show, under the conditions that the skeptic lays down, that one has the knowledge one thinks one has, one is not entitled to claim that one has knowledge. This condition of entitlement implies an internalist conception of knowledge and justification. But since nothing the skeptic says shows or even tends to show that Moore did not have the knowledge he claimed to have in the conditions in which he delivered his proof, the anti-skeptic should not accept conditions of argument that

2 "What is seen to be true from a detached 'external' standpoint might not correspond to what we take to be the truth about our position when we consider it 'internally,' from within the practical contexts which give our words their social point" (Stroud, 1987, p. 81).

13

Hume's Riddle of Induction

Hume on the Foundations of Knowledge

Hume is the most radical skeptic in modern philosophy, and in this chapter we shall explore his most famous skeptical thesis – his doubts about inductive inference – as he formulates it in his *Enquiry Concerning Human Understanding*. He himself does not use the term "induction"; his preferred term is "conclusions from experience." But I shall use "induction" instead as the term most frequently used in subsequent discussions of the issue Hume raised.

Hume begins by distinguishing two types of human inquiry. The first – *relations of ideas* – takes mathematics and logic as its object, and its method of verification is either through intuition (for self-evident truths) or through demonstration (for those truths the knowledge of which depends upon their being deduced from self-evident truths). "Propositions of this kind are discoverable by the mere operation of thought, without dependence on what is anywhere existent in the universe. Though there never were a circle or triangle in nature, the truths demonstrated by Euclid would for ever retain their certainty and evidence" (Hume, 1748, p. 25). Hume is here building upon the view of Descartes in the First Meditation when he claims that the elementary truths of arithmetic and geometry cannot be falsified by anything that experience can bring. Such truths are known *a priori*, independently of experience. Hume claims that such truths do not bring with them any ontological commitments; they imply nothing about any existing objects; the mind, operating independently of experience, has no way of gaining access to any objects at all.

The second set of objects of inquiry consists of *matters of fact*; these are real existents that can be verified *a posteriori* by experience and that imply ontological commitments. These are neither intuitive nor demonstrable because their existence is contingent. The question Hume undertakes to answer in his discussion of inductive inference is how inquiries into matters of fact proceed.

Just as our knowledge of relations of ideas is based upon a foundation of intuitive knowledge, together with intuitively apprehended principles of demonstrative or deductive inference, so our knowledge of matters of fact is grounded upon facts immediately presented through the senses and memory:

> In a word, if we proceed not upon some fact, present to the memory or senses, our reasonings would be merely hypothetical; and however the particular links might be connected with each other, the whole chain of inferences would have nothing to support it, nor could we ever, by its means, arrive at the knowledge of any real existence. If I ask you why you believe any particular matter of fact, which you relate, you must tell me some reason; and this reason will be some other fact, connected with it. But as you cannot proceed after this manner *in infinitum*, you must at last terminate in some fact, which is present to your memory or senses; or must allow that your belief is entirely without foundations. (Hume, 1748, p. 46)

Hume here presents a powerful argument in favor of this understanding of the foundations of human knowledge. If our justifications failed to terminate in matters of fact given by the memory or the senses, we would have no reason to think that we were apprehending any real existence; a system of belief that was internally coherent but not based upon sense impressions or memory would be indistinguishable from fiction. Moreover, without such terminating judgments we would generate an infinite regress that would fail to justify anything. What is missing from Hume's argument is some reason for thinking that perceptual and memory judgments constitute a sufficient basis for human inquiry into matters of fact.

In any case, in these passages he presents us with a neat version of a conception of human knowledge that has come to be called *foundationalism*. In order for justification to be possible, the regress of reasons must terminate in judgments that either are self-evident or are reports of sense impressions or memories. These are the *basic beliefs*. The claim is that all of our justified beliefs either are basic beliefs or can be derived from them by valid inferences.

The Causal Inference

The matters of fact that we have knowledge of or justified belief about are those perceived and remembered and whatever others can be validly inferred from them. For Hume, the causal connection and only the causal connection does the work of grounding the inference. Given some event E, I am entitled to infer the existence of some other event or object T if and only if I have reason to believe that T is either the cause or effect of E.

> The hearing of an articulate voice and rational discourse in the dark assures us of the presence of some person: Why? Because these are the effects of the human make and fabric, and closely connected with it. If we anatomize all the other reasonings of this nature, we shall find that they are founded on the relation of cause and effect. (Hume, 1748, p. 27)

Moreover, our knowledge of what causes what is founded upon experience alone, and the particular type of experience that we suppose justifies a belief in a causal connection is the past conjunction of objects and events. It is only because previous occasions of rational discourse were accompanied by the presence of human persons that I am led to believe that this rational discourse would not have occurred without the presence of a person.

In some cases the causal inference depends upon the supposition of "an intricate machinery or secret structure of parts" (Hume, 1748, p. 28). For example, if I think that this bread will be nourishing for the reason that bread of this type has always turned out to be nourishing in the past, I presuppose that there is an explanation of why bread of this type is nourishing that lies in the "secret structure" of its parts, an explanation which I assume but usually do not know. Hume here recognizes that in everyday life and in science we suppose that there is more to objects and events than what we can gather directly from the senses, and that this something more is a causal factor in determining the specific sequence of events that we happen to observe. The supposition of "intricate machinery or secret structure of parts" is itself based upon a causal inference, but not one that is directly generated by the observable conjunctions of objects and events in the past; we are likely to believe in underlying unobservables when none of the items we observe are necessary or sufficient to produce the changes we observe; given that we also believe that every event has a cause, the absence of an observed cause makes us think that there must be an unobserved one.

The causal inference, then, is thought to justify beliefs about the past when past events are inferred as causes of present ones, and beliefs about the future when present events are thought to cause future ones, and unobservable events in the "secret structure of parts" when nothing observable is found to cause an observed change. In addition, when we have reason to believe that there is a strict constant conjunction between two distinct types of events that holds throughout all time in the past, present, and future, then we think we are justified in believing in the existence of a law of nature.

For Hume, the causal inference is incapable of identifying "the ultimate cause of any natural operation." We may explain how A causes E by discovering intervening events B, C, and D that connect A to E. And we may explain how A causes B by discovering intervening events X, Y, and Z in the "intricate machinery or secret structure of parts" that connects A to B. But once we have identified events that are contiguous and leave no room for further intervening events, we come upon brute inexplicable facts and the best we can do is to say: this is just the way that nature works.

> It is confessed, the utmost effort of human reason is to reduce the principles, productive of natural phenomena, to a greater simplicity, and to resolve the many particular effects into a few general causes, by means of reasonings from analogy, experience, and observation. But as to the causes of these general causes, we should in vain attempt their discovery; nor shall we ever be able to satisfy ourselves, by any particular explication of them. These ultimate springs and principles are totally shut up from human curiosity and enquiry. . . . The most perfect philosophy of the natural kind only staves off our ignorance a little longer. (Hume, 1748, pp. 30–1)

The Riddle of Induction

I see a flame and expect that if I approach it closely enough I will feel heat. My reason for forming this expectation lies in the past conjunctions of flame and heat that I have observed. My expectation is based upon an inference from the past to the future. This is a particular instance of the causal inference. Can it be justified?

The inference is not demonstrative. That past flames have always been conjoined with heat does not entail logically or necessarily that this flame will also be conjoined with heat. The connection between past and future cannot be established by *a priori* reasoning alone. The events of the past on which my expectation is based are totally distinct from the events of the future that my expectation predicts. "Why this experience should be extended to future times, and to other objects, which for aught we know, may be only in appearance similar; this is the main question on which I would insist" (Hume, 1748, pp. 33–4). What is the "medium" Hume asks that connects the past to the future and that serves to justify the inductive inference? That is the riddle of induction. If we can identify the medium, we can solve the riddle.

Samples and Populations

We can think of the observed events that form the basis of an inductive infer-ence as a sample selected from a larger population. The observed flames that happen to be accompanied by heat constitute our sample of flames, on the basis of which we wish to form a rational belief about other members of the population not included in the sample. I may wonder whether this flame, not included in my sample, will similarly be accompanied by heat or whether the flame, not included in my sample, with which Nero burnt down Rome was accompanied by heat, or whether there is a law of nature that all flames are accompanied by heat. An inductive inference is simply an inference from an observed sample to some members of the population not included in the sample or to all members of the population when a law of nature is in ques-tion. Hume's riddle of induction, then, is the question: what justifies an in-ference from a sample to the character of objects entirely distinct from those included in the sample?

One might say that such an inference is justified only if the sample is cho-sen at random and is sufficiently large. In that case, we have reason to be-lieve that it is representative in the sense that, statistically, it matches the population or comes close to matching it. Suppose that someone who is at-tempting to predict an election polls a sample of voters and finds that 52 percent say they will vote for candidate A and 48 percent say they will vote for B. If the pollster judges his sample large enough and selected in a random manner, he will conclude that 52 percent of the whole population of voters will vote for A and 48 percent for B. Here the pollster is following the rule: if a sample S is selected at random from a population P and if the sample is sufficiently large, then you may infer that the sample is representative and that the population matches it statistically with regard to the character in question. Let us call this *the standard rule*. It tells us to project the statistical makeup of a large random sample upon the population. Hume's riddle of induction asks: what, if anything, justifies our use of the standard rule?

The Uniformity of Nature

To return to Hume's example, how do particular judgments that report that the flames I observed in the past were accompanied by heat serve to justify my present expectation that this present flame will be found to be accompa-nied by heat as well? Is there some general principle that serves to connect the past to the future? Hume thinks that we make use of a principle of the uniformity of nature: "All our experimental conclusions proceed upon the supposition that the future will be conformable to the past" (Hume, 1748, p. 35). Or, in more general terms, all our experimental conclusions proceed upon the supposition that the character of a large random sample tells us about the character of other members of the population.

Hume points out that this principle is not self-evident or true *a priori* because "there is no contradiction that the course of nature may change" (Hume, 1748, p. 35). To attempt to prove it inductively by appealing to the premise that, in the past, the future turned out to conform to the past is a fallacious circular argument since it depends upon that very principle. Since both *a priori* and *a posteriori* arguments fail, and since there seems to be no other basis for justifying induction, it follows that inductive inference is not justified by rational means.

A point that Hume failed to make is that the assumption of uniformity that he takes to underlie our use of the standard rule isn't even true. Even if 52 percent of the voters sampled said they would vote for A, it would not be surprising if A failed to win the election. Samples, even large and randomly selected samples, frequently fail to match the population. We recognize that induction is precarious, that we should not risk too much on the expectations that it generates, and that its results are provisional and liable to be overturned by subsequent observation.

Nature may be uniform in the sense that every change is an instance of a strict law. When it suits his argument (as in his discussion of miracles), Hume relies upon this deterministic supposition (Hume, 1748, p. 114). But the fact that samples frequently fail to match their populations shows that there is no inductive basis at all for this supposition, and recent science seems to have discarded it. Today, the supposition of universal law-like determinism appears to be an out of date conjecture that has no bearing on the question of the validity of inductive inference.[1]

Hume is also interested in the question of why the size of the sample should matter.

> It is only after a long course of uniform experiments of any kind, that we attain a firm reliance and security with regard to a particular event. Now where is that process of reasoning which, from one instance, draws a con-

---

1   See Peirce's paper "The Doctrine of Necessity Examined" (1892), reprinted in his *Collected Papers* (1965, volume 6), for an incisive critique of the deterministic assumption as well as for a pragmatic justification of induction.

clusion, so different from that which it infers from a hundred instances that are nowise different from that single one? . . . I cannot find, I cannot imagine any such reasoning. (Hume, 1748, p. 36)

Merely increasing the size of the sample fails to explain the medium by which, in induction, we infer something about a different unobserved instance. When Hume concludes by saying "I cannot imagine any such reasoning," he means that although inductive inference is a passage of the mind from premises to a conclusion, he cannot find a basis for showing that any such inference is valid or justified. According to Hume, not only does induction fail to provide certainty, it does not even provide us with a lesser degree of justification.

Hume's Skeptical Solution

Hume does not recommend that we abandon induction. Clearly we use something like the standard rule at every moment of our waking life, and it is likely that our mind is programmed to use it. But the fact that Hume does not abandon it does not show that it is valid. "My practice, you say refutes my doubts. But you mistake the purport of my question. As an agent, I am quite satisfied in the point; but as a philosopher, who has some share of curiosity, I will not say scepticism, I want to learn the foundation of this inference" (Hume, 1748, p. 38). In his characteristic fashion, Hume distinguishes between two points of view. As an agent who is obligated to act in the world, he does not doubt the validity of induction; the expectations that it produces are genuine and the strength of his convictions about what the future will bring continue to depend upon what he has already observed. But as a philosopher, he is interested in assessing our human epistemic situation, and he has discovered that our epistemic condition is quite unsatisfactory. His doubts about induction are the conclusions of philosophical inquiry and are no impediments to action in the world. His brand of skepticism does not require us to abandon any form of reasoning that is well entrenched and unavoidable. In a famous passage, he says:

> Nature will always maintain her rights, and prevail in the end over any abstract reasoning whatever. Though we should conclude, for instance, . . . that, in all reasonings from experience [induction], there is a step taken by the mind which is not supported by any argument or process of the understanding; there is no danger that these reasonings, on which almost all knowledge depends, will ever be affected by such a discovery. (Hume, 1748, p. 41)

The term "nature" here refers to an innate propensity of the human mind to engage in inductive inference no matter how poor are the arguments presented to establish its rationality. Our basic inductive practices are part of the program of the mind, and it would be hopeless even to try to do without them. Unlike Sextus Empiricus and the Pyrrhonist tradition, Hume thinks that it is futile to aim at suspense of judgment with regard to the conclusions of entrenched epistemic practices.

Hume calls the non-rational principle of inductive inference by the name of "custom or habit." "All inferences from experience, therefore, are effects of custom, not of reasoning" (Hume, 1748, p. 43). It is characteristic of his skeptical inquiries that they conclude not by asking us to abandon practices that are not rationally justifiable but by identifying the mental propensities that generate them. His theory of mind is a theory of the non-rational propensities by which the mind, on the basis of sense impressions and memories, constructs the system of beliefs which form our representation of what we take to be an objective world. But we have no reason to think that the system accurately represents things as they are in themselves. Hume's view of our beliefs about matters of fact can be called constructivism because our beliefs about the world we never made are constructed by mental propensities whose operation provides us with no hope of verifying a conformity between what we think there is and what there really is.

Probabilification

A frequent objection to Hume's inductive skepticism is that all he has shown is that inductive inference is not deductive. In a valid deductive inference, the premises entail the conclusion: if the premises are true, then, necessarily, so is the conclusion. If a deductive inference is sound, if it is valid and has true premises, then the conclusion is true. If it is epistemically sound, then we can know the conclusion to be true. But induction is not deduction, and the rules that govern inductive practices cannot yield the same degree of certainty as deductive rules. That does not mean, however, that induction does not have its own special cogency. The problem with Hume's argument, it is said, is that it takes deduction as the standard of all valid reasoning, and when it is shown to fall short of that standard, Hume incorrectly concludes that it is based upon custom rather than reason.

However, this response involves an incorrect interpretation of Hume's argument. He is not merely saying that induction falls short of deductive cogency. He is saying that if it has a cogency of its own, let that be identified and made explicit. The basic thrust of his argument is that no attempt that he is familiar with to discover the rationale of inductive inference succeeds in establishing its validity. The gap between past and future cannot be bridged by any arguments *a priori*, and efforts to establish an *a posteriori* bridge, such as the principle of uniformity, are circular at the very least and, besides that, are simply mistaken.

A possibility that Hume did not examine is that the validity of inductive inference is founded not upon the entailment relation between premises and conclusion explored in deductive logic but upon a weaker relation of *probabilification* between premises and conclusion. Even if statements about the past do not entail beliefs about the future, perhaps they are capable of probabilifying them.

Consider this example. John has a bag that he knows to contain nine black balls and one white one. The balls are alike in every respect but color, and they have been thoroughly mixed together. John draws one ball from the bag without looking at it, holds it in his hand, and, in response to being asked what color it is, he answers "Black, of course." If he has to bet even money on the color, again he says "Black." If he is asked how sure he is that it is black, he says, "I am not completely certain that it is black, but I have a high degree of confidence that it is. It is quite probably black. In fact, I can even provide a numerical measure of my degree of confidence: I am 90 percent sure that it is black."

J. L. Mackie characterizes this example in this way:

> This kind of reasoning seems cogent. (Most people admit that, in the ninety-nine-to-one case, if their lives depended upon a correct answer, they would say that the ball was black.) Yet it is not deductive. Nor is it inductive. . . . It makes no extrapolation from observed to unobserved cases. . . . There is no appeal to Hume's uniformity principle or to any specific causal judgments. . . . Induction may be rationally justified by showing that in each such inference the conclusion is probabilified by the premises or evidence in accordance with the apparently cogent sort of reasoning illustrated by the example of the balls in the bag. (Mackie, 1979, pp. 118–19)

One way of interpreting Mackie's argument is that he is claiming that there is a logical relation between the premises that formulate the evidence ("Nine of the ten balls are black, one is white, and they have been thoroughly mixed together, etc.") and the conclusion ("The ball I am holding in my hand is black"). This relation is weaker than entailment; even if the premises are true, it is possible that John is actually holding a white ball. But it is rationally stronger than mere custom, for it actually justifies John in saying that the ball is black. This is the relation of probabilification. According to Mackie's argument, one could say, against Hume, that the premise that all observed flames have been accompanied by heat probabilifies the conclusion that this flame is likewise accompanied by heat. Probabilification is the medium Hume was in search of to connect past observations with expectations about the future.

The alleged relation of probabilification is, I think, an artifact of a verbal maneuver. Given the premise about the color composition of balls in the bag together with the assumption that each of the ten possible selections is equally probable (the principle of indifference), it follows logically that it is probable (more probable than not, 90 percent probable) that the selected ball is black. It follows in virtue of the concept of probability involved in the inference: there are ten possible draws; nine of the ten are black; all the draws are equally probable; therefore it is 90 percent probable that this ball is black. This is a deductive inference. In order to provide the illusion that there is a relation of probabilification or weak entailment between the premises and conclusion, the advocate of this approach drops the probability prefix ("it is 90 percent probable") from the conclusion and incorporates it into the relation between premises and conclusion. Since such relations are reducible to or analyzable in terms of deductive relations, the theory of probabilification introduces no new idea.

Probability and Belief

Hume aimed at demonstrating that our inductive inferences not only do not provide certainty, they do not provide probability either. But even if the theory of probabilification fails to discover the medium to connect premises to conclusion, it leads us to conclude that certain premises entail the probability of certain conclusions. Doesn't this dispose of Hume's argument?

In the example just considered, in order to conclude that it is 90 percent probable that this draw is black, John had to assume that each of the ten possibilities was equally probable. For suppose the prior probability of a white draw is 95 percent; then the conclusion certainly does not follow. Can this assumption be justified? There are two ways of attempting to do this. The first is to appeal to the principle of indifference, which assigns *a priori* equal probability to the prior possibilities when there is no known reason for doing otherwise. But it is difficult to understand why one should have any opinion about probabilities in the face of ignorance; the assignment of equal probabilities just seems arbitrary; why the preference for the same probability in each case? One might just as well assign different probabilities at random. Ignorance is, well, just ignorance.

The other way is to justify the assignment of equal probabilities on *a posteriori* grounds. Our past experience of things that resemble the thoroughly mixed balls in the bag situation gives us reason to believe that there is no bias favoring any ball over any other, that there is as good a chance of any ball being drawn as any other. But if we apply this past experience to the present case, we are making use of inductive inference, the very type of inference whose validity is in question. We can, therefore, use induction to determine probabilities in specific cases, but if our question is whether we can establish the validity and probability of induction without assuming its validity and probability, then, to use the words of Quine, "the Humean predicament is the human predicament" (Quine, 1969, p. 72). The rational determination of probabilities in actual cases depends upon our use of inductive inference and cannot serve to justify any belief unless the validity of induction has already been established.

The Limits of Hume's Inductive Skepticism

What exactly has Hume's argument shown? That attempts to justify induction have failed. Moreover, the failure is systematic. Any attempt must incorporate a premise that is known either *a priori* or *a posteriori*. But no such premise is known *a priori*, for none of those suggested are either self-evident or demonstrable from premises that are self-evident. And no such premise is known *a posteriori*, for any attempt to justify any one of them is fallacious because it depends upon induction. Is it reasonable to conclude, then, that no one knows the conclusion of any inductive inference? Is it true that I do not know that this flame will be observed to give off heat?

G. E. Moore does not think that the skeptical conclusion follows:

> We must, I think, grant the premiss that, from the fact that two things have been conjoined, no matter how often, it does not strictly *follow* that they *always* are conjoined. But it by no means follows from this that we may not *know* that, as a matter of fact, when two things are conjoined sufficiently often, they are *always* conjoined. We may quite well *know* that two things are causally connected, although this does not logically follow from our past experience, nor yet from anything else that we know. And, as for the contention that our belief in causal connections is merely based on *custom*, we may, indeed, admit that custom would not be a sufficient *reason*, for concluding the belief to be true. But the mere fact (if it be a fact)

that the belief is only caused by custom, is also no sufficient reason for concluding that we can *not* know it to be true. Custom *may* produce beliefs which we do know to be true, even though it be admitted that it does not *necessarily* produce them. (Moore, 1909, p. 161)

According to Moore, the skeptical conclusion that I do not know that this flame will be observed to give off heat does not follow from the fact that the argument that supports it is not deductive. Nor does it follow from the fact that it is caused by custom or habit. According to Moore, we *may* know things that are caused by custom and that do not follow deductively from anything else we know.

But, as we saw, Hume's argument was stronger than merely remarking that induction is not deduction and that custom is not reason. Hume challenged the friends of induction to discover some positive justification for induction, and we have seen that none is forthcoming.

We will, however, go a step beyond what Moore actually says here to suggest that from the fact that an inference is not deductively valid, it does not follow that it is not valid, and from the fact that an inference is caused by custom, it does not follow that it is not valid. Moreover, from the fact that we cannot show by a valid argument that a form of inference is valid, it does not follow that the form of inference is not valid. So it is possible that I do know that this flame will be observed to give off heat. Let us turn to the notion of validity to examine these contentions.

Validity

The reason why validity is a desirable feature of inferences and arguments is that a valid argument transmits truth from the premises to the conclusion. Thus, if our aim is truth and when the means to attain it is via inference, validity is an intellectual virtue. When the argument is deductively valid, we know that the truth of the premises guarantees, through the force of logical necessity, that the conclusion is true. Inductive arguments from the past to the future or from a sample to other members of the population are not deductively valid. The question is whether there is a broader notion of validity that includes deductive validity as a special case and allows some inductive arguments to be valid as well.

Charles Sanders Peirce developed a theory of rational inference that fits this requirement. In "The Fixation of Belief" he explains:

The object of reasoning is to find out, from the consideration of what we already know, something else which we do not know. Consequently, reasoning is good if it be such as to give a true conclusion from true premisses, and not otherwise. Thus, the question of validity is purely one of fact and not of thinking. A being the facts stated in the premisses and B that concluded, the question is, whether these facts are really so related that if A were B would generally be. If so, the inference is valid; if not, not. It is not the least the question whether, when the premisses are accepted by the mind, we feel an impulse to accept the conclusion also. . . . The conclusion would remain true if we had no impulse to accept it; and the false one would remain false, though we could not resist the tendency to believe in it. (Peirce, 1965, volume 5, para. 365)

For Peirce, validity is an objective affair; it concerns simply the tendency of premises of a certain type to yield conclusions of a certain type. For example, arguments of the type that are specified by the formal structure "All A are B; x is A; therefore x is B" invariably and necessarily produce true conclusions from true premises. But Peirce's notion of validity requires only that truth generally and not necessarily and invariably be the result. Let us say that a type of inference is valid if it reliably produces true conclusions from true premises. Deductively sound inferences are not only reliable; they are super-reliable, since truth is the invariable result of starting from truth. If a type of inductive inference, then, generally or quite frequently produces truth from true premises that are descriptive of the members of the observed sample, it qualifies as valid under Peirce's conception. Moreover, there is nothing in his conception that requires that we be in a position to provide a non-fallacious proof or argument that a form of inference is valid in order for it to be valid. In fact, we may even believe of a valid inference that it is not valid, and this does not affect its validity.

Peirce does not agree with Hume that an inference caused by custom or habit is not rational. Consider his discussion of the concept of a guiding principle of inference:

That which determines us, from given premisses, to draw one inference rather than another, is some habit of mind, whether it be constitutional or acquired. The habit is good or otherwise, according as it produces true conclusions from true premisses or not; and an inference is regarded as valid or not, without reference to the truth or falsity of its conclusions, but according as the habit which determines it is such as to produce true conclusions in general or not. The particular habit of mind which governs this or that inference may be formulated in a proposition whose truth depends on the validity of the inferences which the habit determines; and such a formula is called a *guiding principle* of inference. (Peirce, 1965, volume 5, para. 367)

An inference may be an expression of a habit, acquired perhaps during the years the child learns language. Later, after guiding principles have been formulated through the study of logic, a person's inferences may frequently be the result of the application of an explicit guiding principle. Consider, for example, the standard rule that tells us to predict the character of unobserved members on the basis of a representative sample. At first, the rule operates within us without being explicitly formulated. Later, our statistical inferences may be guided by an explicit formulation. But our inferences are valid or invalid, as the case may be, whether the guiding principles operate as habits or as explicit rules. We are rational when and to the extent that our guiding principles are such as to transmit truth reliably from given truths. The nature of the mental cause does not affect the question of validity.

From an externalist point of view, a belief fixed in a person by a reliable process is justified to the extent to which the process is reliable. An example discussed earlier in the examination of Moore's proof of an external world is the process of fixing beliefs based upon perception. When the belief is true and the process is extremely reliable or even super-reliable, then the individual has knowledge of its truth. Hume's skeptical argument works only on internalist assumptions: if it is necessary to be in a position to offer a nonfallacious argument to establish the reliability of inductive inference in order for induction to provide knowledge or even justified belief as the internalist requires, then Hume's skeptical conclusion that induction fails to provide knowledge and justified belief is correct. But if the aim of the skeptic is to show that we do not have the knowledge and justified belief that we think we have, then his argument fails, at least on externalist grounds (see Levin, 1993, 1997; Landesman, 1997, pp. 139–43).

Inductive inference, thus, may be valid and may provide knowledge, and nothing that Hume and his skeptical followers have said contradicts that. And once we accept induction as valid, we can see that it builds its own support. We can use inductive inference, for example, to establish that our samples are chosen at random and are sufficiently large, and we can use the conclusions of previous inductions to support the conclusions of new inferences. That, of course, is not an argument against the skeptic since he will point out that it is circular and fallacious if we are aiming to justify induction generally. The basic argument against the inductive skeptic is that he has failed to show that, even if his arguments against the possibility of justifying induction are correct, they do not prove what he set out to prove, namely that induction fails to provide knowledge and rational belief.

Reliability

Now for a brief remark about reliability. A process of fixing belief is reliable provided it gives more truth than falsehood. But reliability is a matter of degree, and so is the justification it provides. If the process is super-reliable it provides certainty and knowledge. Suppose, for example, that there are no exceptions whatever to the conjunction of flame and heat. Therefore, the inductive inference from observed past conjunctions of flame and heat to the prediction that this flame will be observed to give off heat is an instance of a super-reliable procedure, and my belief that this flame will give off heat is something I know to be true.

The externalist claims that a belief fixed by a reliable process is justified and, under some circumstances, counts as knowledge even if one cannot establish by valid non-fallacious arguments that the process in question is reliable. Under the influence of Hume's arguments, a person may accept that his belief that this flame will give off heat does not count as knowledge, although he really does know it. Just as one can think one knows something and be mistaken, so one can think one does not know something and be mistaken. If externalism is correct, that is the usual condition of the skeptic.

In explaining what counts as a reliable procedure, one must take into account the fact that a process of fixing belief may appear to be reliable even though it is a product of accident or chance. For example, suppose I am presented with a list of propositions and determine my agreement or disagreement with them by flipping a coin: heads I affirm it and tails I deny it. It may turn out that 52 percent of the beliefs fixed in this way are true and 48 percent are false, and thus the method is, or appears to be, reliable. But one would not agree that this procedure provides any justification whatever, since I was merely guessing.

Such an accidental method of fixing beliefs should not be considered a reliable method; one would not act on beliefs arrived at in this way. The example given of an accidental procedure may appear far-fetched, but a true to life one is not hard to find. Peirce mentions the method that fixes men's beliefs by reference to the authority of political and religious leaders and by threats when the appeal to authority fails.

But in the most priest ridden states some individuals will be found who . . . cannot help seeing that it is the mere accident of their having been taught as they have, and of their having been surrounded with the manners and associations they have, that has caused them to believe as they do and not far differently. Nor can their candour resist the reflection that there is no reason to rate their own views at a higher value than those of other nations and other centuries; thus giving rise to doubts in their minds. (Peirce, 1965, volume 5, para. 381)

For Peirce, the method of authority is to be rejected, for it provides no assurance that our opinions will coincide with facts; even if the authorities should happen to teach what is true, that is a mere accident. What are wanted are methods that assure that our beliefs will regularly correspond with fact. Peirce recommends the method of science because it fixes belief by procedures that place us in contact (via the senses) with the facts we aim at knowing (Peirce, 1965, volume 5, para. 384).

For this reason, we shall consider a procedure to be reliable not only if it arrives at truth more often than not but if it does so non-accidentally and without guesswork. One may wonder how inductive inference fits this description; after all, my belief that this flame will be observed to give off heat is about some event in the future with which I could have no direct contact when I made the prediction. But the contact could be indirect. After all, the "intricate machinery or secret structure of parts" of the flames that I have observed in the past are present in this flame as well and will be supposed to have the same effects. We can understand how inductive inference indirectly places us in contact with events in the future via events of the same type in the past that have caused our observations to be what they are. Of course, this explanation makes use of induction, but there is no circularity here since we are not trying to justify it but to explain the nature of the access to reality it provides.

14

Descartes' *Cogito* and the Problem of Self-knowledge

I Think, therefore I Exist

At the outset of the Second Meditation, Descartes reviews the doubts about the truth of his beliefs that he had generated in the First Meditation primarily by means of the arguments from dreams and from the evil demon. He stands now on a platform of solipsism: "I will suppose then, that everything I see is spurious. I will believe that my memory tells me lies, and that none of the things that it reports ever happened. I have no senses. Body, shape, extension, movement and place are chimeras. So what remains true? Perhaps just the one fact that nothing is certain" (Descartes, 1985, II, p. 16). He then turns to himself. If nothing is certain, then he is not certain about himself either. Perhaps even solipsism cannot be sustained, for that requires at the very least that one knows of the existence of one's own self, even though everything else is placed in doubt. He asks "Does it not follow that I too do not exist?" and, in his answer, introduces his most famous idea, the *cogito*:

> No: if I convinced myself of something then I certainly existed. But there is a deceiver of supreme power and cunning who is deliberately and constantly deceiving me. In that case I too undoubtedly exist, if he is deceiving me; and let him deceive me as much as he can, he will never bring it about that I am nothing so long as I think that I am something. So after considering everything very thoroughly, I must finally conclude that this proposition, *I am, I exist*, is necessarily true, whenever it is put forward by me or conceived in my mind. (Descartes, 1985, II, p. 17)

Descartes reformulates this argument on a number of occasions when he replies to objections, in his letters, and in his various writings. I shall focus mainly on the version of the argument as it is presented in this passage; other passages will be used for purposes of clarifying this one.

His initial response to the question is that he certainly exists if he convinces himself of something. The French version adds ". . . or thought anything at all." How does the fact that he thinks anything at all or convinces himself of anything at all prove that he exists? The answer obviously is that his existence is a necessary condition of his thinking anything at all, and his thinking anything at all is a sufficient condition of his existing.

Why is that? Because only an existing thing can think. In fact, in order for anything to do anything at all it must exist. "I act, therefore I exist." Fictional beings or merely imaginary beings may be imagined to act, but they cannot really act for that requires an existing subject.

What then is so special about thinking? If any action will do the job, why does Descartes select thinking and its various forms to play this role of bringing his doubts to an end? After all, the *cogito* plays a central role in the drama that Descartes is unfolding: "Archimedes used to demand just one firm and immovable point in order to shift the entire earth; so I too can hope for great things if I manage to find just one thing, however slight, that is certain and unshakable" (Descartes, 1985, II, p. 16). The one thing, however slight, is the fact that he thinks and therefore exists. It is this that initiates the downfall of skepticism and is the starting point for his proofs of God's existence and the distinction of mind from body. Since, in the First Meditation, Descartes was able to bring himself to doubt that he had a body, he could not rely upon any bodily action; he could rely only upon actions whose existence he cannot doubt, and these are acts of thinking. That is why thinking is destined to be the Archimedean lever that defeats skepticism.

He suddenly remembers, however, that he has earlier established the possibility of deception by an evil demon. The demon works by causing him to have certain thoughts that are not true. So if he is actually being deceived, then he is actually thinking certain thoughts, and consequently exists. The validity of the passage from "I think" to "I exist" is independent of the truth value of his thoughts.

Descartes' conclusion introduces a new idea. Up to this point, he has spoken of his existence as a necessary condition of any of his acts of thinking. But now he switches to consider the truth of the proposition "I am, I exist." He must make this transition because his investigation is epistemic and is concerned with the question of whether he knows anything with certainty. "I am, I exist" is the verbal expression of the Archimedean lever that establishes that something can be known with certainty, that there is a limit to doubt, that there is a truth that can be grasped.

The proposition "I am, I exist" is conclusively verified by his mere act of entertaining it, for his entertaining it is a form of thinking, and his thinking is a sufficient condition of its truth. So now we have moved from Descartes' act of thinking being a sufficient condition of his existing to his act of thinking being a sufficient condition of the truth of the proposition "I am, I exist."

There is one final step in the argument that is missing from its initial formulation but is supplied by Descartes in other contexts. He is concerned not merely with the fact of his existence but with his knowledge and certainty of that fact. His actually thinking something is a state of affairs sufficient for the truth of "I am, I exist," but in order for the doubts of the First Meditation to be terminated it is not enough that its verifier exist, it must be known to exist. He must know that he is thinking, and that knowledge must explain how he knows the truth of "I am, I exist."

The Inference from Thought to Existence

For this reason, Descartes frequently characterizes the *cogito* argument as an inference from thought to existence. Here is how he formulates it in one of his replies to objections.

> And when we become aware that we are thinking things, this is a primary notion which is not derived by means of any syllogism. When someone says "I am thinking, therefore I am, or I exist," he does not deduce existence from thought by means of a syllogism, but recognizes it as something self-evident by a simple intuition of the mind. This is clear from the fact that if he were deducing it by means of a syllogism, he would have to have had previous knowledge of the major premiss "Everything which thinks is, or exists"; yet in fact he learns it from experiencing in his own case that it is impossible that he should think without existing. It is in the nature of our mind to construct general propositions on the basis of our knowledge of particular ones. (Descartes, 1985, II, p. 100)

Descartes characterizes the move from "I think" to "I exist" as a necessary immediate inference in which the connection of premise to conclusion is self-evident; it is grasped, he says, by "a simple intuition of the mind." In this case, we do not have to rely upon a syllogism with an additional (major) premise because the inference, as it stands, is necessary and may be validated by inspection of the contents of premise and conclusion that reveal that the existence of the thinker is entailed or implied by the fact of his thinking. Not only is the major premise superfluous, but knowledge of its truth depends upon such simple inspections of the mind illustrated by the *cogito* inference. Our grasp of necessary general truths is often mediated by an apprehension of necessity among particulars. We are capable of apprehending the universal in and through the particulars.

The Problem of Epistemic Soundness

A logically sound argument, remember, is one that is deductively valid and has true premises. An epistemically sound argument is one that is logically sound and in which the premises are known to be true. Descartes claims to acquire knowledge of his own existence by inferring it from the fact of his thinking. If the *cogito* is to be epistemically sound, not only must his thinking entail his existing, he must know that he is thinking; that is, the argument must be epistemically sound. In addition, he claims to move from knowledge of the premise to knowledge of the conclusion via an intuition of the mind that tells him that the latter is entailed by the former, that the content of the latter is already included in the content of the former. The *cogito* simply analyses the content of "I think" and extracts "I exist" from it. And because Descartes extracts it in that way, he knows with certainty that he exists.

I shall call an argument that is epistemically sound and in which one comes to know with certainty the truth of the conclusion by inferring it from the premises in virtue of one's knowledge that the premises entail the conclusion *a perfectly sound epistemic argument*. Descartes' claim is that the *cogito* is an epistemic argument that is perfectly sound. Is his claim correct? There are two issues (at least) that need to be investigated. Is Descartes correct in supposing that he knows with certainty that "I think" entails "I exist"? This is *the transition problem*. And does Descartes know with certainty the truth of "I think?" This is *the problem of self-knowledge*.

The Transition Problem

In the First Meditation, Descartes recalls that there are certain truths – "two and three added together are five, and a square has no more than four sides" are his examples – that cannot be called into question by the possibility of his dreaming. These are things known *a priori*. They are "transparent truths." How can they be doubted? But if God is a deceiver or if there is an evil demon of enormous power intent upon deceiving him, "may I not similarly go wrong every time I add two and three or count the sides of a square, or in some even simpler matter, if that is imaginable?" (Descartes, 1985, II, p. 14).

The *cogito* inference is *a priori* as well. That "I exist" follows from "I think" alone is verified by inspection of the contents of these propositional thoughts without appealing to the senses. In the *cogito* passage in the Second Meditation, Descartes affirms the truth of "I exist" because it follows from "I think." Yet he is hesitant to affirm the truth of "two and three are five" and "a square has no more than four sides." These may be doubted. Why is the *cogito* different? Why doesn't it fall before the onslaughts of the evil demon as well?

The *cogito* has a special role to play in Descartes' reflection. He knows that he exists, and this knowledge is derived from the fact of his thinking and only from that fact, for everything else has been doubted. To the question that he then poses about the nature of the "I" or self whose existence he is now certain of, he answers that this "I" is a thinking thing. Whether this "I" is also identical with a body is a question Descartes puts aside until the Sixth Meditation; at this point he is restricting himself only to what he knows. He knows nothing of bodies, but he does know without any doubt that he thinks (Descartes, 1985, II, pp. 18–19).

Having arrived at the first truths that he takes himself as completely justified in asserting, Descartes finds himself in a position to identify a criterion of truth.

> I am certain that I am a thinking thing. Do I not therefore also know what is required for my being certain about anything? In this first item of knowledge there is simply a clear and distinct perception of what I am asserting; this would not be enough to make me certain of the truth of the matter if it could ever turn out that something which I perceived with such clarity and distinctness could be false. So I now seem to be able to lay it down as a general rule that whatever I perceive very clearly and distinctly is true. (Descartes, 1985, II, p. 24)

Here is another example of apprehending the universal through the particulars. The general criterion of clear and distinct perception is apprehended as that which convinces Descartes beyond all doubt of these first truths. It is that which verifies the transition from "I think" to "I exist." It is also that which is exemplified in "I am a thing that thinks."

But Descartes remembers that he had earlier succeeded in doubting his mathematical beliefs because of the possibility that God or an evil genius is deceiving him, so he is led to reconsider whether he can trust the reliability of the criterion of clear and distinct perception. The doubts of the First Meditation cannot be canceled by appeal to this criterion because the same reasons for doubting apply to the *cogito* and the criterion as well. They apply also to Descartes' efforts to remove these doubts by proving that God exists and is not a deceiver; as we saw in chapter 11, the whole effort rests upon the fallacy of arguing in a circle. Descartes recognizes that the *cogito* argument is in the same epistemic boat as simple mathematical truths (Descartes, 1985, II, p. 25), so he is no more justified in appealing to a standard implicit in the *cogito* than he is in appealing to the same standard implicit in "two and three are five."

Sextus Empiricus confined his doubts to things that are non-evident. The achievement of Descartes' use of skepticism is to show that radical doubt applies even to things that are evident. The possibility of an evil genius forces him to distinguish between the self-evidence of a proposition or inferential connection and the appearance of self-evidence. The evil genius may cause falsehoods to appear self-evident to him. This possibility spills over into the *cogito*, the proofs of God's existence, and even the criterion of truth implicit throughout. Simply put, intuitions of the mind are susceptible to error; therefore, the absolute certainty that Descartes seeks cannot be attained, at least by anything he has placed before us. A doubt remains, even though it is "very slight."

The Problem of Self-knowledge

In order for the *cogito* inference to constitute an epistemically sound argument, Descartes must know its premise "I think" with certainty. Why don't the doubts of the First Meditation apply in this case as well? Descartes refuses to extend his doubts to the contents of the mind. Even though we may be mistaken about what we see, we cannot be in error about the sensory appearances: "For example, I am now seeing light, hearing a noise, feeling heat. But I am asleep, so this is false. Yet I certainly *seem* to see, to hear, and to be warmed. This cannot be false; what is called 'having a sensory perception' is strictly just this, and in this restricted sense of the term it is simply thinking" (Descartes, 1985, II, p. 19). And in his reply to Arnauld's objections, Descartes states more generally that "we cannot have any thought of which we are not aware at the very moment when it is in us. . . . We are always actually aware of the acts and operations of our minds" (Descartes, 1985, II, pp. 171–2).

Freud frequently complained that philosophers arbitrarily identified mind with consciousness. He denied that the mind is transparent, claiming that most ideas, thoughts, and emotions are unconscious. Peirce notes that Descartes in particular "is taking it for granted that nothing in his nature lies hidden beneath the surface" (Peirce, 1965, volume 5, para. 382n). Moreover, Descartes' version of the transparency of mind generates a vicious infinite regress: each thought generates an awareness of itself which generates a further awareness of itself, and so on. But even if the assumption of transparency is unjustified in general, all that the *cogito* argument requires is that Descartes has knowledge and certainty of just some of his thoughts, not all of them.

The basis of self-knowledge, for Descartes, is self-awareness. I know that I am thinking, for example, that I may be deceived by an evil demon because I am aware of just that thought. I have a thought, I am aware of it, and this awareness is the ground of my coming to know that I have it. Moreover, I cannot be mistaken about any of the thoughts I am aware of. There is just no room for error here.

One of the thoughts which the possibility of dreams casts doubt upon in the First Meditation is "I am here in my dressing gown, sitting by the fire." Descartes is referring to a particular place, a particular dressing gown and fire. Simply doubting the truth of that belief does not itself raise doubts about that place, that dressing gown and that fire. If that belief is entirely false, then he is not in that place, dressed in that dressing gown, sitting by that fire. But the place, dressing gown and fire are not called into question just by negating the thought. Whether the thought is true or false, it contains an ontological commitment to the existence of these three things. If he is to succeed in doubting the existence of an external world, he must not merely apply negation to his thoughts, he must reformulate their content to rid them of their existential presuppositions. Thoughts do not exist in their entirety in the recesses of subjectivity; they reach out into the world. If one really doubts the world, then one cannot have many of the thoughts that one's formulations seem to express. He cannot be thinking "I am here in my dressing own, sitting by the fire" and simultaneously doubting the external world, doubting the existence of these three things, for the very expression of that thought commits him to their existence whether the thought is true or false. Instead he requires a formulation such as "It seems to me that I am in a certain place and that there is a certain dressing gown I am wearing and that there is a fire in that place." Prefixing "It seems to me" to the thought cancels the commitment to the existence of these three items.

Thus, the consistent application of the method of doubt requires Descartes to question the very contents of his thoughts; his doubt cannot be restricted just to things beyond himself because his acts of thinking purport to bring those things into the mind's own contents. When we speak of the contents of our thoughts, we are already in the world, and we cannot consistently doubt it. Perhaps that is what Heidegger means when he says: "The perceiving of what is known is not a process of returning with one's booty to the 'cabinet' of consciousness after one has gone out and grasped it"; and "The question of whether there is a world at all and whether its being can be proved, makes no sense if it is raised by *Dasein* as Being-in-the-world; and who else would raise it?" (Heidegger, 1927, pp. 89, 246–7).

The consistent application of the method of doubt requires not merely placing a question mark next to one's thoughts but also purging them of all existential commitments to the external world. The task of identifying the inner content of thought and purging it of its reference to outer things cannot be just a matter of simple awareness; it involves first the analysis of each thought expression to identify its existential presuppositions, and second the reformulation of those thought expressions that do imply the existence of an outer reality into expressions in which such implications are absent. Surely this cannot be a process in which there is no room for error. The identification of our own thoughts is as susceptible of error as is the identification of external things. Descartes is simply mistaken when he claims that "I can achieve an easier and more evident perception of my own mind than of anything else" (Descartes, 1985, II, pp. 22–3). There is no reason to think that Descartes is entitled to greater certainty of the premise of the *cogito* argument than Moore has of "Here is one hand and here is another."

The Transition from Thinking to the Thing that Thinks

For Descartes, when one knows one's own thoughts, one knows that one is *thinking*, that thinking is an *act of mind*, that one's thoughts have an identifiable *content*, that this act of thinking with this content is produced by a certain *agent*, and, furthermore, that this agent or "I" is *oneself*. Adopting the terminology of the Aristotelian tradition, Descartes classifies this "I" as a substance; this means that it is a subject of attributes, though not itself an attribute, and that it is an agent that acts, though not itself an act. One knows a substance through knowledge of its attributes. "We do not have immediate knowledge of substances. . . , We know them only by perceiving certain forms or attributes which must inhere in something if they are to exist" (Descartes, 1985, II, p. 156). If, in the *cogito*, Descartes perceives certain acts of thought, if he has immediate knowledge of his thinking and its contents, how does he come to know the "I" that is doing all this work? Here is his answer:

> It is certain that a thought cannot exist without a thing that is thinking; and in general no act or accident can exist without a substance for it to belong to. But we do not come to know a substance immediately, through being aware of the substance itself; we come to know it only through its being the subject of certain acts. (Descartes, 1985, II, p. 124)

Since, in the *cogito*, Descartes is not acquainted both with his act of thought and with himself as the agent performing this act, his knowledge of "I think" cannot be based upon a simple inspection of both the "I" and the thinking that grasps their connection. Rather he must rely upon a particular metaphysical principle (*the act–substance principle*): "no act or accident can exist without a substance for it to belong to." Armed with this principle and acquainted with his act of thinking, Descartes is in a position to infer "I think."

So his knowledge of "I think" is not immediate or direct, but involves an inference from thinking to self, with the act–substance principle as a major premise. Perhaps Descartes might reply much as he did to those who claimed that the *cogito* itself needed as a major premise "Whatever thinks exists": that the general principle is known through the particular case. But in the *cogito*, he did not need the general principle to move from "I think" to "I exist" because all he needed to do was to inspect the contents of both and discern that the content of the latter is included in the content of the former. But in the move from thinking to self, although the former is available for inspection, the latter is not; the connection between them cannot be immediately known. Reliance upon the act–substance principle cannot be avoided.

The certainty of the *cogito* depends, therefore, upon the certainty of the act–substance principle. But this principle is no more immune to the onslaughts of the evil demon argument than are the simple truths of arithmetic and geometry. So Descartes is not justified in imputing a special epistemic status to the *cogito* that he denies to these other simple truths. If these truths are undermined by the evil demon, so is the *cogito*.

In Search of the Self

Given the difficulties that Descartes encountered in discovering an Archimedean point to bring skeptical doubts to an end, philosophy did not have to wait long for a philosopher to attempt to develop their full implications and to bring into question our basic framework of thought. At the outset of his *A Treatise of Human Nature*, Hume cast doubt upon the legitimacy of the category of substance:

> If it [the idea of substance] be convey'd to us by our senses, I ask, which of them; and after what manner? If it be perceiv'd by the eyes, it must be a colour; if by the ears, a sound; if by the palate, a taste; and so of the other senses. But I believe none will assert, that substance is either a colour, or a sound, or a taste. The idea of substance must therefore be deriv'd from an impression of reflexion, if it really exist. But the impressions of reflexion resolve themselves into our passions and emotions; none of which can possibly represent a substance. We have therefore no idea of substance, distinct from that of a collection of particular qualities, nor have we any other meaning when we either talk or reason concerning it. (Hume, 1739, p. 16)

Neither the perception of external objects nor the reflective or introspective awareness of the contents of our own minds reveals a substance distinct from the collection of qualities that experience presents. Unlike Descartes, Hume does not introduce his own version of the act–substance principle because we have no idea of substance. Thus, when we predicate a quality of a thing, all that we can mean is that the quality belongs to a collection of related qualities. To suppose that there is, in the words of Locke, "a something I know not what" that exemplifies the qualities but is distinct from them and imperceptible as well is, according to Hume, to have recourse to a meaningless fiction.

It would be of no use to try to legitimize the category of substance by claiming, as Descartes did, that it is an innate idea. Perhaps our propensity to predicate qualities of something or other rather than leave them standing as separate existents is innate, but that is no proof of the existence of "a something I know not what."

Hume's attack on substance was not entirely original. Berkeley led the way by arguing that we have no conception of material substance. The real novelty in Hume's argument was to apply Berkeley's argument to mental substance. Both Berkeley and Hume took as their starting point Descartes' admission that we have no direct acquaintance with substance. For Hume, when we turn our gaze within to inspect the contents of our minds, we come upon a stream of impressions and ideas and nothing else. We have no reason to assent to the act–substance principle that Descartes uses to prove the existence of a substantial self; it has no basis in experience, and it is not self-evident. There is nothing to be said in its favor. We need nothing outside the stream of conscious experiences to glue its elements together; discernible relations among the elements will do the job.

> For my part, when I enter most intimately into what I call *myself*, I always stumble upon some particular perception or other, of heat or cold, light or

shade, love or hatred, pain or pleasure. I never can catch *myself* at any time without a perception, and never can observe any thing but the perception. . . .[Individual persons] are nothing but a bundle or collection of different perceptions, which succeed each other with an inconceivable rapidity, and are in a perpetual flux and movement. . . . The mind is a kind of theatre, where several perceptions successively make their appearance; pass, re-pass, glide away, and mingle in an infinite variety of postures and situations. (Hume, 1739, pp. 252–3)

But what is the glue that ties the elements of each bundle together? After all, I am different from you, and that means that there must be a connection among the elements of my bundle that constitutes them a unified self and a connection among the elements of yours that constitutes them a unified self distinct from me.

In reflecting upon his account of the self in the appendix to the *Treatise*, Hume conceded that nothing that he could think of satisfactorily answers the question. He could find no way of individuating selves that is immune from devastating objections. "But all my hopes vanish when I come to explain the principles, that unite our successive perceptions in our thought or consciousness. I cannot discover any theory, which gives me satisfaction on this head. . . . I must pretend the privilege of the sceptic, and confess, that this difficulty is too hard for my understanding" (Hume, 1739, pp. 635–6). Descartes was able to resist this dissolution of the self because he rather uncritically accepted the traditional framework of substance and attribute. But Hume found this framework to be just a prejudice that has no justification in experience or in metaphysical argument.

But a puzzle remains. Hume says: "I never can catch myself . . ." Doubts about the self emerge because it cannot be caught, but what about the self that fails to catch itself. Don't Hume's own words reinstate the very self that the same words lead us to doubt?

The Self as a Grammatical Habit

In his account of Wittgenstein's lectures, G. E. Moore tells us that Wittgenstein "quoted with apparent approval, Lichtenberg's saying 'Instead of "I think" we ought to say "It thinks"' ('it' being used, as he said, as 'Es' in 'Es blitzer' [it rains])" (Moore, 1993, pp. 100–1). Nietzsche, who was familiar with Lichtenberg's writings, developed this insight in his *Beyond Good and Evil*. Using the pretensions of Descartes' *cogito* as one of his examples, Nietzsche attacks the whole Cartesian project:

There are still harmless self-observers who believe that there are "immediate certainties"; for example, "I think," or as the superstition of Schopenhauer put it, "I will"; as though knowledge here got hold of its object purely and nakedly as "the thing in itself," without any falsification on the part of either the subject or the object. But that "immediate certainty," as well as "absolute knowledge" and the "thing in itself," involve a *contradictio in adjecto*, I shall repeat a hundred times; we really ought to free ourselves from the seduction of words! (Nietzsche, 1968, p. 213)

According to Nietzsche's fallibilism, even those beliefs that seem to us to be most secure are products, not of direct access to the facts themselves, but of understandings founded upon unproven and unprovable frameworks of interpretation. He goes on to attack the *cogito* directly:

When I analyze the process that is expressed in the sentence, "I think," I find a whole series of daring assertions that would be difficult, perhaps impossible to prove; for example, that it is *I* who think, that there must necessarily be something that thinks, that thinking is an activity and operation on the part of a being who is thought of as a cause, and there is an "ego," and finally, that it is already determined what is to be designated by thinking – that I *know* what thinking is. For if I had not already decided within myself what it is, by what standard could I determine whether that which is just happening is not perhaps "willing" or "feeling"? In short, the assertion "I think" assumes that I *compare* my state at the present moment with other states of myself which I know, in order to determine what it is; on account of this retrospective connection with further "knowledge," it has, at any rate, no immediate certainty for me. (Nietzsche, 1968, p. 213)

The whole of the *cogito* consists of a problematic interpretation of mental life, even in characterizing the act as one of thinking. Even if something should be given, how best to characterize it is not itself given, for every characterization is an interpretation that applies past knowledge of fact and of words and meanings to present items. Nietzsche goes beyond the skepticism of the Pyrrhonist tradition by rejecting the category of the evident, and he goes beyond the skepticism of Descartes by rejecting all attempts to overcome skeptical doubts in order to reinstate this category. Like the poet John Keats, Nietzsche is willing to live with *negative capability*, "when man is capable of being in uncertainties, *Mysteries*, doubts, without any irritable reaching after fact and reason" (Keats, 1970, p. 43). Nietzsche's negative capability is a willingness to live without any immediate certainty whatever, something quite foreign to the spirit of Descartes' quest for certainty.

Finally, Nietzsche comments on Lichtenberg's aphorism as follows:

A thought comes when "it" wishes, and not when "I" wish, so that it is a falsification of the facts of the case to say that the subject "I" is the condition of the predicate "think." *It* thinks, but that this "it" is precisely the famous old "ego" is, to put it mildly, only a supposition, an assertion, and assuredly not an "immediate certainty." After all, one has even gone too far with this "it thinks" – even the "it" contains an *interpretation* of the process, and does not belong to the process itself. One infers here according to grammatical habit: "Thinking is an activity; every activity requires an agent, consequently –" (Nietzsche, 1968, p. 214)

Descartes' metaphysical act–substance principle is just a grammatical habit, a reification and objectification of the convention of grammar that language generally requires a subject for a verb. Lichtenberg does not go far enough, for he sees a need to substitute "it" for "I" and does not realize that even this substitution simply reflects a grammatical convention.

Nietszche's view even transcends solipsism, for it denies any metaphysical standing to the self and its thoughts. For Nietszche, the metaphysical temptation is merely the urge to project our grammar upon reality, a temptation motivated by the human need for stability amidst the flux of experience. Western philosophy and the quest for certainty is the intellectual expression of this search for permanence amidst change. We can see in the thought of both Hume and Nietszche how skepticism about substance, mind, and matter rejects this need and urges upon us the acceptance of change and a willing submission to uncertainty.

In his *Tractatus Logico-Philosophicus*, Wittgenstein draws this critique of the *cogito* to its logical conclusion:

There is no such thing as the subject that thinks or entertains ideas. . . . Where *in* the world is a metaphysical subject to be found? . . . Solipsism, when its implications are followed out strictly, coincides with pure realism. The self of solipsism shrinks to a point without extension, and there remains the reality co-ordinated with it. (Wittgenstein, 1921, 5.631)

But Wittgenstein does not intend to jettison the self entirely. For although the subject is not *in* the world, it is a limit of the world:

The subject does not belong to the world: rather, it is a limit of the world. . . . What brings the self into philosophy is the fact that "the world is my world." The philosophical self is not the human being, not the human body, or the human soul, with which psychology deals, but rather the metaphysical subject, the limit of the world – not a part of it. (Wittgenstein, 1921, 5.632, 5.641)

What Wittgenstein means by the limit of the world is quite obscure; nevertheless he finds a reason to preserve the self, if not as a substance, then as a limit.

There is a reason, however, to think that we should not too quickly accept Lichtenberg's "It thinks." For the analogy with "It rains" must be considered in the light of a certain dissimilarity. We can see that the "it" in "It rains" refers to nothing because quantifying over it leads to nonsense: we would reject as semantically anomalous the claim that "There is an x such that x rains," whereas it is not anomalous to say "There is an x such that x thinks." Given what it is to rain, we do not require a subject. Raining is not an act though "rains" is a verb. We are not at the mercy of syntax, and we can be saved by semantics. We can have insight into what we are talking about that overrides superficial grammatical forms. Wittgenstein recognized this when he said that "it was Russell who performed the service of showing that the apparent logical form of a proposition need not be its real one" (Wittgenstein, 1921, 4.0031).

Lichtenberg's aphorism settles nothing. I shall try to answer the skeptic by leaning upon a particular insight of Kant's.

The Unity of Consciousness

In the section of the *Critique of Pure Reason* called "The Paralogisms of Pure Reason," Kant undertakes a critical examination of Descartes' *cogito* for the purpose of unmasking its pretensions to reveal the true nature of the self. Kant agrees with both Hume and Descartes that when we look within our stream of thought, we do not discover a distinct object that we can identify as the self. The term "I" in "I think" does not pick out a discernible entity that we can observe. In fact, we know nothing of the self that is alleged to underlie and possess the experiences we ascribe to it. "It is known only through the thoughts which are its predicates" (Kant, 1781, A346). Neither the perception of external objects nor the reflective observation of our inner life reveals the real nature of the "I." Thus, Descartes' effort to develop a rational psychology that establishes *a priori*, by reflecting upon the implications of "I think," the permanence, identity, and possible immortality of a non-physical mental substance cannot be successful.

On the other hand, Kant would agree neither with Hume in his denial that the stream of thought includes nothing for the "I" to represent nor with Lichtenberg in his claim that the "I" can just as well be replaced by "It." When Hume says "I never can catch *myself* at any time without a perception, and never can observe any thing but the perception," his very formulation indicates the indispensability of the "I" as something attached to any perception even though it is not distinguishable as a separate observable item amidst the flux of experience. Perceptions and thoughts do not exist as independent entities; every thought is accompanied by "I think," in which the term "I" represents "the unity of self-consciousness." The "I" is a "bare consciousness which accompanies all concepts." It is "a mere thought." "The 'I' is merely the consciousness of my thought." It is merely an abstract representation of whatever it is that owns its thoughts and has no other content whatsoever (Kant, 1781, A364, A346, B413, B428–9).

For Kant, the real self is elusive; it escapes any attempt to characterize it in concepts; any attempt to catch itself requires itself to maneuver in the background as something not yet caught. "The subject of the categories cannot by thinking the categories acquire a concept of itself as an object of the categories. For in order to think them, its pure self-consciousness, which is what was to be explained, must itself be presupposed" (Kant, 1781, B422). When I think something, I am conscious of myself as thinking that thought. But the consciousness is present to itself merely as a consciousness of that thought and nothing more. So no philosophically interesting claims are implied by the fact of consciousness. True, Kant thinks that *something* is conscious, that *something* is the owner of the thoughts it thinks, but what that something is, how it is related to the body, how it preserves its identity through time, and how it produces the consciousness that accompanies its thoughts cannot be extracted by reflection upon the content of "I think" as Descartes believed.

The way that Kant formulates these insights is by saying that the term "I" in "I think" does not refer to a discernible object but instead represents "a form of representation in general." It is a form rather than an object because it accompanies each thought as our consciousness of it; that is, our being conscious of our thoughts and our thoughts being owned by a thinker is the way we have thoughts; every thought has "I think" attached to it (Kant, 1781, A346, A348). Thoughts are not free-floating entities, and it makes no sense to depersonalize them as Lichtenberg does with his "It thinks."

The Depths of Our Ignorance

By self-knowledge, I mean knowledge of propositions prefixed by "I think," where "think" is short for any mode of thought, such as judgment, belief, assent, denial, and so forth. My knowledge that I *believe* that two and three are five is an example of self-knowledge. How is it possible that in my thinking that two and three are five I not only come to know that two and three are five but also come to know that I am thinking that two and three are five?

You ask me whether I believe that two and three are five, and since I already have a fixed belief, I reply right off that I do. If you should ask me how I know that I believe that two and three are five, I will reply that I have no idea. I know that I believe it; that is a fact about me. I once learned this mathematical fact, but I do not remember when or how. If you ask me how I know that two and three are five, that is a request for a justification of my belief; but when you ask how I know I have the belief, you are not asking for a justification of what is believed but a justification of my claim that I *believe* that. We are frequently able to report right off our propositional attitudes: thoughts, desires, intentions, and so forth. Perhaps some of these are unconscious as Freud thought, but there is no trouble about access to many others. How do we do it? Our ability to do it does not usually depend upon evidence; when you ask whether I believe that two and three are five, I do not search for evidence that I do, and if I did search for it, I would not know where to look. Nor does it appear that my knowledge of my having this belief is grounded in the way that perceptual beliefs are. How do I know this is an apple? Well, "I see it" or "It looks like one" or "It tastes like one" are possible answers and good ones, but there is nothing comparable in the case of propositional attitudes. So the first point I wish to make here is that we do not know anything about the underlying mechanisms which make self-knowledge possible. I am frequently able to tell anyone who asks about my beliefs what they are without going to any trouble at all, but I have no idea how I manage it. One's knowledge of one's own thoughts or propositional attitudes generally is ungrounded. Kant claimed that the underlying mechanisms are unknowable; I rest content with the more modest claim that they are unknown.

But our ignorance about how self-knowledge comes about runs even deeper than this. I claim to know that I believe that two and three are five. Included in this claim is a claim about myself, that *I* believe this, a claim about the content of the belief, that what is believed is *that two and three are five*, and a claim about the way in which I am related to this content, namely in the way of *belief*. But what is the nature of this "I" that I claim to know about? How does this content manage to become represented by this "I"? And what does belief amount to, and how do I identify this state of mind as belief rather than as denial or intention or desire? Philosophical theories have been proposed to answer all of these questions, but turn to the philosopher sitting next to you and you will probably find that his theory is nothing like yours.

The only assurance we have about the nature of self-knowledge is that we frequently are able to make claims about our states of mind with little difficulty while feeling sure that they are things we know. But how we know these things if we do, and how this knowledge is possible, and what is the nature of the items of which we claim to have knowledge, all these questions we approach as through a glass darkly. Perhaps Hume went too far in claiming that there was nothing here to know about; perhaps Kant went too far in stating that these questions are in principle beyond our powers to answer. But our understanding of the most elementary facts about self-knowledge is shrouded in ignorance and uncertainty.

How Self-knowledge Is Possible

But then do we have any self-knowledge? Can anything be said in favor of my knowing that I believe that two and three are five?

It can be said that none of the skeptical reflections reviewed here imply that we do *not* have such knowledge. Suppose that all of those judgments about my beliefs that are sincere and made without any difficult soul searching are true. Then these judgments are reliable, perhaps super-reliable. I know nothing about the underlying mechanism that makes this possible, except that it is a reliable source of belief. Let us suppose that this mechanism is connected to our belief forming faculty in a way that provides it access to the existence and content of our beliefs, so that its reliability is not accidental. The reliability of our beliefs is evidence that this supposition is true even if we have no idea whatsoever about the nature of this mechanism, about the belief forming faculty, and about the mechanism's access to the faculty. We can know something about the function even though we do not know anything about how it is implemented.

Because this class of judgments about what I believe is produced by a super-reliable non-accidental process, each member of this class is known to be true. That is how self-knowledge is possible. Self-knowledge can comfortably coexist alongside the shroud of ignorance and uncertainty. Hume, Nietszche, and Kant have convinced me how little we know about the process. We have no reason at all to respect Descartes' optimism about our capacity for understanding our mental life; neither can his view that the mind is transparent to itself, that it is better known than the body, and that introspection reveals all that there is to know about mental activity any longer be sustained. But these successful skeptical attacks against Descartes' claim to self-understanding and to the supposed wealth of insights contained in the *cogito* fail to undermine more modest claims to possess knowledge of oneself.

But how can one have knowledge that one cannot justify? If one cannot explain how one knows something, it may be said, if one cannot offer a justification, if one cannot defend one's claims when challenged, then one is lacking the credentials of knowledge. Reliably obtained true belief is quite insufficient, it is said, because without something more, one cannot sustain or prove or establish that these beliefs are indeed true.

This objection comes from an internalist epistemology that insists that being able to offer an account, a reason, a justification, that having access to and knowledge of the grounds of one's belief, is necessary for knowledge. But in this very sentence, the circularity of internalism becomes apparent. If having an account entails knowing something, then the internalist's definition of what it is to know something includes the very concept being defined.

Our claims to know various things can often be supported by other claims to know various things. To this extent, internalism captures an important component of our epistemic condition. But to claim that this component is the invariable and inescapable component of all knowledge undermines every one of our knowledge claims. A consistent internalism leads either to an infinite regress – this claim must be justified by some other claim which must be justified still further, *ad infinitum* – or to a circular argument. So if any of our beliefs count as knowledge, then some of them may be grounded upon facts that are not themselves beliefs (as in "This is an apple" is grounded in its tasting like an apple), and some of them may be grounded upon nothing at all. Ungrounded true beliefs produced by a reliable process count as knowledge if anything does. Internalism cannot be the whole story if knowledge is possible.

The Modest Triumph of Skepticism

During this debate between internalism and externalism, the skeptic has been sitting on the sidelines, smiling with contentment. When the defeated internalist departs, he approaches the victorious externalist and points out that though he has won the battle, he has not won the war. After all, the debate has been conducted under the common assumption that there is knowledge. Externalism wins because if there is knowledge at all, some of it must consist of reliably produced true beliefs. The skeptic smugly asserts that he would like to be given some reason for accepting that assumption. He requests that the externalist provide him with a proof or at least a persuasive argument that any beliefs about oneself count as knowledge. Even if there is a mechanism that produces them in a systematic and coherent form, it does not follow that one knows them to be true or even that they are true. The skeptic may even accept the externalist's conception of the sufficient conditions of knowledge, but wonder whether he has been given any non-circular reason for thinking that these conditions have been satisfied.

Global skepticism has two sides. On the one hand, it claims to have established by argument that we lack the knowledge we think we have, and, on the other, it challenges the non-skeptic to show that he has the knowledge he claims to have. But it fails in its first claim because all the difficulties it points out are compatible with our having knowledge; it fails to show that knowledge is not possible; and since global skepticism presents itself as being a rationally defensible position established by arguments that it knows to be sound, it is incoherent because its denial of knowledge is based upon knowledge.

However, it is successful in its second claim because the non-skeptic cannot establish by non-question begging arguments that he is in possession of all the knowledge he claims to have. But even this victory is limited, because the failure of the non-skeptic is not due to any inherent flaw in his claims to know or some fundamental error in his belief system, but to a basic feature of our epistemic condition, namely that knowledge emerges from circumstances and processes that are not themselves cases of knowledge and that these can only be shown to be productive of knowledge by appealing to what we already know about them.

A Note on Empiricism

Empiricism is the claim that all our knowledge and/or justified belief is based or grounded upon experience. Sense experience reveals facts about the external world. But what of the internal world of the self and its thoughts? Here empiricists often cite inner experience as the foundation for self-knowledge. For example, Locke speaks of "the *Perception of the Operations of our own Minds* within us." He entitles this capacity "reflection" and says of it that "though it be not Sense, as having nothing to do with external Objects; yet it is very like it, and might properly enough be call'd internal Sense" (Locke, 1690, book II, pp. i, 4). Locke's calling reflection internal sense suggests that just as our knowledge of outer objects is grounded upon sense experience, our knowledge of inner objects must be grounded upon an experience of the operations of our own minds.

Yet the argument of this chapter showed that much of our self-knowledge is ungrounded, that there is no inner experience of our mental operations on which to ground it. There is no perception of mental operations that corresponds to the perception of bodies. So classical empiricism is mistaken in its conception of self-knowledge. Moreover, Locke appealed to reflection not only as the basis of the knowledge of our own mental operations but also as the source of our ideas or conceptions of our mental operations; I know, for example, what thinking is because I have experienced it via reflection. So if there is no inner experience, his theory of ideas is radically mistaken.

Because there is no inner experience of propositional attitudes corresponding to sensory perception of external things, some of the questions that arise about our knowledge of the external world do not arise for knowledge of states of mind. For example, there is no issue about how to establish the validity of a shaky inference from experience to object. There is no evidence corresponding to the evidence of the senses that supports our beliefs about mental operations. It looks as if a reliabilist and externalist account of self-knowledge is the only alternative remaining once the empiricist picture has been shown to be incomplete.

15

The Problem of Knowledge

The man who is presumptuous of his knowledge does not yet know
what knowledge is. (Montaigne)

The Foundations of Knowledge

The dominant conception of human knowledge in the Western philosophical tradition (*classical foundationalism*) identifies basic justified beliefs as those whose justification arises from a source other than inference from beliefs already established. Some of these may be self-evident (truths of logic and mathematics), others are grounded in the senses, and others may possess their own form of intrinsic credibility, such as memory beliefs and beliefs about one's own mental acts. Justified beliefs that are not basic are inferred from basic beliefs by valid rules of inference that transmit justification from the premises to the conclusion.

The version of classical foundationalism that has received the most attention (*knowledge-based foundationalism*) is satisfied with nothing less than knowledge. The only justified beliefs that matter are those that are known to be true. There is an excellent reason for this. To say that a belief is justified is compatible with its being false. So it is logically possible for every one of the beliefs in a person's belief system to be justified yet false. Mere justification fails to satisfy the pursuit of truth that is intrinsic to the very practice of forming beliefs about the world; after all, believing a proposition is equivalent to believing that it is *true*. Since knowledge entails truth, possessing knowledge is superior to possessing a justification that falls short of certainty with regard to the pursuit of truth. We want to end up with a system of beliefs that satisfy the requirements of knowledge-based foundationalism; that is the ideal implicit in our cognitive practices.

Most of the philosophical systems that endorsed knowledge-based foundationalism also accepted realism, the idea that what we aim at knowing is a world that exists independently of our beliefs and mental activities.

Thinking does not make it so. Our inquiries will end only when we have grasped the full nature of things as they are in themselves, not merely how they appear to us. This is realism in Kant's transcendental sense, the very realism that Kant rejected because he could see no way to refute the arguments of the skeptics. Beliefs that are merely justified but fall short of knowledge are provisional and uncertain and may fall by the wayside as inquiry proceeds.[1] The task of inquiry is to make sure that the world as it is represented by the mind corresponds to the world as it really is.

Implicit in the program of classical and knowledge-based foundationalism is a distinction between our manner of acquiring beliefs (*the context of discovery*) and their mode of justification (*the context of justification*). Descartes realized that the ways in which he acquired his opinions failed to convince him that they counted as knowledge. Our ordinary procedures are too unsystematic and wayward to satisfy the highest standards of inquiry or to guarantee the truth about important matters. Therefore, it is necessary at periodic intervals to conduct a review of our beliefs to determine which should be retained and which discarded and to organize them so that their logical relations and sources of credibility may be marked – this is the context of justification. To borrow a phrase from Carnap, what Descartes was after was a *rational reconstruction* of his belief system. But he wanted even more than this. He wanted to replace our ordinary unsystematic practices with a method that would guarantee that inquiry would invariably produce truth if conducted carefully and systematically. He wanted the context of discovery to be so transformed that it would coincide with the context of justification. This was the ideal he put forward. Whether it could ever be realized in practice was another question. But as an ideal, it could be used to evaluate our cognitive practices and to redirect them when they stray from the correct method.

Skepticism and the Search for Foundations

Skeptical arguments have been employed to undermine knowledge-based foundationalism. Although Hume did not question the possibility of knowledge based upon immediate sensation, nevertheless he argued that we have no reason to think that truth is transmitted by such premises to conclusions

---

1　Beliefs that are certain may also be rejected because we are misled in some way or other. In that case the rejection is in error.

arrived at by inductive inference. Moreover, certainty of the principles of mathematics is purchased, according to Hume, at the cost of their failing to provide knowledge of anything that exists. They are, in the language of Kant, mere analytic truths whose negation implies a contradiction. Hume also attempted to undermine the legitimacy of the basic categories we use to interpret our experience, such as substance and attribute, cause and effect, and self-identity.

In order to gain knowledge of things as they are in themselves, it is necessary to be able to advance from the ways things appear to objective knowledge of their mind-independent attributes. Reflections in early modern philosophy on the status of secondary qualities led to the idea of "the great deception of sense," according to which the ways things appear fail in important ways to represent the ways they really are. Moreover, the arguments used to establish "the great deception" showed that theoretical considerations can be used to undermine perceptual judgments. There is no straight line, as classical foundationalism claims, from perception to theory. The distinction between basic and derived beliefs becomes murky. If our beliefs about the appearances are basic, we need to advance via inferences to the true character of the things that appear. Descartes and Berkeley demonstrated how difficult it is to show that inferences from appearance to reality are truth preserving.

Doubts arise even as to whether we have knowledge of appearances. Even in the case of appearances, thinking does not make it so. That something looks in a certain way is one thing, that I describe it using such and such concepts is a separate and distinct thing. There is no guarantee that the act of applying concepts to sense experience is immune from error. Moreover, the very idea of sense experience is problematic. When I say of something that it looks red, I do not imply that it or anything else really is red. There is no reason to posit the existence of sense-data as carriers of sensible qualities. So the concept red does not apply to my experience of something's looking red. There is nothing red in the experience itself. But then what exactly are we doing when we use this concept in our description? What is the nature of the fact being reported? The difficulties of answering such questions have led philosophers to speak of *the myth of the given*. The traditional claim that we have privileged access to the sensory contents of our own minds has been undermined because the very idea of mental sensory contents is deeply problematic or, at the very least, not well understood.

Living with Skepticism: The New Academy

The quest for certainty assumed the form of a foundationalist approach in epistemology. Classical foundationalism was the way in which philosophers explained how our cognitive faculties operated to provide us with "windows on the world" that enable us to apprehend things as they are in themselves. Although the quest for certainty has taken quite a beating in twentieth-century philosophy, the philosophers of ancient Greece and Rome were quite well aware of the difficulties standing in the way of attempting to grasp the nature of things in themselves. The skeptical among them thought that there are no windows on the world, and that our theories and beliefs are merely dogmatic conjectures that do not deserve the title of knowledge. Here is Cicero's account of the views of Arcesilas, one of the founders of the New Academy:

> It was entirely with Zeno, so we have been told . . . that Arcesilas set on foot his battle, not from obstinacy or a desire for victory, as it seems to me at all events, but because of the obscurity of the facts that had led Socrates to a confession of ignorance, as also previously his predecessors Democritus, Anaxagoras, Empedocles, and almost all the old philosophers, who utterly denied all possibility of cognition or perception or knowledge, and maintained that the senses are limited, the mind feeble, the span of life short, and the truth (in Democritus's phrase) is sunk in an abyss, opinion and custom are all-prevailing, no place is left for truth, and all things successively are wrapped in darkness. Accordingly, Arcesilas said that there is nothing that can be known, not even that residuum of knowledge that Socrates had left himself – the truth of this very dictum ["We do not even know that nothing can be known"]: so hidden in obscurity did he believe that everything lies, nor is there anything that can be perceived or understood. (Cicero, 1961, I, p. xii)

It is interesting to note that Cicero presents the skepticism of Arcesilas not as just one among many ancient schools of thought but as the culmination of the epistemological reflections of many of "the old philosophers." Cicero even suggests that the New Academy is continuous with the Old Academy founded by Plato because Plato himself is really a skeptic "in whose books nothing is stated positively and there is much arguing both *pro* and *contra*, all things are inquired into and no certain statement is made" (Cicero, 1961, I, p. xii).

How shall we live if all things are wrapped in darkness? The answer of Arcesilas is suspension of judgment, a response similar to the one we earlier noted in Sextus Empiricus:

For these reasons, he [Arcesilas] said, no one must make any positive statement or affirmation or give the approval of his assent to any proposition, and a man must always restrain his rashness and hold it back from every slip, as it would be glaring rashness to give assent to a falsehood or to something not certainly known, and nothing is more disgraceful than for assent and approval to outstrip knowledge and perception. His practice was consistent with this theory – he led most of his hearers to accept it by arguing against the opinions of all men, so that when equally weighty reasons were found on opposite sides on the same subject, it was easier to withhold assent from either side. (Cicero, 1961, I, p. xii)

But if we are forbidden from assenting to any proposition, how, then, shall we live? According to Cicero, since we lack a criterion of knowledge, Carneades suggested that we should live by probability. "But if for instance he [a wise man] were setting out from here to Puteoli, a distance of four miles, with a reliable crew and a good helmsman and in the present calm weather, it would appear probable that he would get there safe" (Cicero, 1961, II, p. xxxi).

Implicit in this defense of probability as the guide to life is a distinction between giving assent to a proposition and ascribing probability to it. Assent is acceptance with full conviction that what is said is true, whereas probability withholds full conviction but follows wherever the evidence happens to lead. Thus the reason why the wise man thinks that it is probable that he will arrive safely in Puteoli is that the crew is reliable, the ship has a good helmsman, and the weather is calm.

It is not, however, coherent to combine skepticism with a reliance upon probability. For, according to Cicero, the skeptic holds that "no sense-presentation has such a character as a false presentation could not also have without differing from it at all" (Cicero, 1961, II, p. xxxi). Since the true is not intrinsically different from the false, there is no mark or criterion of truth intrinsic to the presentation itself. So we must rely on external factors embodied in the statements of evidence. But these external factors, such as the fact that the weather is calm, are themselves made accessible through presentations which may very well be false. Since the ascription of probability to an opinion is relative to the truth of the evidence on which it is based and since we have no more reason to have confidence in the evidence than on the proposition for which it is evidence, there are no valid grounds for saying of any belief that it is more probable than its contrary. So skeptical arguments undermine not only full conviction but also reliance upon probability. It seems as if the New Academy cannot help us live under the condition that all things are wrapped in darkness. Cicero portrays an opponent of

Academic skepticism as saying that "by doing away with all assent they have done away with all movement of the mind and also with all physical activity; which is not only a mistake but an absolute impossibility" (Cicero, 1961, II, p. xix). Is there any way of being a skeptic other than by withdrawing from all activity?

Living with Skepticism: Hume

The most eloquent formulation of the problem of how to live as a skeptic is contained in the last chapter of book 1 of Hume's *Treatise*. For Hume, since belief is involuntary, suspension of judgment is not a live option. If perception produces the conviction that, for example, the object before me is an apple, there is nothing I can do to rid myself of that belief; of course I may lose it in the future if new experience convinces me that I was then undergoing a hallucination. Belief is sensitive to evidence, and emotion may cause us to assign weight to evidence that it does not deserve. But belief is not directly under the control of the will.

Of course, the ancient philosophers who advocated suspension of judgment did not necessarily assert that one can produce or suspend judgment at will. Sextus Empiricus, for example, claimed that it is appropriate to suspend judgment between a proposition and its negation when the course of argument shows that the reasons for and against the one are equal to those for and against the other. Thus he implicitly conceded that belief is controlled by evidence. In ancient skepticism, belief sneaks back into the mind in the form of probability or in the recommendation that we submit to our natural inclinations. So life goes on in spite of philosophical argument.

Hume, on the other hand, was not inclined to avoid the difficulty by reintroducing belief in another guise. Having reflected upon the force of his skeptical reflections in the preceding chapters of book 1, he describes himself as being in the condition of a man who has "narrowly escaped ship-wreck" and is now sailing in the ocean of philosophy in a "leaky weather-beaten vessel" (Hume, 1739, p. 263). His skeptical arguments have convinced him that his faculties are too feeble for the further philosophical explorations that he has planned. "The wretched condition, weakness, and disorder of the faculties I must employ in my enquiries, encrease my apprehensions." The fact that these faculties cannot be repaired drives him to despair and he falls into the deepest melancholy (Hume, 1739, p. 264).

Hume is driven to what Santayana called the "solipsism of the present moment," in which the only existents he is able to accept are those perceptions "which are immediately present to consciousness." He speaks of the "forlorn solitude, in which I am plac'd in my philosophy," and predicts, correctly as it turned out, "the enmity of all metaphysicians, logicians, mathematicians, and even theologians" because he has declared his "dis-approbation of their systems" (Hume, 1739, p. 264).

Hume realizes that his radical skepticism can be turned against his own reasonings. He had claimed that custom or habit, not reason, is the guide of human life in inductive inference, and he recognizes that habit is what leads him to accept his own skeptical conclusions. It is the imagination that confers assent, not reason. Even if he should have hit upon the truth, he has no criterion to assure him of his success (Hume, 1739, p. 265).

He refers to the "manifold contradictions and imperfections in human reason" that he has uncovered in his philosophical ruminations, and he now "can look upon no opinion even as more probable or likely than another."

> Where am I, or what? From what causes do I derive my existence, and to what condition shall I return? Whose favour shall I court, and whose anger must I dread? What beings surround me? and on whom have I any influence, or who have any influence on me? I am confounded with all these questions, and begin to fancy myself in the most deplorable condition imaginable, inviron'd with the deepest darkness, and utterly depriv'd of the use of every member and faculty. (Hume, 1739, pp. 268–9)

It is interesting how the metaphor of darkness used by both Arcesilas and Hume to describe our epistemic condition is able to span two millennia of philosophical reflection.

This "total skepticism" is barely noticed in common life, which knows little or nothing of philosophy and in which the difficulty produced by skeptical arguments is "seldom or never thought of." Common life is built on illusions, and the philosopher naturally worries about to what extent "we ought to yield to these illusions" (Hume, 1739, pp. 267, 268). But the despair, melancholy, and worry that philosophy causes can be removed, at least temporarily:

> Most fortunately it happens, that since reason is incapable of dispelling these clouds, nature herself suffices to that purpose, and cures me of this philosophical melancholy and delirium, either by relaxing this bent of mind, or by some avocation, and lively impression of my senses, which obliterate all these chimeras. I dine, I play a game of back-gammon, I converse, and am merry with my friends; and when after three or four hours' amusement, I wou'd return to these speculations, they appear so cold, and

strain'd, and ridiculous, that I cannot find in my heart to enter into them any farther. (Hume, 1739, p. 269)

Here then is how one lives with skepticism. "I find myself absolutely and necessarily determin'd to live, and talk, and act like other people in the common affairs of life." For "the current of nature" produces a "blind submission" to "the general maxims of the world." Because this submission is "blind," i.e. not based upon reason, "I shew most perfectly my sceptical disposition and principles" (Hume, 1739, p. 269). The philosopher can combine skepticism with living as others do because, although he cannot resist the current of nature, he does not confuse this instinctive compulsion with the deliverance of his rational faculty. He lives amidst the darkness, recognizing it as darkness. "In all the incidents of life, we ought still to preserve our scepticism. If we believe, that fire warms, or water refreshes, 'tis only because it costs us too much pains to think otherwise. Nay if we are philosophers, it ought only to be upon sceptical principles" (Hume, 1739, p. 269). Hume does not, however, intend to give up philosophy even though the current of nature causes him to live as others do. He remains curious to understand the principles that regulate the judgments and actions of mankind. He feels ambitious to instruct mankind and gain fame for his philosophical discoveries. Moreover, philosophy is the basic weapon to combat the dangers of religious superstition. "The errors in religion are dangerous; those in philosophy only ridiculous" (Hume, 1739, pp. 271, 272). Hume intends to continue his study of human nature, his "science of man," side by side with his skeptical principles to remind him to avoid the "dogmatical spirit" that one finds in other systems of philosophy.

On the one hand, Hume is a skeptic and continues to be one; he accepts the arguments and reasoning that produce doubts about any claim (except claims about current sense impressions). On the other hand, one cannot leave the study and enter common life with these doubts remaining active in the mind. They do not disappear but lie dormant and function not as real active doubt (for that clashes with the requirements of common life) but as an epistemic verdict upon the beliefs that the current of nature forces upon us. One can also remove oneself from common life, re-enter the study, and resume philosophical reflection. When that happens skepticism functions as a principle of restraint, as a warning against dogmatism, and a way of becoming immunized against both religious superstition and chimerical systems of philosophy.

Living with Skepticism: Quine

Those of you who are acquainted with Quine's philosophy may be surprised to find him labeled a skeptic. After all, in his many books and articles, he has developed a wide-ranging, many sided, coherent philosophical system, and it would appear that his works belong among the great systems in the history of philosophy rather than among the anti-philosophical skeptics aiming to undermine the systems of the past as chimeras and illusions.

On the other hand, Quine has commented: "I do not see that we are farther along today than where Hume left us. The Humean predicament is the human predicament" (Quine, 1969, p. 72). Quine's philosophical system is post-Humean. A post-Humean philosophy is one that fundamentally agrees with Hume's skeptical arguments and attempts to construct an epistemology that is impervious to skeptical criticisms. It attempts not to refute Hume but to explore the alternatives that remain once skepticism has been assimilated.

I see Kant's Copernican revolution in philosophy in this light. His transcendental idealism accepts skepticism in claiming that things as they are in themselves are unknowable as they are in themselves. Kant repudiated traditional metaphysics and relabeled epistemology as transcendental psychology, whose aim is to understand how the mind works over and organizes the sensory input.

If I may put forward what seems to be a paradox, Hume was also a post-Humean philosopher. His skepticism was a conclusion from his efforts to establish a science of man, a science concerned to understand the principles or basic modes of action followed by the mind in responding to the impressions of sense. As we saw, Hume did not see his skeptical conclusions as requiring him to give up philosophy or cease inquiring into human nature. He continued his inquiries in book 2 of the *Treatise* on the passions and book 3 on morality and politics. Skepticism for him as for other post-Humean philosophers was a framework within which philosophical activity could be pursued. As a framework, skepticism means that philosophical inquiry cannot attain certainty, that it is fallible, that it should reject efforts to comprehend the world *a priori*, and that it should focus upon the activities of the human subject. This is what Hume called mitigated skepticism; inquiry is constrained by the limitations of the human faculties. We have a mind that works in a certain way upon a certain form of sensory input. We are competent to investigate the workings of the human mind because we have access to that; the rest is conjecture.

There is one major relevant difference in the historical situation of the ancient world where skepticism originated and the modern world just before and after Hume: the rise of science. When the ancient skeptics studied the theoretical activity of their own times, they found that by and large it consisted of a bunch of dogmatic systems disagreeing with each other in major ways, and they had no hope of discovering rational means of resolving disputes over fundamentals. Endless controversy was what they expected, and no system could be shown to be better than any other system. But modern science in its many specialties is a form of thought in which the community of inquirers is capable of coming to agreement on fundamental matters and in which there is hope that such agreements, provisional though they may be, represent genuine approximations to the correct understanding of things as they are in themselves.

Just this morning (May 9, 2000), the newspaper reported the discovery of astronomers that the Andromeda galaxy, fourteen billion billion miles away, and the Milky Way are speeding towards one another at more than 250,000 miles per hour. The article tells us of the work of several scientists using computer simulations to predict what might happen should these galaxies collide. Although there is no certainty in their predictions, what prompts us to take such inquiries seriously and not dismiss them as dogmatic conjectures is that the methods by which scientists gather the data on which their predictions are founded appear to put them in contact with the very objects they are studying; moreover, before the results of scientific inquiries are deemed provisionally acceptable, they must be scrutinized by the relevant community of scientists and replicated if possible. The procedures of science and the ways that scientists are educated are designed to eliminate wishful thinking, prejudice, and ungrounded conjectures and to encourage the use of the most advanced methods and technologies. In comparison, philosophical conjectures about the existence and nature of God, the immortality of the soul, and the freedom of the will (the three main topics that Kant thought provided the problematic of traditional metaphysics) appear to be just guesses, no guess being better than another. Moreover, the fact that science confirms theories that explain the behavior of enormous objects at vast distances and minute objects undetectable with the naked eye appears to support realism. When scientists speak of galaxies billions of miles away, they are referring not merely to how they appear to us but to how they are in themselves, although it is via the appearances and the instruments that produce a variety of new appearances that their data are gathered.

For this reason, Quine thinks that the a task of philosophy is to understand the workings of science. When Quine says that "the Humean predicament is the human predicament," what he means is not only that Descartes' quest for certainty is "a lost cause" but that it is futile to think "of grounding natural science upon immediate experience in a firmly logical way" (Quine, 1969, p. 74). Even so, one cannot abandon sense experience because "whatever evidence there is for science is sensory evidence. . . . The stimulation of his sensory receptors is all the evidence anybody has had to go on, ultimately, in arriving at his picture of the world" (Quine, 1969, p. 75).

Quine confronts us with a Humean understanding of scientific inquiry: science is ultimately based upon experience, although the way it is based on experience is not "firmly logical." Moreover, the theories we form on the basis of sensory evidence outrun the data of the senses; they are undetermined by our sense impressions. The senses provide us with a "meager input" on the basis of which science delivers as a "torrential output" a representation "of the three-dimensional external world and its history" (Quine, 1969, p. 83). We have here the insinuation of a skeptical thought, for if the input is so meager and the output so torrential, what chance do we have of establishing that our representations approximate to things as they are in themselves?

However, Quine does not stay to answer this question, perhaps because he believes there is no good answer to it, given the Humean condition under which we live. Since the foundationalist project is unfeasible, since science cannot be firmly grounded in sense experience, we should surrender our efforts at rational reconstruction. For rational reconstruction was part of the foundationalist project; since the project is hopeless, the effort to reorder and reorganize our system of beliefs to identify those that are basic and those that are justified logically by being derived from them is futile. We should stop "dreaming of deducing science from observations" (Quine, 1969, p. 77).

What, then, becomes of epistemology, the philosophical attempt to understand human inquiry? Instead of attempting to reorder the system of beliefs constructed on the basis of the meager input, Quine asks: "Why not just see how this construction really proceeds? Why not settle for psychology? . . . Better to discover how science is in fact developed and learned than to fabricate a fictitious structure to a similar effect" (Quine, 1969, pp. 75, 78). Epistemology is naturalized; that is, it is replaced by the science of psychology. "Epistemology still goes on, though in a new setting and a clarified status. Epistemology, or something like it, simply falls into place as a chapter of psychology and hence of natural science. It studies a natural phenomenon, viz., a physical human subject" (Quine, 1969, p. 82). In its traditional form, epistemology contained an important normative component: it told us how we *ought* to proceed in order to gain knowledge. In naturalized epistemology, the normative component is shifted into the background as the understanding that science is a successful practice that deserves to be comprehended. Other types of philosophical inquiry, such as traditional *a priori* metaphysics, either drop by the wayside or, where they contain an empirical component, become assimilated to science.

In Quine's earliest and most influential formulations of naturalized epistemology, the question of knowledge almost entirely disappears and is replaced by an effort to understand the conditions under which theories are accepted, modified, and replaced. Epistemology becomes an account of theory change. There is a shift toward pragmatism according to which "the conceptual scheme of science [is] a tool, ultimately, for predicting future experience in the light of past experience" (Quine, 1961, p. 44). Theories are wanted for the sake of prediction, and they are changed or replaced in order to acquire better means to that end.

Although, historically, science emerged from myth, Quine employs the metaphor of myth to characterize any theory that introduces unobservable entities.

> Physical objects are conceptually imported into the situation as convenient intermediaries – not by definition in terms of experience, but simply as irreducible posits comparable, epistemologically, to the gods of Homer. . . . The myth of physical objects is epistemologically superior to most in that it has proved more efficacious than other myths as a device for working a manageable structure into the flux of experience. (Quine, 1961, p. 44)

What make one myth better than another are the "differences in degree to which they expedite our dealings with sense experiences" (Quine, 1961, p. 45)

Two conditions motivate and control theory change. One is simplicity: "we adopt, at least in so far as we are reasonable, the simplest conceptual scheme into which the disordered fragments of raw experience can be fitted and arranged." The main objective of the "elaborate myths or fictions" of science is "the simplicity of laws." The second is the conservative principle, "our natural tendency to disturb the total system as little as possible." Whereas the simplicity of laws provides manageable premises on which to base our predictions, the conservative principle discourages changes which further no end (Quine, 1961, pp. 16, 45, 44).

Because theories cannot be logically deduced from experience, the sensory input controls theory change in a loose way, leaving us with "much latitude of choice as to what statements to reevaluate in the light of any single contrary experience" (Quine, 1961, pp. 42–3).

Any statement can be held true come what may, if we make drastic enough adjustments elsewhere in the system. Even a statement very close to the periphery [of experience] can be held true in the face of recalcitrant experience by pleading hallucination or by amending certain statements of the kind called logical laws. Conversely, by the same token, no statement is immune from revision. (Quine, 1961, p. 43)

Although the fit between experience and theory is loose, the requirements of the simplicity and conservative principles limit and control the changes that are actually introduced.

Note the difference in atmosphere between Quine's naturalized epistemology and Moore's defense of common sense. Whereas Moore is interested in defending the claim that we *know* certain things to be true, Quine seldom speaks of knowledge. Whereas Moore speaks of our knowing various things with certainty, Quine is a fallibilist about every statement, insisting that "no statement is immune from revision." Whereas Moore claims that he knows of the existence of, say, his hands, Quine would speak of his hands as myths or posits introduced to facilitate prediction of the future. Quine, but not Moore, is a post-Humean philosopher.

Quine's pragmatism is consistent with realism. The verbal formulations of the theories that we accept frequently commit us to the existence of unobservable entities ("On What There Is," in Quine, 1961). Although unobservables are posited in order to improve our ability to predict the future, the acceptance of a theory that refers to them commits us to their inclusion within our ontology. But the realism is tinctured by skepticism. Unobservables are not known to exist; they are merely convenient posits or myths. Realism is inescapable because the characteristics attributed to these posits by our theories are incompatible with their being mere products of our own minds. Although our theories are constructed by us in order to predict and control the future, the entities to which our theories commit us are not constructed by us. If our theories are true, those entities really exist. Quine's skepticism is not a denial of realism; it is merely a recognition of the fact that, in our Humean condition, there is no non-circular way of proving the reliability of the methods of science.

Knowledge and Belief

The examples of Hume and Quine show that it is possible to combine a skeptical outlook with constructive philosophical activity. Acceptance of skeptical arguments does not require that we become speechless and motionless. But the validity of skeptical doubts about the possibility of knowledge depends upon the nature of human knowledge. What do we mean, anyhow, when we claim to know something? I shall now say a few words about our concept of knowledge, approaching this topic by comparing knowledge with belief.

Knowledge and belief are alike in having the same objects. Consider a proposition P that I claim to know. Someone else may claim to believe rather than to know the very same proposition. Both belief and knowledge take propositions as objects. Moreover, implicit in each is a reference to truth. When someone says "I believe that P" or "I know that P" he implies that he believes or knows that P is true.

But their relation to truth is different. The fact that I believe that P is compatible with P's being false. There is no logical incoherence in the idea of false belief. But if I know that P is true, then P is true. If it turns out that it isn't, my claim to know it is mistaken: I merely believed it after all. "False knowledge" represents a self-contradictory concept. Having knowledge is a kind of achievement, the successful apprehension of truth.

Knowledge and belief are also different in their communicative role. In saying to someone that I know that P, I am giving him my word that P is true, and I am expressing confidence that it is true. But saying that I believe that P is a weaker claim; it does not communicate as high a level of conviction of its truth.

Knowledge, then, entails truth. Does it also entail belief? If I know that P, does it follow that I believe that P? Belief comes in degrees. People may differ in the degree of confidence or strength of conviction with which they believe something. Since my saying to someone that I know that P communicates a high degree of confidence in the truth of P, it would seem that knowledge entails strong belief in P and hence belief in P. However, this is not conclusive. Strength of conviction is communicated by *saying* that one knows. But it does not follow that it is implied just by knowing without saying so. I may have knowledge without realizing it and so may not feel much confidence when questioned. For example, suppose someone asks whether there are more than three million people in Guatemala. I may reply that I do not know, that I have no idea. Later I remember that I once did research on Guatemalan demographics and that I found that there were indeed more than three million people. I knew it all along, although I did not remember I did. A person may be unsure and confused about what he really knows. Just as he may be mistaken when he claims to know something, so he may be mistaken when he claims not to know something. So lack of inner conviction is compatible with having knowledge, although when one becomes aware that one knew it all along, one's conviction tends to become stronger. But even if knowledge does not entail a high degree of conviction, it may entail belief to some degree or other anyhow. This is suggested by the fact that one may ask, as did Descartes: which of the things that I believe to be true do I really know to be true? This question presupposes that the things that I know form a subset of the things that I believe.

In characterizing the structure of belief, one must distinguish between the proposition believed and the fact that it is believed. The proposition may be believed by many, as Frege pointed out. It is not a state of mind of an individual person. But those who believe it are in a certain state of mind; they accept, to one degree or another, that it is true. I shall call this state of mind *acceptance*; it includes a representation of the proposition believed as well as a willingness to assent to its truth when the question of assent arises. Since at any given time a person is not conscious of all the propositions he believes, acceptance is mostly unconscious. And since the mind is neither consciously nor unconsciously assenting at any one time to everything believed, acceptance is also mostly dispositional. It is a disposition to assent, either in inward thought or in outward speech and action when the question of the truth of the proposition believed arises.

The question then is: does knowledge that P entail acceptance that P is true? In bygone ages, when a person learned something, what he learned later became available to him because he remembered it, and what he remembered of his having learned he would say he believed or knew, as the case may be. What he learned was stored within himself, the place of storage being called the memory, and when he needed something he had learned, he retrieved it from storage; that is, he remembered it. For that reason we have become accustomed to associate knowledge with belief and think of knowledge as including an individual state of mind. That leads us to suppose that knowledge entails belief or acceptance.

But this individualist conception of knowledge is belied by the development in subsequent ages of modes of storage of acquired information external to the individual. The invention of writing, the production of books, the growth of libraries, the invention of printing, and now of computers allows us to speak of objective knowledge. I do some research; I store the information obtained on index cards; I am asked whether so and so is true; I retrieve the relevant card and answer the question. We had become accustomed to associate knowledge with belief when the only form of storage available was personal, in the individual mind or brain, in the form of memory. But that association is now out of date. The brain is too limited in space and function to store everything we human beings have learned and wish to retain. Human memory is too weak and fallible to be the sole repository of the cognitive achievements of human civilization. We should speak, as does Karl Popper, of objective knowledge (Popper, 1973, chapters 3 and 4). If we continue to think of belief and acceptance as individual states of mind, then knowledge does not entail belief. On the other hand, if we expand the notion of belief to include those items of information we have stored for our own use outside our memory, then, in that sense, knowledge entails belief and acceptance. The concept of objective knowledge brings along with it the concept of objective mind. Knowledge, then, entails true belief when belief is properly understood in the objective sense.

A person may have true belief without knowledge, as when one accidentally hits on the truth. I am firmly convinced that a certain horse will win the race; my reason is that I like his name; the horse does win the race: a lucky guess. By no means could it be said that I knew ahead of time that he would win the race. What, then, must be added to true belief to have knowledge? Some philosophers have suggested a psychological feature, an inner mark of knowledge that can be discerned introspectively: clear and distinct ideas, the light of nature, inconceivability of the opposite, feeling sure have been suggested. But since knowledge entails truth, and truth implies correspondence with things as they are, there is no reason to suppose that some mental feature can guarantee truth. One might reply that it is not necessary for it to guarantee truth; rather, given that the proposition is true, what else is required to yield knowledge? But again an inner mark will not do; when someone challenges our claim to know something, we do not mention a psychological fact about ourselves but provide reasons for thinking our assertion is true. So perhaps knowledge equals true belief supported by reasons.

Knowledge and Justification

Giving reasons is a process of providing justification to others. For that reason, a common definition of knowledge offered in the philosophical literature is that knowledge is justified true belief. But this cannot be the whole story because there are cases in which a belief is both true and justified but is not known to be true.[2] For instance, we usually contrast knowledge with

---

2   See Gettier (1963) for the classical discussion of the issue.

probability. I may have reasons for thinking that some proposition is quite probable; if the reasons are very strong, then it is justified – we have good reason to accept it. But it is not known to be true. For example, I am shown a bag with eighty red and twenty green marbles in it and am asked to predict the color of the next marble to be drawn from the bag. I would be justified in predicting red, and if a red marble is drawn, then my prediction is true and justified, but no one would claim that I knew it to be true.

But what if the probability is extremely high? Suppose I buy a lottery ticket for a dollar; a million others have also bought tickets. The probability that I will not win the lottery is 99.9999 percent. Don't I know that I will not win? If I say yes, I fall into a contradiction. For everyone else who purchased a ticket has the same reason to say that they know that they will not win as I do. Consider, the winner W. He knows he will not win. But he does win, so he was mistaken – he did not know it. So by the assumptions of the example, he knows and does not know he will win, a contradiction. So probability excludes knowledge; knowledge entails certainty where certainty is here interpreted to exclude mere probability. Or, if you like, certainty is 100 percent probability. Certainty here is not the same as feeling certain. The latter is a psychological state and is irrelevant, as we have seen. Certainty is an objective relation between a proposition and the strength of the reasons there are for asserting it.

In the light of this discussion, perhaps knowledge should be defined as true belief that is fully justified where full justification is justification that provides certainty. If we cannot show to someone that what we believe is certain, we have no right to claim knowledge. Our right to claim knowledge, it would appear, depends on our ability to defend what we assert according to the highest standards.

One must be careful, however, because one is at the brink of another logical error. Suppose I think of a person's having a full justification of a proposition P as consisting of his being able to defend his belief successfully against all challenges. His defense consists of his giving reasons and providing evidence in favor of P. His reasons consist of other assertions R, S, T, etc. But in order for R, S, T, etc. to establish the certainty of P, they too must be certain for him; that is, he must know them to be true. According to this account of being fully justified, knowledge consists of providing reasons to support the certainty of a belief, reasons that one knows to be true. This internalist account of justification is circular. Of course, we often justify beliefs in the light of other beliefs we know to be true. But in order to avoid circularity, one must develop a concept of justification that avoids incorporating the concept of knowledge into its essential content.

Being Justified

There is a difference between being justified and providing a justification to others. Providing a justification to others is usually, though not always, a verbal affair. But one can justify one's own thoughts to oneself without speaking out loud. One can formulate the reasons in words in inner speech without having the slightest intention to communicate what one knows to others.

But one can have a reason or a justification without using words at all, inner or outer. The members of Moore's audience knew that his utterance "Here is one hand and here is another" is true because they saw his hands. Their seeing them justified their belief in the sense that their seeing them explained how they knew what Moore said was true. The answer to the question "How do you know that is true?" need not always mention a verbal state of affairs, although the answer may be given in words.

Suppose someone asks: "How do you know that the liquid in that test tube is an acid?" You answer: "The litmus paper turned red." That the litmus paper turned red is your reason in the sense that it explains how you know that is true. Another question may be, "How do you know that it turned red?" to which you may answer, "I saw it." It is your seeing it, not your saying you saw it, that was your reason that explains how you know it. Notice that the answer to the first question mentions an objective state of affairs and mentions nothing about what you have seen, whereas the answer to the second brings seeing into the picture. Both are equally good answers, for different questions. Of course, the second answer is important because it explains how you were in a position to answer the first.

Consider now a third question: "How do you know that you *saw* the litmus paper turn red?" This is a puzzling question, and it requires the offering of a context to make sense of its being asked. Perhaps there is a question about whether it was really litmus paper. Perhaps it is thought that you are color blind, so maybe others would not agree that it was red. Or perhaps there is little confidence in your trustworthiness, so there is a question of whether you really saw what you say you saw. An answer to the first would be "I took the paper from a fresh container of litmus paper"; to the second "I am not color blind, you know"; and to the third "Are you questioning my honesty?"

But suppose someone who had epistemological interests pressed you on the third understanding of the question. After all, you appealed to your sense of sight as the basis of your knowledge that it is red. How do you know that it was your *seeing* the color of the litmus paper that explains it? Given that seeing it consists of its appearing in a certain way to you, you can answer by saying: "Well it certainly looks red to me. Doesn't it to you?" (Put the question of color skepticism aside for the moment.)

But our epistemologist is not yet satisfied in his effort to understand the basis of human knowledge. Persisting, he asks: "How do you know that it looks red? How do you know that it is as if something red is appearing to you?" It is hard to know how to answer this query. The litmus paper and its color are made evident via the way they look. That they look that way is not made evident to you by any further conscious state of mind. Frege used to speak of the mode of presentation of an object. The mode of presentation of objects in the external world is through sense-experience, how things look, feel, sound, taste, and smell. One is frequently in a position to characterize one's own sense experience in the language of appearance and to acquire knowledge of its character; but there is no further mode of presentation of experiences other than the experiences themselves. Let us call the occurrence of a sense experience a *self-presenting state of mind*. Philosophers have often spoken of immediate perception or awareness, an awareness not mediated by some further fact. Our sense experiences, then, are objects of immediate awareness.

Notice that although the answering of these questions is a verbal affair, the items mentioned in the answers (e.g. that the litmus paper is red, and that it looks red to me) are not verbal affairs. Ultimately justification of our knowledge of the external world leads back to sense experience; that is, to self-presenting states. If one is in the right self-presenting state, one is thereby justified in having a certain belief. One can thereby be justified even if one does not say so, to oneself or others. What one says to oneself and others reports circumstances that are taken to justify, but it is the circumstances, not the reporting of them, that do the justifying.

I believe that the litmus paper is red on the basis of my sense experience. Is my having that experience enough or must I know that I have it? Of course, if one is attending to the color of the litmus paper, it is difficult to avoid knowing that it looks red. But the question is whether knowing it is an essential component of being justified. I want to argue that it is not an essential component. Consider the fact that we often know how something is on the basis of how it looks, even though it looks differently from the way it is. I may learn, for example, that a piece of paper is white because it looks gray in this dim light. I compensate for the poor lighting by applying knowledge of how white things look under varied circumstances. Later on, I remember the color of the paper without remembering how it looked to me. This is not unusual since our experiences are fleeting and we are usually more interested in the objective features of things than in the ways they appear. So I am now justified in thinking it white although I cannot report the experience that justified it.

In general, our self-presenting experiential states are capable of becoming known, although for the most part they come and go without being attended to. They most often operate not as verbally formulated premises from which we make inferences but as causes that trigger perceptual judgments. They count as reasons for these judgments in the sense that their occurrence is included in the explanation of how we know them to be true.

Justification and Reliability

Not only are our experiences reasons for our perceptual judgments, but they are usually thought of as good reasons, reasons that succeed in justifying them. As Quine said, "whatever evidence there *is* for science *is* sensory evidence." Perhaps we should qualify this formulation by saying that whatever evidence there is for our beliefs about the external world is, *ultimately*, sensory evidence. After all, that the litmus paper turned red is evidence for the liquid's being an acid, and the evidence here does not incorporate reference to sense experience. What brings in sense experience as the ultimate evidence is asking the question "How do you know?" over and over again.

But what makes sense experience not only a reason, but a good reason? How does it justify our beliefs in the external world? As Quine has pointed out, sense experience constitutes a rather meager input on which to base the torrential output that constitutes the totality of our beliefs about things as they are in themselves. It is certainly not the intrinsic character of the experiences, not some interior mark of veridicality, that does the trick. Descartes has cured us of that illusion. The answer, I think, appeals to reliability. We not only accept but are justified in accepting the propositional constituents of our perceptual judgments to the extent that perceptual experience is reliable, and it is reliable to the extent that it usually produces true belief in a non-accidental manner. Experience is trustworthy to the extent it is reliable.

But how reliable is it? Earlier I argued in favor of the great deception of sense. Our common sense judgments about color and other secondary qualities are mostly false; useful, though false. Because they are false, they are unreliable as far as truth is concerned. Because they are useful, they are reliable as far as satisfying our desires is concerned. Let us put aside utility and focus upon truth. Taking sense experience as a whole, we cannot say that it is very reliable. But as we gain knowledge of the relation between experience and things as they are in themselves, we can isolate certain aspects of sense experience that we have reason to believe are reliable. Experiences of primary qualities are more reliable than are those of the secondary. We often have good reason to think that something is square, whereas we never have good reason, all things considered, to think that something is red. So a large proportion of our perceptual judgments are justified, although it is difficult if not impossible to calculate exactly how large a proportion this is.

Do any of our perceptual judgments count as knowledge? This is equivalent to asking whether any of those that are true are ever fully justified. Remember that to be fully justified excludes probability and implies certainty. Is there any class of perceptual judgments that are super-reliable, that are true 100 percent of the time?

I am now in broad daylight holding something before my eyes that I judge to be a pencil. I look carefully and attend to what I am looking at. There is nothing wrong with my eyes; they have been operating normally. Again I see it as a pencil. I check again and again, and always arrive at the same verdict. I ask others to look as well, and they all agree that it is a pencil. I operate with it to make sure it behaves like a pencil. In general, perceptual judgments arrived at in such a manner, excluding such judgments that we know on other grounds to be mistaken, such as judgments about color, are super-reliable. The process of checking and rechecking and calling on others to report what they see excludes the very possibility of error. Thus not only am I justified in believing that this is a pencil, I know it to be a pencil.

Excluding Irrelevant Alternatives

Descartes' response to this account would be to call to mind various possibilities: I may be dreaming; I may be deceived by an evil demon. Others would say that it is possible I am a brain in a vat. In order to grapple with this issue, consider a different type of example. I am assured that all the marbles in this bag are red. Do I know that the next one that will be drawn is red? The skeptic says: "Even though they are all red while in the bag, it is possible that the next one drawn will change its color as it encounters light; so it is possible that it won't be red after all; so you do not know that it will be red."

If the concept of possibility in "It is possible that it won't be red" is logical possibility, then all that the statement asserts is that "It won't be red" is not self-contradictory; but this is compatible with my knowing that it will be red. More likely the intended meaning is epistemic; it is epistemically possible for it not to be red means "You do not know that it will be red." But that is not a reason for thinking that I do not know that it will be red; instead it is simply the negation of my claim to know that. In fact, I do know that it will be red, and I can exclude the possibility of its changing color because I also know that the world does not work that way; I know that the next marble will not change its color as it hits the light.

In reply to Descartes, we can now say that I know that I am not dreaming, I know that I am not being deceived by an evil demon. I know that the world does not work in these ways. We can exclude these ideas as irrelevant because they are canceled on the basis of our prior understanding of the way the world works; they are not even possibilities in the required sense.

The skeptic will answer, of course, that I am not entitled to make use of my knowledge of how the world works in excluding these alternatives because I have no right to claim that I really know these things. After all, in epistemology, we are attempting to examine the foundations of all knowledge, and we must bracket all claims about the external world to determine whether any knowledge of it is possible on the basis of sense experience. And since sense experience contains no intrinsic mark of truth, and since appealing to so-called knowledge of the external world to interpret sense experience simply begs the question, the obvious conclusion is that we have no knowledge of the external world.

The problem with this reply is that the arguments from dreams and from the evil demon are supposed to constitute reasons for bracketing our prior beliefs about the external world, for putting them out of operation, for raising doubts whether they actually count as knowledge. But the appeal to the possibility that I am dreaming or that I am being deceived by an evil demon is incapable of requiring me to bracket my prior beliefs because, as an argument that these beliefs do not count as knowledge, it simply begs the question.

Clearly, if I am to bracket my beliefs about the external world in order to examine the possibility of human knowledge, then skepticism wins. There is no non-circular argument against the skeptic once you enter the territory in which he is operating. But it is incumbent upon the skeptic to provide good and sufficient reasons to enter upon his domain of operation, and the traditional Cartesian arguments fail to do the trick, since they assume the very point at issue.

In this chapter, I have argued for a concept of knowledge as true belief fixed by a reliable process that is externalist in character. A person may have knowledge even if he does not recognize that he has it. In fact, philosophical skeptics actually know most of the things that they say they do not know. A person may have knowledge even if he has no idea how he has acquired it, even if he is totally unable to defend his claim to know to another.

Of course, there are certain contexts in which the ability to explain how one knows and to defend one's claim to know are absolutely essential: science, philosophy, public debates about controversial political and ethical issues are salient examples. One cannot enter these arenas bereft of argument, unless one expects an early knockout. But the particular demands of these contexts are not constitutive of our concept of knowledge in general.

Quine's naturalized epistemology is not quite as naturalized as he thinks it is. He wants to replace epistemology with psychology. He wants to use what we already know about the human mind and its interaction with the external world and its input and output to explain how the processes of arriving at our theories about the world actually work. So far so good. But these efforts at explanation also have a normative function; they show that many of our beliefs about the world are actually justified, and that many of them constitute knowledge.

For example, consider a description of how induction actually works. In induction, what we need is a representative sample, so that our predictions about what we will encounter in the future will be reliable. Not all samples are representative, so we have to use our prior information to determine, for example, whether the sample we are using is selected at random and whether it is a fair sample. We cannot determine representativeness without employing a great deal of information about the objects being studied. Suppose now we have achieved a representative sample; then our predictions are justified and most will turn out to be true. So we can justify inductions about particular classes of objects making use of knowledge we have obtained from prior inductions. Induction builds up its own support over time and can be genuinely productive of knowledge.

Take another example. Quine and others have pointed out the important role that simplicity plays in the acceptance of theories. Some philosophers have argued in favor of anti-realism on this ground. After all, they say, what has simplicity got to do with the way the world is? The world in itself may or may not conform to our simplest theories. So to the extent to which simplicity plays a role in theory acceptance, to that extent we must surrender our claims that science provides knowledge about the external world. Yet anti-realism does not follow from the use of the simplicity criterion. Suppose that selecting the simplest theory is a reliable procedure helping us gradually to approximate in our theories to the actual constitution of the world. Perhaps the methods of theory acceptance inherent in our mental makeup will yield truth in the long run. In that case, scientific knowledge or at least justified belief is not only possible, it is actual. Even if we cannot prove that the criterion of simplicity is truth tending, the arguments of the anti-realists do not show that it isn't. We may have knowledge that we cannot prove we have.

What Is Wrong and What Is Right with Skepticism

One conclusion that seems well supported by the argument of this book is that the arguments put forward by skeptics from ancient times to the present day fail to show that we do not have the knowledge that we think we have. Human knowledge is possible, and the arguments against the criterion, from dreams, from the evil demon, and so forth fail to demonstrate that knowledge is impossible. We do not have to be in a position to prove that we have knowledge in order to have knowledge. So one basic claim of global skepticism is mistaken, namely that human knowledge is impossible.

But there is another basic claim of global skepticism that is, I think, quite correct, namely that we cannot prove that we have knowledge without using knowledge already in our possession. So arguments intended to prove that we actually know something beg the question because they must rely upon background information. For example, I can prove that I am not dreaming, I think, by pinching myself. But, the skeptic replies, can you prove that you are pinching yourself as distinct from merely dreaming you are pinching yourself? No, I cannot provide an argument that will satisfy the skeptic. Ultimately we rely upon procedures that are reliable, even though we cannot prove they are reliable without relying upon these very procedures. So even though the skeptic fails to prove that knowledge is impossible, the non-skeptic cannot prove that he actually has knowledge without begging the question.

Philosophical skepticism, then, is partly wrong and partly right. Can we live with that? Moore pointed out long ago that we cannot prove to be true everything that we know to be true. We do not have to surrender our claims to possess knowledge just because we are in no position to convince the skeptic that we do. We are not obliged to accomplish an impossibility. But we do not have to fall back upon Santayana's animal faith or existentialism's blind commitment. Fideism is out.

But skeptical arguments do justify the verdict: not proven. Like Hume, we should enter the affairs of life with that verdict in the back of our minds, recognizing our fallible condition and being wary of speculative claims. Our claims to knowledge should be constrained by an understanding of the limits of our ability to prove the reliability of the procedures we use to get in contact with the external world.

Bibliography

Baldwin, Thomas (1990) *G. E. Moore.* New York: Routledge.

Berkeley, George (1709) *An Essay towards a New Theory of Vision.* Collected in Berkeley, *Philosophical Works* (1993).

Berkeley, George (1710) *A Treatise Concerning the Principles of Human Knowledge.* Collected in Berkeley, *Philosophical Works* (1993).

Berkeley, George (1713) *Three Dialogues between Hylas and Philonous.* Collected in Berkeley, *Philosophical Works* (1993).

Berkeley, George (1993) *Philosophical Works, Including the Works on Vision* (ed. Michael R. Ayers). London: Everyman.

Boswell, James (1791) *The Life of Samuel Johnson LLD.* Reprinted New York: The Modern Library.

Burnyeat, M. F. (1983) Can the skeptic live his skepticism? In Myles Burnyeat (ed.), *The Skeptical Tradition.* Berkeley: University of California Press.

Chisholm, Roderick (1963) The theory of appearing. In Max Black (ed.), *Philosophical Analysis.* Englewood Cliffs, NJ: Prentice Hall.

Chisholm, Roderick (1982) The problem of the criterion. In *Foundations of Knowing.* Minneapolis: University of Minnesota Press.

Cicero (1961) *Academica* (trans. H. Rackham). Cambridge, MA: Harvard University Press.

Curley, E. M. (1978) *Descartes Against the Skeptics.* Cambridge, MA: Harvard University Press.

Davidson, Donald (1986) A coherence theory of truth and knowledge. In Ernest Le Pore (ed.), *Truth and Interpretation.* Oxford: Basil Blackwell.

DeRose, Keith and Warfield, Ted A. (eds) (1999) *Skepticism: A Contemporary Reader.* New York: Oxford University Press.

Descartes, René (1976) *Descartes' Conversation with Burman* (trans. John Cottingham). Oxford: Clarendon Press.

Descartes, René (1985) *The Philosophical Writings of Descartes* (trans. John Cottingham, Robert Stoothoff, and Dugald Murdoch). Cambridge: Cambridge University Press.

Dewey, John (1938) *Logic: The Theory of Inquiry*. New York: Henry Holt and Co.

Diogenes Laertius (1991) *Lives of Eminent Philosophers* (trans. R. D. Hicks). Cambridge, MA: Harvard University Press.

Dummett, Michael (1996) *The Seas of Language*. Oxford: Clarendon Press.

Galileo Galilei (1623) *The Assayer*. Collected in *Discoveries and Opinions of Galileo* (trans. Stillman Drake). New York: Doubleday, 1957.

Gettier, Edmund (1963) Is justified true belief knowledge? *Analysis*, 23, 121–3.

Goldman, Alvin (1979) What is justified belief? In George Pappas (ed.), *Justification and Knowledge*. Dordrecht: Reidel.

Grice, H. P. (1989) *Studies in the Way of Words*. Cambridge, MA: Harvard University Press.

Groarke, Leo (1997) Ancient skepticism. In *Stanford Encyclopedia of Philosophy* (http://Plato.Stanford.edu/archives/win1997/entries/scepticism-ancient).

Heidegger, Martin (1927) *Being and Time* (trans. John Maquarrie and Edward Robinson). London: SCM Press, 1962.

Hill, Christopher (1999) Process reliabilism and Cartesian scepticism. In K. DeRose and T. A. Warfield (eds) *Skepticism: A Contemporary Reader*. New York: Oxford University Press.

Hobbes, Thomas (1641) *Leviathan*. Oxford: Clarendon Press, 1967.

Hobbes, Thomas (1650) *The Elements of Law* (ed. Ferdinand Tonnies). Cambridge: Cambridge University Press, 1928. (Hobbes completed the manuscript about 1640.)

Hume, David (1739) *A Treatise of Human Nature* (ed. L. A. Selby-Bigge). Oxford: Clarendon Press, 1951.

Hume, David (1748) *Enquiry Concerning Human Understanding*. Collected in *Enquiries Concerning Human Understanding and the Principles of Morals* (ed. L. A. Selby-Bigge). Oxford: Clarendon Press, 1985.

Husserl, Edmund (1960) *Cartesian Meditations: An Introduction to Phenomenology*. The Hague: Martinus Nijhoff.

James, William (1907) *Pragmatism: A New Name for Some Old Ways of Thinking*. New York: Longman, Green and Co., 1949.

Kant, Immanuel (1781) *Critique of Pure Reason* (trans. Norman Kemp Smith). New York: St Martin's Press, 1965.

Kant, Immanuel (1783) *Prolegomena to Any Future Metaphysics that Will Be Able to Come Forward as Science* (trans. James W. Ellington). Indianapolis: Hackett Publishing Co., 1983.

Keats, John (1970) *Letters of John Keats* (ed. Robert Giddings). Oxford: Oxford University Press.

Kripke, Saul A. (1982) *Wittgenstein on Rules and Private Language*. Cambridge, MA: Harvard University Press.

Landesman, Charles (1989) *Color and Consciousness: An Essay in Metaphysics*. Philadelphia: Temple University Press.

Landesman, Charles (1997) *An Introduction to Epistemology*. Oxford: Blackwell.

Levin, Michael (1993) Reliabilism and induction. *Synthese*.

Levin, Michael (1997) You can always count on reliabilism. *Philosophy and Phenomenological Research.*

Locke, John (1690) *An Essay Concerning Human Understanding* (ed. P. H. Nidditch). Oxford: Clarendon Press, 1975.

Lovejoy, Arthur (1929) *The Revolt Against Dualism.* La Salle, IL: Open Court.

Mackie, J. L. (1979) A defense of induction. In G. F. Macdonald (ed.), *Perception and Identity.* Ithaca, NY: Cornell University Press.

Mates, Benson (1996) *The Skeptic Way: Sextus Empiricus's Outlines of Pyrrhonism.* New York: Oxford University Press.

Matson, Wallace I. (1991) Certainty made simple. In A. P. Martinich and Michael J. White (eds), *Certainty and Surface in Epistemology and Philosophical Method: Essays in Honor of Avrum Stroll.* Lewiston, NY: The Edwin Mellon Press.

Montaigne, Michel de (1965) *The Complete Essays of Montaigne* (trans. Donald M. Frame). Stanford, CA: Stanford University Press.

Moore, G. E. (1909) Hume's philosophy. In *Philosophical Studies.* London: Routledge and Kegan Paul, 1922.

Moore, G. E. (1953) *Some Main Problems of Philosophy.* New York: Collier Books, 1962. (Based upon lectures delivered in 1910–11.)

Moore, G. E. (1968) A reply to my critics. In Paul Arthur Schilpp (ed.), *The Philosophy of G. E. Moore.* La Salle, IL: Open Court.

Moore, G. E. (1970) *Philosophical Papers.* London: George Allen and Unwin.

Moore, G. E. (1993) Wittgenstein's lectures in 1930–33. In Ludwig Wittgenstein, *Philosophical Occasions* (ed. James Kluge and Alfred Nordmann). Indianapolis: Hackett.

Nietzsche, Friedrich (1968) *Basic Writings of Nietzsche* (trans. Walter Kaufman). New York: The Modern Library.

Nozick, Robert (1981) *Philosophical Explanations.* Cambridge: Cambridge University Press.

Peirce, Charles Sanders (1965) *Collected Papers of Charles Sanders Peirce* (ed. Charles Hartshorne and Paul Weiss). Cambridge, MA: Harvard University Press.

Peirce, Charles Sanders (1997) *Pragmatism as a Principle and Method of Right Thinking* (ed. Patricia Ann Turisi). Albany: State University of New York Press. (Peirce gave these lectures in 1903.)

Popkin, Richard (1968) *The History of Skepticism from Erasmus to Descartes.* New York: Harper and Row.

Popper, Karl (1973) *Objective Knowledge: An Evolutionary Approach.* Oxford: Clarendon Press.

Price, H. H. (1954) *Perception.* London: Methuen.

Price, H. H. (1969) *Belief.* London: George Allen and Unwin.

Quine, W. V. (1961) *From a Logical Point of View.* New York: Harper and Row.

Quine, W. V. (1969) *Ontological Relativity and Other Essays.* New York: Columbia University Press.

Rorty, Richard (1991) *Objectivity, Relativism, and Truth: Philosophical Papers,*

Volume I. Cambridge: Cambridge University Press.

Russell, Bertrand (1912) *Problems of Philosophy.* Oxford: Oxford University Press.

Santayana, George (1923) *Scepticism and Animal Faith.* New York: Dover, 1955.

Schmitt, C. B. (1983) The rediscovery of ancient skepticism in modern times. In Myles Burnyeat (ed.), *The Skeptical Tradition.* Berkeley: University of California Press.

Sextus Empiricus (1955) *Outlines of Pyrrhonism* (trans. R. G. Bury). Cambridge, MA: Harvard University Press.

Sosa, Ernest (1991) The raft and the pyramid: coherence vs foundations in the theory of knowledge. In *Knowledge in Perspective.* Cambridge: Cambridge University Press.

Strawson, P. F. (1959) *Individuals: An Essay in Descriptive Metaphysics.* London: Methuen and Co.

Stroll, Avrum (1994) *Moore and Wittgenstein on Certainty.* New York: Oxford University Press.

Stroud, Barry (1987) *The Significance of Philosophical Scepticism.* Oxford: Clarendon Press.

Tarski, Alfred (1933) The concept of truth in formalized languages. In *Logic, Semantics, and Metamathematics: Papers from 1923 to 1938* (trans. J. H. Woodger). Indianapolis: Hackett Publishing Co., 1983.

Whitehead, Alfred North (1925) *Science and the Modern World.* New York: The Free Press, 1967.

Williams, Michael (1996) *Unnatural Doubts: Epistemological Realism and the Basis of Skepticism.* Princeton, NJ: Princeton University Press.

Wittgenstein, Ludwig (1921) *Tractatus Logico-Philosophicus* (trans. D. F. Pears and B. F. McGuinness). New York: Humanities Press, 1972.

Wittgenstein, Ludwig (1953) *Philosophical Investigations* (trans. G. E. M. Anscombe). New York: Macmillan, 1968.

Wittgenstein, Ludwig (1969) *On Certainty* (trans. Denis Paul and G. E. M. Anscombe). New York: Harper and Row.

Index